THE COMPLETE COLLECTION OF LEGAL FORMS FOR EMPLOYERS

All-Inclusive Sample Contracts, Forms and Checklists
for Hiring, Firing, and Day-to-Day Employment

By
Steven Mitchell Sack
Attorney at Law

Legal Strategies
PUBLICATIONS

THE COMPLETE COLLECTION OF LEGAL FORMS FOR EMPLOYERS

All-Inclusive Sample Contracts, Forms and Checklists for Hiring, Firing, and Day-to-Day Employment

By Steven Mitchell Sack
Attorney at Law

Copyright © 1996 by STEVEN MITCHELL SACK.
All rights reserved.
This publication may not be reproduced, stored in a retrieval system, or transmitted in whole or in part, in any form or by any means, electronic, mechanical, photocopying, recording, or otherwise, without the prior written permission of Legal Strategies Inc., 1795 Harvard Avenue, Merrick, NY 11566. Telephone (516) 377-3940.

This publication is designed to provide accurate and authoritative information in regard to the subject matter covered. It is sold with the understanding that the publisher is not engaged in rendering legal, accounting, or other professional services. If legal advice or other expert assistance is required, the services of a competent professional person should be sought. *From a Declaration of Principles jointly adopted by a Committee of the American Bar Association.*

Library of Congress Catalog Number: 96-75385
ISBN: 0-9636306-4-4
Printed in the United States of America
1 2 3 4 5 6 7 8 9 0

LEGAL STRATEGIES PUBLICATIONS is an organization devoted to providing employers in all industries throughout the United States with important legal information through books, seminars and special reports.

AUTHOR'S NOTE

The forms, agreements, checklists and documents contained in this book are provided to assist the human resource professional, business owner, executive and attorney. These documents are not intended to provide legal advice per se, because laws vary considerably throughout the fifty states and the law and agreements can be interpreted differently depending upon the particular facts of each case. Furthermore, since it is important that agreements and documents be reviewed and drafted clearly so that they specifically refer to the facts at hand, it is important to consult experienced counsel regarding the applicability of any document or point of information contained herein whenever you are utilizing or implementing these forms.

This publication is sold with the understanding that the publisher is not engaged in rendering legal, accounting or other professional services. If legal advice or expert assistance is required, the services of a competent professional must always be sought.

Finally, any fictitious names that are used throughout the work having any similarity to actual persons, places or events are purely coincidental.

ACKNOWLEDGMENTS

Due to the size and complexity of this book, there are many people I wish to thank.

I am grateful to Donald W. Hawk, Director of Reports and Electronic Media at BRP Publications, Inc., for encouraging me to produce this book. Don assisted me in most phases of the book's planning and publishing and I applaud his knowledge, skills and support.

Kudos are given to my executive secretary, Alison Achor, for her assistance in designing and in-putting the human resource forms, and to Carolyn Porter and Alan Gadney of ONE-ON-ONE BOOK PRODUCTIONS for their aid in production and marketing.

I offer thanks to friend and fellow attorney Stanley M. Spiegler, who taught me more about the practice of labor law than he could ever realize. I also acknowledge the friendship and expertise of Shirley and Larry Alexander, who helped me acquire an understanding of the publishing industry and who introduced me to BRP Publications, Inc.

Thanks are extended to Chicago attorney, James J. Oh for permitting me to include his valuable checklist for sexual harassment investigations.

Of course, personal thanks are extended to Dr. Subhi Gulati, my brother and law partner Jonathan Scott Sack, Esq., Joan and Sidney Pollack, my mother Judith and my extended family for their constant love and encouragement.

I wish to express my love to my wife Gwen, who put up with my long hours in creating and writing this book and to my sons Andrew and David for future dreams. Finally, as always, I wish to express my appreciation and gratitude to my father, Bernard, whose insights and dreams helped make this book a reality.

ABOUT THE AUTHOR

Steven Mitchell Sack is a nationally known attorney who devotes substantial time to labor problems and employment litigation avoidance. Since 1980, he has maintained a private law practice in New York City devoted primarily to representation in contract negotiations, disputes and litigation, and general labor law.

A prolific writer, Mr. Sack is the author of sixteen books on legal subjects. Since 1986, his advice on labor issues regularly appears in The Legal Brief column carried in NAPL's *Printing Manager Magazine*. He has also authored numerous articles in business publications which discuss many labor subjects including hiring and firing salespeople, anti-trust issues, and avoiding age and sex discrimination problems.

In addition to conducting a private law practice, Mr. Sack serves as General Counsel for many trade associations, presides in commercial arbitrations as an arbitrator for the American Arbitration Association, and has conducted corporate seminars for companies throughout the United States both in-house and with the American Management Association.

A Phi Beta Kappa graduate of Stony Brook University and a graduate of Boston College Law School, he is a member of the American Bar Association (Labor and Employment Division), New York County Lawyer's Association, New York State Bar Association, and is admitted to practice before the United States Tax Court.

Mr. Sack's advice about company exposure to employment-related litigation has appeared nationally in such publications as *The New York Times, The Wall Street Journal, Alert* (published by the Research Institute of America), and many other business journals. He has appeared on hundreds of radio programs and national television including *The Oprah Winfrey Show* and *The Salley Jesse Rapheal Show*. His recent books in the consumer market include *The Salesperson's Legal Guide* (Prentice Hall, 1981), *Don't Get Taken* (McGraw-Hill, 1985), *The Complete Legal Guide to Marriage, Divorce, Custody and Living Together* (McGraw-Hill, 1987), *The Employee Rights Handbook: Answers To Legal Questions From Interview to Pink Slip* (Facts on File, Inc., 1991), *The Lifetime Legal Guide* (Book-of-the-Month Club, 1996), and *The Hiring & Firing Book: A Complete Legal Guide for Employers* (Legal Strategies Inc., 1993), from which some of the agreements, contracts, forms and documents in this book have been adopted.

Mr. Sack is president and CEO of Legal Strategies, Inc.

BOOKS BY STEVEN MITCHELL SACK

- **The Lifetime Legal Guide** (Book-of-the-Month Club, 1996)

- **The Hiring & Firing Book (Revised Edition):** A Complete Legal Guide for Employers (Legal Strategies, 1996)

- **The Complete Collection of Legal Forms for Employers:** All-Inclusive Sample Contracts, Forms, and Checklists for Hiring, Firing, and Day-to-Day Employment (Legal Strategies, 1996)

- **Don't Get Taken:** Protect Yourself Legally from Common Abuses and Rip-Offs! (Legal Strategies, 1996)

- **From Hiring to Firing:** The Legal Survival Guide for Employers in the 90's (Legal Strategies, 1995)

- **Legal Documents for Employers**: Sample Contracts, Forms and Checklists for Hiring, Firing and Day-to-Day Operations (Legal Strategies, 1995)

- **Legal Documents for HR Professionals** (Legal Strategies, 1994)

- **The Hiring & Firing Book:** A Complete Legal Guide for Employers (Legal Strategies, 1993)

- **Don't Get Taken:** How to Avoid Common Consumer Rip-offs (Consumer Reports Books, 1993)

- **The Employee Rights Handbook:** Answers to Legal Questions From Interview to Pink Slip (Facts on File, 1991)

- **Sales Rep Strategies for Dealing With Principals Successfully**: Negotiations, Contracts, Working Relationships and Terminations (Sales Reps Advisor, 1991)

- **Employment Law:** A Printer's Handbook on Hiring & Firing (NAPL, 1991)

- **The Complete Legal Guide to Marriage, Divorce, Custody, and Living Together** (McGraw-Hill, 1987)

- **The NAPL Employee Handbook** (NAPL, 1986)

- **Don't Get Taken:** A Preventative Legal Guide to Protect Your Home, Family, Money and Job (McGraw-Hill, 1984)

- **The Salesperson's Legal Guide** (Prentice Hall, 1981)

TABLE OF CONTENTS

How to Use This Book xi

Section One: Pre-Hiring Considerations

Checklist of Important Pre-hiring Concerns 3
Checklist of Legal and Illegal Hiring Questions 6
Sample Job Applicant Summary Review Forms 8
Comparison Form 9
Clerical Appraisal 10
Sample Employment Application 11
Applicant Consent Form to Investigate and Disclose Data 13
Reference Check Form 14
Optional Reference Inquiry Form 15
Telephone Reference Inquiry Form 17
Anticipated Job Requirements Summary 19
Short Form Job Description 21
Job Hiring Progress Summary 23
List of Acceptable Documents for Immigration Control & Reform Act 24
Sample Rejection Letter to Job Applicant 25
Sample Rejection Letter from Unsolicited Resume 26
Checklist of Important Hiring Concerns 27
Employment Negotiating Checklist 29
Sales Employment Checklist 30
Checklist of Important Points to Follow Regarding Contract Execution 32
Twenty Factor Checklist to Determine Independent Contractor V. Employee Status 33
Checklist to Determine Overtime Liability under the Fair Labor Standards Act 37
Hiring Results Summary Form 39
Letter Confirmation of Job Offer 40
Confirmation of At-Will Employment Form 41
Sample Confidentiality and Non-Competition Agreement 42
Standard Employment Agreement 45
Sample Employment Agreement—Long Version 50
Sample Employment Agreement—Alternative Long Version 56
Sample Sales Employee Agreement—Long Version 62
Sample Sales Employee Agreement—Short Version 71
Sample Employment Agreement—Short Version 74
Sample Employment Agreement—Letter Version 77
Sample Sales Employee Agreement—Letter Version 79
Sample Consulting Agreement 84
Sample Employment Agreement When Hiring Outside Consultants
    and Independent Contractors 87

Sample Independent Sales Representative Agreement 91
Sample Independent Sales Representative Agreement, Short Version 104

Section Two: Day-to-Day Operations

Sample Code of Ethics Policy Statement 113
Receipt of Idea 120
Trade Secret Concerns Checklist 121
Sample Statement on Trade Secrets 123
Sample EEO Compliance Statement and Plan 125
Checklist of Important On-the-Job Policies to Follow 134
Receipt of Employee Handbook Form 136
Comprehensive Checklist Regarding Drugs and Alcohol in the Workplace 137
Release and Disclaimer from Drug Testing 141
Security Investigation Consent and Release, Version One 142
Security Investigation Consent and Release, Version Two 143
Consent to Medical Examination 144
Interrogation Confirmation and Release Form 145
Financial Disclosure Form 146
Lie Detector Disclaimer and Release Form 147
Request to Review Employee Records Form 148
Leave of Absence Request Form 149
Vacation Request Form 150
Direct Deposit Consent Form 151
Sample Time Report 152
Sample Job Log 153
Sample Attendance Log 154
Business Voucher Receipts Form 155
Expense Report 156
Authorization for Payroll or Other Deductions Form 157
Salary Recommendation Form 158
Employee Status or Fact Change Form 159
Self Performance Review Evaluation Form 160
Sample Performance Appraisal 165
Alternative Performance Review 167
New Hiring Job Appraisal Summary 171
Orientation Period Employee Performance Review 172
Objective Employee Improvement Evaluation 174
Numerical Employee Evaluation Form 176
Transfer/Promotion Log 179
Employee Referral Policy and Award 180
Accident/Work Injury Report 181
Checklist to Minimize Workplace Accidents 182
Checklist for Sexual Harassment Investigations 185
Personnel Action Form 187

Section Three: Separation Documents

Reducing Lawsuit Exposure: Eleven Things Your Company Should Know 191
Pre-Termination Consideration Checklist 192
Model Disciplinary Warning 195
Final Disciplinary Warning 196
Sample Leave of Absence Letter 197
Sample Notice of Termination 200
Sample Job Elimination Notification 201
Sample Separation Agreement and Release 202
Preliminary Payment Calculation Sheet 205
Sample Separation Agreement and Release 206
General Release—Version One 211
General Release—Version Two 213
Cover Letter and Release 215
Termination Log Summary 218
Sample Exit Interview Form 219
Checklist of Employee Termination Action 221
Final Supervisor's Approval for Termination Checklist 223
Voluntary Resignation by Employee Form 225
Confidential Settlement Agreement, Mutual Release, and Covenant Not to Sue 226
Settlement Agreement and Mutual Release 230
    Negotiable Promissory Note 234
    Personal Guaranty 237
    Affidavit for Judgment by Confession 238
    Judgment Pursuant To Affidavit for Judgment by Confession 240
Sales Rep Protection Statutes 242

Section Four: Business Formation

Sample Partnership Agreement 249
Sample Shareholder Agreement 262
Stock Purchase Agreement 271
    Consulting Agreement 274
    Non-Solicitation Agreement 277
Sample Purchase Agreement 279
    Bill of Sale 286
Technical Employment Agreement and Related Documents with a Foreign Employer 288
    Action of the Incorporator of XYZ, Inc. 288
    Written Consent of the Board of Directors of XYZ, Inc 289
    Certificate of Incorporation of XYZ, Inc. 291
    By-Laws of XYZ, Inc. 292
    Application for Authority of XYZ, Inc. under Section 1304
    of the Business Corporation Law 299
    Shareholder's Agreement 300

    Non-negotiable Demand Promissory Note 308
    Assignment and Bill of Sale 309
    Distribution and License Agreement 310
    Management, Administrative and Technical Services Agreement 318
    Employment Agreement 321
Option and Purchase Agreement 326

Section Five: Glossary Of Terms

Glossary of Terms 345
Index 357

HOW TO USE THIS BOOK

This book of forms, agreements, checklists and documents was written to save your company money and aggravation.

Beginning in the 1960s, some state legislatures began scrutinizing the fairness of the employment-at-will doctrine. Under this traditional rule of law, employers hired workers at will and were free to fire them at any time, with or without cause and with or without notice. From the nineteenth to mid-twentieth century, employers could discharge individuals with impunity. But beginning in the 1960s, courts began handing down rulings to safeguard the rights of non-unionized employees, and Congress passed specific laws pertaining to occupational health and safety, civil rights and freedom to complain about unsafe working conditions.

Thirty years later, there has been a gradual erosion of the employment-at-will doctrine in many areas. For example, some states have enacted public policy exceptions which make it illegal to fire workers who wish to perform jury duty or military service. Some courts have ruled that statements in company manuals, handbooks and employment publications constitute implied contracts which employers are bound to follow. Other states now recognize the obligation of companies to deal in fairness and good faith with longtime workers. This means, for example, that they are prohibited from terminating workers in retaliation when an employee tattles on abuses of authority (i.e., whistle-blowing), or denying individuals an economic benefit (e.g., a pension that is vested or about to vest, commission, bonus, etc.) that has been earned or is about to become due.

Most employers are unaware that in the past thirty years, the amount of employment-related litigation has increased more than 2000 percent. The average jury verdict in wrongful discharge cases now exceeds $500,000, and the amount of litigation stemming from discrimination charges has sky-rocketed, due in part to the more liberal amendment to Title VII in the form of the Civil Rights Act of 1991 and the Americans With Disabilities Act. From pre-hiring considerations to on-the-job rights of privacy, freedom from lie detector tests, and enhanced rights upon discharge, new rulings are emerging every day that give employees greater rights.

Federal and state laws are continually being passed that grant employees access to their personnel records, prohibit companies from firing pregnant employees or females on maternity leave, make it more difficult to fire workers who are performing inadequately, permit union employees to be represented by union delegates when accused of disciplinary violations and protect employees in many other ways.

In the past, employers could fire workers with or without cause or notice, with little fear of legal reprisal. This has changed. More and more terminated workers are successfully arguing and proving that company promises made at the time of the hiring interview are binding on the employer. Years ago, terminated employees would merely bow their heads and shuffle out the door after hearing they had been fired. Now, terminated workers are questioning these decisions and negotiating better severance packages and other post-termination benefits. In fact, the guiding maxim I offer to personnel executives, recruiters and owners of businesses is, "No good deed out of kindness goes unpunished." If you think about this apparent contradiction for a moment, you will begin to understand the problems employers currently face.

No company, regardless of its size or industry, is immune from this growing trend. The evolution of new laws, and the philosophy that a job is an integral part of a person's life and not just a vehicle for earning a living, is creating problems for employers and giving workers ammunition with which to fight back. Thousands of independent salespeople are also receiving protection from principals who fail to pay commissions due them in a timely fashion. In the past few years, 31 states have enacted sales rep protection laws which guarantee prompt payment of commissions upon termination or resignation and award double and triple damages, plus reasonable attorney fees and costs of litigation, in the event companies fail to comply with the appropriate provisions of each applicable state law.

Statistics indicate that 3.8 of every 100 employees are fired or resign from their jobs each month. Experts suggest that more than 350,000 workers are terminated unjustly or illegally each year, exposing their employers to hundreds of millions of dollars in potential damages, not including lost manpower costs and bad publicity, and tens of millions of dollars in unnecessary legal fees and expenses. A story in *The New York Times* reported that "in almost every industry, unfair discharge litigation has proliferated and the amount of money involved in settlements runs into hundreds of millions of dollars annually." *The Wall Street Journal* confirmed in a 1987 article that more than one-third of the New England companies interviewed indicated they were involved in legal actions with terminated employees, which in most cases were settled for cash payments ranging from $1,000 to $50,000, not including other benefits.

The Complete Collection of Legal Forms for Employers evolved from the variety of services I perform as legal counsel. In the mid-1980s, I was invited to address a major industry forum at a dinner in New York City. My topic was how to hire and fire employees properly in view of recent, drastic changes in the law. After the meeting, I was invited to create a special full-day seminar to cover the wide spectrum of legal issues and problems currently faced by printing companies. Following the seminar, I was commissioned to write a sample manual, complete with checklists and forms, for 3,700 printing company members belonging to the National Association of Printers & Lithographers entitled *Employment Law: A Printer's Handbook On Hiring And Firing*. This manual was written to give company executives charged with interviewing, hiring, disciplining and firing employees an overview of and assistance in understanding the multitude of court rulings, regulations and laws which protect workers.

Based on the manual's positive impact I decided to write a major, comprehensive book for employers in *all* industries throughout the country which would combine up-to-the minute changes in the law with the expertise gained in my professional experience as a practicing labor lawyer.

That book, *The Hiring & Firing Book: A Complete Legal Guide for Employers*, was published in 1993 and is now published in a revised edition. Many of the thousands of employers, human resource professionals and attorneys who purchased the book called or wrote to compliment me on the forms contained throughout the book and in the appendix. Some suggested that I continue to cull through my law firm files and include other agreements and documents in a separate book.

This book is a compendium of important documents that should be used by business owners, lawyers and human resource professionals in all phases of their dealings with employees. In this litigious age, it is *crucial* that employers take a preventive approach. By implementing the checklists, letters, forms, and agreements contained in this work, you can significantly reduce the chances that your company will be successfully sued by a former or current employee. Many of the self-protective steps outlined herein can enable your business to avoid ongoing disruption due to claims of sexual harassment, discrimination, invasions of privacy, breach of contract and unfair firings.

Regardless of the number of workers your company employs, its location or industry, the documents contained in this book offer hundreds of preventive strategies your company can take to avoid such problems. The agreements handle pre-hiring and post-hiring considerations as well as the traditional problems associated with the hiring and firing stages essential to minimizing litigation. In fact, most lawsuits that arise after a firing could have been avoided by proper planning long before the hiring stage. With these documents as your guide, you will be able to implement new policies within your company if none already exist, and alter current policies and agreements where warranted. Obviously, while these forms suggest what company policy should be, they are not a per se statement of a particular policy. Rather, the forms provide various strategies which can be modified and implemented as required.

These materials can reduce the odds of your company being sued unfairly and assist you and your lawyer in minimizing claims if you are sued. For example, some states allow terminated workers to sue in tort (as opposed to asserting claims based in contract) and recover punitive damages and money for pain and suffering arising from the firing. Employees who assert tort claims for wrongful discharge sometimes recover large six-figure and more jury verdicts as a result. Also, innovative lawyers are asserting federal racketeering (RICO) claims seeking criminal sanctions and treble (triple) damages against companies. This is in addition to fraud and misrepresentation claims against individuals responsible for making wrongful termination decisions. By utilizing these forms, you may be in a better position to tell if an individual is able to assert such theories and reduce your company's exposure to such claims.

The Complete Collection of Legal Forms for Employers contains the actual contracts and documents I prepare for my employer clients but at a small fraction of the cost. As you can see, the forms are divided into four essential areas to maximize their use.

Section One: Pre-Hiring Considerations, provides employers with many useful forms for interviewing, selecting and properly hiring job applicants as well as recommended employment contracts and other agreements when hiring executives, employees, outside consultants, and sales representatives. Pay special attention to the comprehensive checklist of legal and illegal hiring questions; most employers are not knowledgeable as to what questions cannot be asked at the job interview and may be sued as a result.

Section Two: Day-to-Day Operations, contains numerous suggested documents that should be prepared by all employers.

Section Three: Separation Documents, contains recommended agreements and forms that should be adapted and used when terminating employees in a wide variety of circumstances.

Section Four: Business Formation, provides a host of documents essential when creating the employer entity, such as a model comprehensive Partnership or Shareholder Agreement.

It is hoped that all of these forms will provide your company with the materials necessary to properly prepare for and defend against unfair discharge, breach of contract, and other common lawsuits frequently asserted today by disgruntled employees and ex-employees. The body of employment law has been created to further fairness and justice, but it will not help unless you participate in your own defense, know how to detect improprieties, and take active measures to avoid common labor problems. Studying, revising, incorporating, and implementing the documents, agreements, and forms in this book can go a long way towards protecting your company.

Steven Mitchell Sack, Esq.
New York City, New York

SECTION ONE:
Pre-Hiring Considerations

CHECKLIST OF IMPORTANT PRE-HIRING CONCERNS

Remember: Avoid litigation through proper planning and execution. The time to defend against the termination lawsuit begins <u>before</u> you hire.

A. Before Hiring:

1. Be sure that advertisements and help-wanted ads are not discriminatory.

2. Avoid using descriptions in advertisements and brochures implying that the job being offered is secure (i.e., listing words such as "long-term growth," "permanent," "secure," or "career path."

3. Minimize the inference that long-term tenure is being given in advertisements and brochures by using preferred words such as only "full-time" or "regular."

4. Save copies of all ads and record the number of responses and the number of hires.

5. Avoid asking discriminatory questions during job recruiting and selection.

6. Instruct all personnel in charge of hiring never to tell or admit to an older applicant that they are "overqualified" or lack "formal education credits."

7. Scrutinize all job requirements to insure that your company is not inadvertently screening out qualified disabled applicants.

8. Review your hiring policies regarding disabled applicants to comply with the ADA.

9. Avoid making guaranteed earning claims you don't intend to keep.

10. Properly investigate an applicant's references and statements on the employment application but be careful not to violate defamation or privacy rights when investigating references.

11. When preparing job criteria, do not set a higher requirement than is needed for the job simply to attract a better caliber of applicant to avoid discriminating against a particular class of applicant.

12. Review employment applications, personnel manuals and work rules likely to be involved in a termination lawsuit.

13. Regulate statements that recruiters, interviewers and other intake personnel make to new or prospective employees.

14. Do not institute affirmative action policies without conducting a thorough statistical analysis of your workforce.

15. Be familiar with the technical aspects of The Immigration Reform and Control Act of 1986 and comply with all aspects of this law when hiring workers.

16. Do not impose pre-employment physicals even if all applicants are required to take physicals in the screening process.

17. Do not request applicants to take lie detector or polygraph tests.

18. Tread carefully before thinking about offering stress tests, psychological tests, and other honesty tests to applicants.

19. Understand the distinction between employee and independent contractor status to comply with IRS requirements.

20. Clearly understand the arrangement your company has with employment agencies and confirm the placement fee and other conditions in writing to avoid potential disputes.

21. Contact your nearest office of the Department of Labor to be sure your company complies with all appropriate benefits laws affecting part-time workers.

22. Be cautious when seeking to investigate an applicant's medical history.

23. Always have applicants sign release forms that approve reasonable background checks on credit, criminal and work histories.

24. Carefully evaluate "English-only" language rules before implementing such rules within your workforce to avoid potential EEOC violations.

25. Always refrain from asking for photos of applicants before hiring.

26. Avoid asking for clergy references before hiring.

27. Avoid asking questions of females that you would not ask of males.

28. Pay special attention when inquiring into arrests (not convictions) since arrests are often overcome by acquittal, dismissal, or withdrawal of charges and such questions in most cases are illegal.

29. Understand that the Fair Debt Credit Reporting Act restricts employers from using credit reports for hiring or employment decisions.

30. Instruct all officers to avoid making any remarks regarding lifetime employment.

31. If you decide to screen applicants for drug or alcohol use, adopt a plan and record it in work rules, policy manuals, employment contracts and/or collective bargaining agreements.

32. Understand that lawsuits commenced by employers to enforce restrictive covenants in employment agreements are not always successful.

33. To increase the chances of enforcing a restrictive covenant, be sure the clause is clearly drafted in writing, is short in terms of geographic location and time constraints (i.e., no more than one year) and additional consideration was offered as a fair inducement for the employee to sign a contract containing such a clause.

CHECKLIST OF LEGAL AND ILLEGAL HIRING QUESTIONS

Subject	You May Ask	You May Not Ask
IDENTITY	What is your full name? Have you ever used an alias? If so, what was the name you used? What is the name of your parent or guardian? (Ask only if the applicant is a minor.) What is your maiden name? (Permissible only for checking prior employment or education.)	Have you ever changed your name by court order or other means? What are the names of friends and relatives working for the company? What kind of work does your mother, father, wife, or husband do? (Do not ask for information about spouses, children, or relatives not employed by the company.)
RESIDENCE	What is your address? How long have you lived in this state/city? What is your phone number?	Do you rent or own your home? How long have you lived in this country? If you live with someone, what is the nature of the relationship? Do you live in a foreign country?
RACE, NATIONAL ORIGIN	Do you speak a foreign language? If so, which one?	What is your skin color? Your ancestry? Your maiden name? Where were you born? What is your mother's native language? What is your native tongue? How did you learn to speak a foreign language? What is your spouse's nationality?
CITIZENSHIP	Are you a citizen of the United States? If not, do you intend to become one? Can you provide documents required to prove that you have a legal right to work in this country?	Of what country are you a citizen? Are you a native-born or naturalized citizen? Your parents? Your spouse? When did you/they acquire citizenship?
CHILD CARE	Do you know of any reason why you might not be able to come to work on time, every day? (Caution: permissible only if the question is put to every applicant, regardless of gender.)	Are there children at home? How many? Their ages? Who looks after them? If you plan to have children later on, who will take care of them while you work?
DISABILITY	Would you be willing to take a company physical if offered the job?	Are you disabled or impaired? Have you ever received compensation for injury or illness? Have you ever been treated for (do not present a checklist). In your last job, how much sick time did you have?
PERSONAL HISTORY	Have you ever been convicted of a crime? Do you hold a valid driver's license? Do you belong to any groups or clubs related to this job or field?	Have you ever been arrested? Have you ever pleaded guilty to a crime? Have you ever been in trouble with the law? To what societies, associations, lodges, etc., do you belong?
AGE	Are you of legal job age? If you are younger than 18 or older than 65, what is your age?	How old are you? When were you born? What makes you want to work at your age?
RELIGION		What is your religion? What church are you a member of? What religious holidays do you observe? Can you work on the Sabbath?

The Complete Collection of Legal Forms for Employers

MARITAL STATUS	What is your marital status?	Are you married, single, divorced, separated, widowed, or engaged? Should we call you Miss, Ms., or Mrs.? Where does your spouse work? What does your spouse do? Is your spouse covered by a medical/health insurance plan? Are you the head of your household? Are you the principal wage earner?
GENDER ISSUES		Do you plan to marry? Will you have children? Do you believe in birth control or family planning? Do you consider yourself a feminist? What do you think about ERA?

SAMPLE JOB APPLICANT SUMMARY REVIEW FORMS
NUMERICAL GRADE FORM

Applicant's Name: _____

Position and Title
Applied For: _____

Date Interviewed: _____

Evaluator's Name: _____

Date Evaluation
Prepared: _____

RATING SCALE:

0	Does not satisfy job needs.
1 - 2	Weak match to job needs.
3 - 4	Average applicant.
5 - 6	Satisfies job needs.
7 - 8	Exceeds job needs.
9 - 10	Very strong candidate.

JOB FUNCTIONS AND NEEDS	IMPORTANCE (in percentage)	X	RATING	=	TOTAL

APPLICANT'S TOTAL: _____

SUGGESTED ACTION:

The Complete Collection of Legal Forms for Employers

COMPARISON FORM

Position & Title
Applied For: _____

Interviewer: _____

RATING SCALE:

A = Satisfies Job Requirements

B = Exceeds Job Requirements

C = Does Not Satisfy Job Requirements

JOB FUNCTIONS & NEEDS	APPLI-CANT 1	APPLI-CANT 2	APPLI-CANT 3	EVALUATOR'S OBSERVATIONS

DATE OF EVALUATION: _____

CLERICAL APPRAISAL

Applicant's Name: _____

Position and Title
Applied For: _____

Date Interviewed: _____

Interviewed By: _____

RATING SCALE:

A = Exceeds job requirements

B = Satisfies job requirements

C = Does not satisfy job requirements

JOB FUNCTIONS AND NEEDS	A	B	C
1. TYPING SKILLS			
2. COMMUNICATION SKILLS			
3. SHORTHAND SKILLS			
4. VOCABULARY & GRAMMAR			
5. DISPOSITION & PERSONALITY			
6. ABILITY TO FOLLOW INSTRUCTIONS			
7. DESIRE TO SUCCEED			
8. MOTIVATION			

OBSERVATIONS AND RECOMMENDATIONS:

CIRCLE DECISION: THIS INDIVIDUAL SHOULD/SHOULD NOT BE HIRED.

SAMPLE EMPLOYMENT APPLICATION

NAME _____ SOC. SEC. NO. _____

ADDRESS _____

TELEPHONE ( ) _____ Are you 18 years or older? YES   NO

If hired, can you provide the documents required to prove that you are
authorized to work in the U.S.?   YES   NO

EDUCATION

Type	Name / Location	Course of Study	No. Years Completed	Degree/ Diploma
Elementary & Jr. High				
High School				
College				
Technical				
Other				

EMPLOYMENT RECORD

	Company Name / Address	Kind of Work	Date Started/ Left	Pay	Reason for Leaving
1.					
2.					
3.					
4.					

Type of Work desired _____ Desired Pay _____

How were you referred to our organization? _____

Is there any information we would need about your name or use of another name for us to be able to check your work record?   YES   NO
Please specify _____

Pre-Hiring Considerations

U.S MILITARY SERVICE

Branch of Service _____

Rank & Type of Service _____

Training/Experience Received _____

REFERENCES

Name	Occupation	Yrs. Known	Address
1. _____
2. _____
3. _____

Please list any additional information such as licenses, professional degrees, that you consider important for the job to which you have applied: _____

I understand that the employer follows an employment-at-will policy, in that I or the employer may terminate my employment any time, or for any reason consistent with applicable state or federal law. I understand that this application is not a contract of employment. I understand that to be employed I must be lawfully authorized to work in the United States, and I must show the employer documents that will prove this if I am offered the job.

I understand that the company will thoroughly investigate my work and personal history and verify all data given on the application, on related papers, and in interviews. I authorize all individuals, schools and firms named within to provide any information requested about me, and I release them from all liability for damage in providing this information.

I certify that all the statements herein are true and understand that any falsification or willful omission shall be sufficient cause for dismissal or refusal of employment.

Signature: _____ Date: _____

APPLICANTS PLEASE DO NOT WRITE BELOW THIS LINE

Interviewed by: (1)_____ (2)_____ (3)_____ (4)_____

Starting Date _____ Rate _____ Classification _____

Agency Fee Arrangements _____

Other Commitments _____

Approved by: (1) _____ (2) _____ (3) _____ (4)_____

APPLICANT CONSENT FORM TO INVESTIGATE AND DISCLOSE DATA

I, (name of applicant), hereby allow ABC Company the right to contact and investigate my former and current employers, and all other pertinent parties, including, but not limited to educational institutions where I enrolled, to fully investigate my background.

I understand that as part of the interview process, since I am applying for the position of (specify), ABC Company requires all applicants to disclose pertinent data concerning previous work history, police and military records, and educational activities.

The purpose and procedures used in this investigation have been fully described to me and I completely understand the reasons and potential uses of such investigations. I authorize ABC Company to use any and all information acquired to make decisions regarding my employment, which may be disclosed to third parties.

I understand and agree that if any material facts are discovered which differ from those facts stated by me on my employment application, at my interview, or at any time prior to my commencing employment at ABC Company (if I am offered a position with ABC Company), I will not be offered the job. Furthermore, I understand and agree that if material facts are later discovered which are inconsistent with or differ from facts I furnished before taking the job, I will be disciplined, including immediate discharge without warning.

The cost of this investigation will be paid by ABC Company. Nonetheless, I hereby indemnify, release and forever discharge and hold ABC Company and its subsidiaries and affiliated companies, agents and employees, as well as all third parties supplying such information, harmless from any and all claims, demands, judgments and legal fees arising out of or in connection with this investigation, the results, or any lawful use of the results or disclosure thereto.

_____
Signature of Applicant

_____
Printed Name of Applicant

Social Security Number:

Date:

Name of Witness:

REFERENCE CHECK FORM

To Whom It May Concern:

                         ☐ has been employed by us
_____   ☐ has applied for employment

and given the following information covering employment in your organization. We have been authorized to communicate with you for verification and such reference information as you care to give us.

(Please check if correct or change if incorrect.)

Employment dates: _____ _____

Position: _____ _____

Last earning rate: _____ _____

Reason for leaving: _____ _____

                         _____ _____

Is applicant eligible for rehire? _____

                                                    _____
                                                    Your signature

                                                    _____
                                                    Title

On the back of this letter we would appreciate any helpful comments you care to make, and will respect your confidence in this matter. The enclosed duplicate is for your own files.

                                                    Sincerely yours,

                                                    Personnel Department

OPTIONAL REFERENCE INQUIRY FORM

Date:

Name of Pertinent Contact
Title
Company Name
Company Address
Company Address

      RE: <u>Name of Applicant</u>

Dear (Name of Pertinent Contact):

(Name of Applicant) has applied for the position of (specify) with our company and has authorized us, in writing, to communicate with you for verification and reference information (copy of written authorization enclosed). Kindly complete the enclosed information sheet and return it to us immediately.

Your assistance is greatly appreciated.

                                                          Very truly yours,

                                                          HR Professional

Enc.

The Applicant provided the following data. Kindly make changes or point out inconsistencies where applicable.

Applicant: _____   S.S. No.: _____

Address: _____   Phone No.: _____

_____

Employed from: _____ to _____.

Reason for leaving:_____

_____

_____

Is the applicant eligible for rehire? ___ Yes ___ No

If not, please explain why. Attach additional sheet(s) if necessary.

Using the rating scale given, please complete the chart below.

RATING SCALE:

A = Exceeded job requirements
B = Satisfied job requirements
C = Did not satisfy job requirements

JOB FUNCTIONS AND NEEDS	A	B	C
1. OVERALL COMPETENCY			
2. COMMUNICATION SKILLS			
3. DISPOSITION & PERSONALITY			
4. ABILITY TO FOLLOW INSTRUCTIONS			
5. DESIRE TO SUCCEED			
6. MOTIVATION			

Date: _____ Name: _____ Title: _____

TELEPHONE REFERENCE INQUIRY FORM

Applicant's Name: _____

PREVIOUS EMPLOYER:

Employer's Name: _____

Interviewee Name: _____

Interviewee Title: _____

Phone No.: _____

QUESTIONS FOR PREVIOUS EMPLOYER

What was Applicant's Job Title?

What were the duties, functions and responsibilities of that job?

What were the Applicant's dates of employment?

What was the Applicant's last rate of pay?

Using the school grading system of "A" through "F", please rate the applicant's performance on the following:

JOB FUNCTIONS AND NEEDS	GRADE	REMARKS
1. Overall Competency		
2. Communication Skills		
3. Disposition & Personality		
4. Ability to Follow Instructions		
5. Desire to Succeed		
6. Motivation		
7. Attendance Record		

Pre-Hiring Considerations

TELEPHONE REFERENCE INQUIRY FORM
PAGE TWO

What was the Applicant's reason for leaving?

Would you re-hire the Applicant?

Are there any other pertinent facts you would like to add regarding the Applicant?

Interviewer's Comments:

Interviewer's Name: _____   Date: _____

ANTICIPATED JOB REQUIREMENTS SUMMARY

Assigned to: (HR Professional's Name)   Date:_____

Job is: ___ Budgeted ___ Not Budgeted

Budget Amount for Recruitment — not to exceed $_____

Departmental Interviewer(s): _____

Job is available as of: _____

_____

Department: _____ Location: _____

Job to be filled by: _____ Supervisor's Name: _____

Starting Salary Range: _____ Job Status: Exempt/Non-Exempt _____

List additional monetary and non-monetary benefits to be offered:

_____

_____

List job functions:

_____

_____

Where applicable, give number and titles of workers to be supervised by this employee.

_____

_____

List any special conditions such as relocation for successful job performance.

_____

List job criteria:

_____

_____

_____

ANTICIPATED JOB REQUIREMENTS SUMMARY
PAGE TWO

On a scale of 0 to 10, where 0 is "not applicable" and 10 is "essential", please indicate the importance of each item to the performance of this job.

General Skills:

Supervision	_____	Writing	_____
Leadership	_____	Reading	_____
Organization	_____	Proof Reading	_____
Creativity	_____	Typing	_____
Diplomacy	_____	Shorthand	_____
Analytical Skills	_____	Accountancy	_____
English Grammar	_____	Math	_____

Computers:

Programming _____ List languages:_____

Literacy _____ List software:_____

Education:

High School _____

Some College _____

Technical Diploma _____ State Type: _____

License _____ State Type: _____

Bachelor's Degree _____ Major: _____

Master's Degree _____ Major: _____

Doctorate Degree _____ Major: _____

Foreign Language _____ Language(s): _____

State any other requirements important to this position's performance on back.

SHORT FORM JOB DESCRIPTION

_____   _____
Title   Department

_____   _____
Status   Location

_____
Salary Range

This job description is written (specify date) by (Name and Title), and is approved by (Name and Title), and covers the job duties, functions and responsibilities as of this date. Changes to these duties, functions and responsibilities may be made for the benefit of the Company as a whole, and therefore, flexibility within this description is required.

_____   _____
(Name/Title)   (Name/Title)

Date: _____   Date: _____

1.   State the primary function of this position.

2.   State the purpose and need for this position.

SHORT FORM JOB DESCRIPTION
PAGE TWO

3. State essential requirements with regards to skills and education, which are necessary for the successful performance of this position.

Filed with Human Resources Department: (Name of HR Professional)

Date: _____

JOB HIRING PROGRESS SUMMARY

Title: _____   Department: _____

Supervisor: _____   Location: _____

Date:

Name of Applicant:

Referred By:

Interviewed By:

Additional Interviews By:

LIST OF ACCEPTABLE DOCUMENTS FOR IMMIGRATION CONTROL & REFORM ACT

LIST A
Documents that Establish Both Identity and Employement Eligibility

1. U.S. Passport (unexpired or expired)

2. Certificate of U.S. Citizenship (INS Form N-560 or N-561)

3. Certificate of Naturalization (INS Form N-550 or N-570)

4. Unexpired foreign passport with I-551 stamp or attached INS Form I-94 indicating unexpired employment authorization

5. Alien Registration Receipt Card with photograph (INS form I-151 or I-551)

6. Unexpired Temporary Resident Card (INS Form I-688)

7. Employment Authorization Card (INS Form I-688)

8. Unexpired Reentry Permit (INS Form I-327)

9. Unexpired Refugee Travel Document (INS Form I-571)

10. Unexpired Employment Authorization Document issued by the INS which contains a photograph (INS Form I-688B)

LIST B
Documents that Establish Identity

1. Driver's license or ID card issued by a U.S. state or outlying possession provided it contains a photograph or information such as name, date of birth, sex, height, eye color, and address

2. ID card issued by federal, state, or local government agencies or entities provided it contains a photograph or information such as name, date of birth, sex, height, eye color, and address

3. School ID card with a photograph

4. Voter's registration card

5. U.S. Military card or draft record

6. Military dependent's ID card

7. U.S. Coast Guard Merchant Mariner Card

8. Native American tribal document

9. Driver's license issued by a Canadian government authority

For persons under age 18 who are unable to present a document listed above:

10. School record or report card

11. Clinic, doctor, or hospital record

12. Day-care or nursery school record

LIST C
Documents that Establish Employment Eligibility

1. U.S. Social Security card issued by the Social Security Administration (other than a card stating that it is not valid for employment)

2. Certification of Birth Abroad issued by the Department of State (Form FS-545 or Form DS-1350)

3. Original or certified copy of a birth certificate issued by a state, county, municipal authority or outlying possession of the United States bearing an official seal

4. Native American tribal document

5. U.S. Citizen ID Card (INS Form I-197)

6. ID Card for use of Resident Citizen in the United States (INS Form I-179)

7. Unexpired employment authorization document issued by the INS (other than those listed in LIST A).

SAMPLE REJECTION LETTER TO JOB APPLICANT

Date:

Name of Applicant
Address

Dear (Name of Applicant):

We appreciate you applying for the position of (specify) at ABC Company.

Unfortunately we interviewed many applicants in the job search process and hired another individual whose credentials and qualifications were better suited for our needs.

Thus we will not be offering you the position, but thank you for your interest.

If a need arises for us to contact you in the future, we will do so and you have our continued good wishes.

Very truly yours,

HR Professional

SAMPLE REJECTION LETTER FROM UNSOLICITED RESUME

Date:

Name of Applicant
Address

Dear (Name of Applicant):

Your recent inquiry and attached resume is noted.

Due to the fact that ABC Company is not hiring at the present time (or is looking for candidates with different skills, qualifications and background), we will not be contacting you for an interview.

I am returning your resume and thank you for your interest in ABC Company.

Good luck in your future endeavors.

Very truly yours,

HR Professional

Enc.

CHECKLIST OF IMPORTANT HIRING CONCERNS

1. Always confirm the employment relationship with the employee in writing after it has been agreed upon.

2. Consider the use of arbitration clauses in your employment agreements.

3. Consider the use of restrictive covenants in your employment agreements.

4. Carefully review all written agreements submitted to your company by employment agencies.

5. Be sure there is a clear understanding with any employment agency as to when a fee is earned.

6. Request reimbursement of the fee if the employee only works a short time and get this guarantee in writing.

7. Always confirm the placement fee in writing.

8. To avoid problems with competing employment agencies, hire only one or two at the same time.

9. Carefully scrutinize all contracts with outplacement firms before hiring and prepare written agreements which discuss how additional fees may be incurred.

10. Contact your nearest The Department of Labor office to be sure your company complies with all appropriate benefits laws affecting part-time workers.

11. Understand the law pertaining to overtime, vacations, lunch breaks and coffee breaks affecting part-time workers.

12. Be sure to explain to part-time workers what fringe benefits are not available to them.

13. Analyze your company's position with respect to shorter holidays, vacations, paid sick leave and other benefits for part-time workers.

14. Understand the distinction between employee and independent contractor status.

15. Draft employee manuals which give employees a clear description of all benefits, states rules for on-the-job behavior, and discusses criteria used for evaluating job performance.

16. Reserve the right in your company manual in conspicuous language to alter benefits without warning or notice where warranted at the company's sole discretion.

17. To avoid exposing your company to an IRS tax audit, or reduce the chances of handling an audit incorrectly, impose compliance rules for reimbursement to directly-related business expenses.

18. Always have a written policy that sets forth record keeping requirements, reimbursement rules for company-related expenses, and penalties the worker may sustain for not following such policies.

19. Understand the impact that the Fair Labor Standards Act has with respect to travel and overtime.

20. Prepare a waiver whenever you are given a valuable money saving idea by an employee to reduce potential litigation; make sure the employee signs the document before accepting the idea for consideration.

EMPLOYMENT NEGOTIATING CHECKLIST

☐ Date employment is to begin.

☐ Length of employment: Is employment for a definite term (e.g., one year) or at-will (e.g., terminable at any time with or without notice)? If a definite term, is the contract renewable after the expiration of the original period? Can one or both parties terminate the agreement prior to the expiration of the term? How much notice must be given before the termination is effective?

☐ Define the employee's title.

☐ Specify employment duties. Will the employee report to a superior?

☐ Number of required working hours, sick days, holidays and vacations. If the employee does not use sick days and holidays, can they be taken in the following year, are they lost, or will the employee be paid for them?

☐ Employment status: Is the individual considered an employee or independent contractor?

☐ Amount of base salary: When is it payable? Specify all deductions from the employee's paycheck.

☐ Are expenses reimbursable? What, when, how and to what extent?

☐ Are bonuses paid? How are they calculated and when are they paid? Are prorated bonuses given if the employee is fired or resigns prior to the natural expiration of his/her contract?

☐ Are commissions paid? If so, specify how they are earned. Is the commission a gross or net amount: If net, what deductions are included?

☐ Are there fringe benefits? For example, does the company offer use of an automobile, free parking, car insurance, gasoline allowances, death benefits, prepaid legal services, medical, dental and hospitalization costs, life insurance, company credit cards, stock options, pension and profit-sharing plans? Be sure to advise the employee of all of the ramifications of the benefit package (e.g., when does the pension or profit-sharing plan vest?).

☐ Possibility of job advancement. Are periodic raises given? What is the procedure for merit raises?

☐ What happens in the event of disability? Define the meaning of temporary and permanent disability.

☐ Discuss the company policy in terms of maternity and paternity leave.

☐ Is a physical examination necessary?

☐ Will relocation ever be required? If so, specify who will pay for it and the manner of reimbursement.

☐ Can the employee have side ventures in a non-competing business or must the employee work exclusively on a full-time basis?

☐ Will the company require the employee to sign an agreement containing a restrictive covenant prohibiting him/her from working for a competitor or setting up a competing business? If so, for how long will the restriction last and what territory will be involved?

☐ Who owns inventions and processes created by the employee during employment?

☐ How will formal notices be communicated by one party to the other?

☐ Can the contract be assigned?

☐ What happens if the company is sold, acquired or merged during the employee's employment?

☐ Will disputes be handled by litigation or binding arbitration?

☐ It is also a good idea to discuss other matters which should be included in the company manual:
    Time clock regulations (if any)
    Rest periods
    Absences
    Safety and accident prevention
    Authorized use of telephone
    Reporting complaints
    Bereavement pay, jury duty, personal days
    Company policy regarding drugs and alcohol
    No solicitation or distribution rules
    Rules of conduct
    Code of ethics and confidential policies

SALES EMPLOYMENT CHECKLIST

COMPENSATION

Salary (usually given to company-employed salespeople)

☐ What is the amount and when is it payable?

Draw (usually given to independent sales reps)

☐ Is it applied against commission?

☐ What is the amount and when is it payable?

☐ The draw can be stopped by the company any time without prior notice when commission earnings do not exceed draw.

☐ The sales rep is personally liable for repayment when draw exceeds commission earnings or when the rep is fired from his job.

☐ The company has the right to set off draw and reduce the amount of commission owed upon termination of the employment relationship.

Bonus (usually given to company-employed salespeople)

☐ Is the bonus gratuitous or enforceable by contract?

☐ What is the amount and when is it payable?

☐ Specify that prorated bonuses will not be given in the event the salesperson resigns or is fired prior to the date when the bonus will be paid. Avoid basing the bonus on a determination of profits because this may give the salesperson the right to inspect your company's books and records.

COMMISSION

☐ Specify the commission rate and when it is payable.

☐ Avoid guaranteed shipping arrangements.

☐ Specify split commission policies if applicable.

☐ Specify all deductions from commission, how and when they are computed? e.g., returns, freight charges, unauthorized price concessions given by the salesperson, billing and advertising discounts, collection charges, failure of the customer to pay.

☐ Specify commission for large orders, special customers, off-price goods, and reorders.

Expenses (usually for company-employed salespeople)

☐ Specify the kind and amount of expenses that are reimbursable.

☐ Specify the kind of documentation the salesperson must supply in order to receive reimbursement.

TERRITORY

☐ Are you giving exclusive or non-exclusive territorial rights? Define the particular territory and customers.

☐ Be sure to discuss all house accounts and document these in writing.

☐ What about products sold in one territory and shipped into another? Determine how this will affect your split commission policy.

☐ Can the salesperson sell in other territories not solicited by other salespeople, e.g., at trade shows?

☐ If exclusive territorial rights are not involved, insure that the salesperson will not receive commission for orders not actually solicited by him.

DUTIES

☐ Exercise best efforts in representing the company and its products or services.

☐ Make no representations, warranties, or commitments binding that company without the company's prior consent.

☐ The salesperson will be personally liable and required to reimburse the company in the event he exceeds his authority.

☐ Forward all field inquiries or complaints in the field to the company immediately.

☐ Must work full-time for the company without any sideline. Especially, must not represent or form a competing business.

DUTIES (cont.)

☐ Must personally solicit the product and cannot hire an associate to represent the company without prior written approval.

☐ Maintain minimum general and automobile liability coverage in excess of $___ per occurrence.

☐ Attend sales meetings, both local and national.

☐ Call on accounts periodically, service accounts, and maintain accurate selling records and lead sheets.

☐ Assist in any collection efforts requested by the company.

☐ Promise to protect all trade secrets, customer lists, and other forms of confidential information acquired while working for the company.

LENGTH OF EMPLOYMENT

☐ Date employment is to begin.

☐ Length of employment. Is employment at-will (the salesperson can be fired any time) or for a definite term, say two years?

☐ If employment is at-will, is notice required?

☐ If so, when must it be sent for the termination to be effective and how must it be sent (e.g., certified or regular mail?)

☐ Never give assurance of job security if you are hiring a salesperson at-will.

☐ If employment is for a definite term, is the contract renewed under the same terms and conditions after the expiration of the original agreement? Must notice be sent to confirm this?

☐ Peg employment to a minimum sales quota if applicable.

TERMINATION

☐ Clarify when commissions stop: e.g., upon termination, upon shipment of an order, upon shipment with a final cut-off date, to eliminate the problem with reorders.

☐ Avoid severance compensation arrangements. Specify when a final accounting will be made.

☐ Limit the right of the salesperson to sue for commission within a specific period.

☐ Specify the prompt return of all samples, customer lists, orders, field information, with a penalty if not complied with.

☐ Include a restrictive covenant for additional protection in writing.

CHECKLIST OF IMPORTANT POINTS TO FOLLOW REGARDING CONTRACT EXECUTION

1. Discuss all employment terms in advance

2. Legal disputes often arise because many companies hire workers on a handshake; thus prepare an employment agreement with each employee to protect your company

3. Remember that your position is strongest before the hiring so include many favorable provisions in the confirmation letter or employment agreement

4. With written contracts you can insert restrictive covenants that are reasonable in terms of geographic scope and time limitations for additional protection

5. Consider arbitration to resolve employment disputes and add this clause to your employment agreements where applicable

6. When employment contracts are issued, be sure that all changes, strikeouts and erasures are initialed by a company officer and the employee

7. Be sure all blanks are filled in if your company uses a standard employment contract

8. If additions are necessary, include them in a space provided or attach them to the contract itself; then note on the contract that addenda have been accepted by both parties

9. Always review and respond in writing to any comments or proposed amendments to the contract you may have received from the potential employee so your lack of notice will not be viewed as an acceptance

10. Be sure your agreement is signed by the employee

11. Always avoid promises of lifetime employment or "jobs for life" for obvious reasons

TWENTY FACTOR CHECKLIST TO DETERMINE INDEPENDENT CONTRACTOR V. EMPLOYEE STATUS

As an aid to determining whether an individual is an employee under the common law rules, twenty factors or elements have been identified as indicating whether sufficient control is present to establish an employer-employee relationship. The twenty factors have been developed based on an examination of cases and rulings considering whether an individual is an employee. The degree of importance of each factor varies depending on the occupation and the factual context in which the services are performed. The twenty factors are designed only as guides for determining whether an individual is an employee; special scrutiny is required in applying the twenty factors to assure that formalistic aspects of an arrangement designed to achieve a particular status do not obscure the substance of the arrangement (that is, whether the person or persons for whom the services are performed exercise sufficient control over the individual for the individual to be classified as an employee). The twenty factors are described below:

☐ **1. Instructions.** A worker who is required to comply with other persons' instructions about when, where, and how he or she is to work is ordinarily an employee. This control factor is present if the person or persons for whom the services are performed have the right to require compliance with instructions. See, for example, Rev. Rul. 68-598, 1968-2 C.B. 464, and Rev. Rul. 66-381, 1966-2 C.B. 449.

☐ **2. Training.** Training a worker by requiring an experienced employee to work with the worker, by corresponding with the worker, by requiring the worker to attend meetings, or by using other methods, indicates that the person or persons for whom the services are performed want the services performed in a particular method or manner. See Rev. Rul. 70-630, 1970-2 C.B. 229.

☐ **3. Integration.** Integration of the worker's services into the business operation generally shows that the worker is subject to direction and control. When the success or continuation of a business depends to an appreciable degree upon the performance of certain services, the workers who perform those services must necessarily be subject to a certain amount of control by the owner of the business. See United States v. Silk, 331 U.S. 704 (1947), 1947-2 C.B. 167.

☐ **4. Services Rendered Personally.** If the services must be rendered personally presumably the person or persons for whom the services are performed are interested in the methods used to accomplish the work as well as in the result. See Rev. Rul. 55-695, 1955-2 C.B.H. 410

☐ **5. Hiring, Supervising, and Paying Assistants.** If the person or persons for whom the services are performed hire, supervise, and pay assistants, that factor generally shows control over the workers on the job. However, if one worker hired supervises, and pays the other assistant pursuant to a contract under which the worker agrees to provide materials and labor and under which the worker is responsible only for the attainment of a result, this factor indicates an independent contractor status. Compare Rev. Rul 63-115, 1963-1 C.B. 178, with Rev. Rul. 55-593, 1955-2 C.B. 610.

☐ **6. Continuing Relationship.** A continuing relationship between the worker and the person or persons for whom the services are performed indicates that an employer-employee relationship exists. A continuing relationship may exist where work is performed at frequently recurring although irregular intervals. See United States V. Silk.

☐ **7. Set Hours of Work.** The establishment of set hours of work by the person or persons for whom the services are performed is a factor indicating control. See Rev. Rul. 73-591, 1973-2 C.B. 337.

☐ **8. Full Time Required.** If the worker must devote substantially full time to the business of the person or persons for whom the services are performed, such person or persons have control over the amount of time the worker spends working and impliedly restrict the worker from doing other gainful work. An independent contractor, on the other hand, is free to work when and for whom he or she chooses. See Rev. Rul. 56-694, 1956-2 C.B. 694.

☐ **9. Doing Work on Employer's Premises.** If the work is performed on the premises of the person or persons for whom the services are performed, that factor suggests control over the worker, especially if the work could be done elsewhere. Rev. Rul. 56-660, 1956-2 C.B. 693. Work done off the premises of the person or persons receiving the services, such as the office worker, indicates some freedom from control. However, this fact by itself does not mean that the worker is not an employee. The importance of this factor depends on the nature of the service involved and the extent to which an employer generally would require that employees perform such services on the employer's premises. Control over the place of work is indicated when the person or persons for whom the services are performed have the right to compel the worker to travel a designated route to canvass a territory within a certain time, or to work at specific places as required. See Rev. Rul. 56-694.

☐ **10. Order or Sequence Set.** If a worker must perform services in the order or sequence set by the person or persons for whom the services are performed, that factor shows that the worker is not free to follow the worker's own pattern of work but must follow the established routines and schedules of the person or persons for whom the services are performed. Often, because of the nature of an occupation, the person or persons for whom the services are being performed do not set the order of the services or set the order infrequently. It is sufficient to show control, however, if such person or persons retain the right to do so. See Rev. Rul 56-694.

☐ **11. Oral or Written Reports.** A requirement that the worker submit regular or written reports to the person or persons for whom the services are performed indicates a degree of control. See Rev. Rul 70-309, 1970-1 C.B. 199, and Rev. Rul. 68-248, 1968-1 C.B. 431.

☐ **12. Payment by Hour, Week, Month.** Payment by the hour, week, or month generally points to an employer-employee relationship, provided that this method of payment is not just a convenient way of paying a lump sum agreed upon as the cost of a job. Payment made by the job or on a straight commission generally indicates that the worker is an independent contractor. See Rev. Rul. 74-389, 1974-2 C.B. 330.

☐ **13. Payment of Business and/or Traveling Expenses.** If the person or persons for whom the services are performed ordinarily pay the worker's business and/or traveling expenses, the worker is ordinarily an employee. An employer, to be able to control expenses, generally retains the right to regulate and direct the worker's business activities. See Rev. Rul. 55-144, 1955-1 C.B. 483.

☐ **14. Furnishing of Tools and Materials.** The fact that the person or persons for whom the services are performed furnish significant tools, materials, and other equipment tends to show the existence of an employer-employee relationship. See Rev. Rul 71-524, 1971-2 C.B. 346.

☐ **15. Significant Investment.** If the worker invests in facilities that are used by the worker in performing services and are not typically maintained by employees (such as the maintenance of an office rented at fair value from an unrelated party), that factor tends to indicate that the worker is an independent contractor. On the other hand, lack of investment in facilities indicates dependence on the person or persons for whom the services are performed for such facilities and, accordingly, the existence of an employer-employee relationship. See Rev. Rul. 71-524. Special scrutiny is required with respect to certain types of facilities, such as home offices.

☐ **16. Realization of Profit or Loss.** A worker who can realize a profit or suffer a loss as a result of the worker's services (in addition to the profit or loss ordinarily realized by employees) is generally an independent contractor, but the worker who cannot is an employee. See Rev. Rul 70-309. For example, if the worker is subject to a real risk of economic loss due to significant investments or a bona fide liability for expenses, such as salary payments to unrelated employees, that factor indicates that the worker is an independent contractor. The risk that a worker will not receive payment for his or her services, however, is common to both independent contractors and employees and thus does not constitute a sufficient economic risk to support treatment as an independent contractor.

☐ **17. Working for More Than One Firm at a Time.** If a worker performs more than de minimis services for a multiple of unrelated persons or firms at the same time, that factor generally indicates that the worker is an independent contractor. See Rev. Rul 70-572, 1970-2 C.B. 221. However, a worker who performs services for more than one person may be an employee of each of the persons, especially where such persons are part of the same service arrangement.

☐ **18. Making Service Available to General Public.** The fact that a worker makes his or her services available to the general public on a regular and consistent basis indicates an independent contractor relationship. See Rev. Rul 56-660.

☐ **19. Right to Discharge.** The right to discharge a worker is a factor indicating that the worker is an employee and the person possessing the right is an employer. An employer exercises control through the threat of dismissal, which causes the worker to obey the employer's instructions. An independent contractor, on the other hand, cannot be fired so long as the independent contractor produces a result that meets the contract specifications. Rev. Rul 75-41, 1975-1 C.B. 323.

☐ **20. Right to Terminate.** If the worker has the right to end his or her relationship with the person for whom the services are performed at any time he or she wishes without incurring liability, that factor indicates an employer-employee relationship. See Rev. Rul. 70-309.

CHECKLIST TO DETERMINE OVERTIME LIABILITY UNDER THE FAIR LABOR STANDARDS ACT
(Executives)

Factors to govern exempt status for Executives:

1. Supervises a division or department;

2. Generally manages the work of subordinates on a consistent basis;

3. Has authority to hire and discharge employees or make personnel decisions;

4. Has the discretion to implement numbers 2 and 3 above;

5. Devotes a small percentage (less than 20%) of time to work unrelated to the above; and

6. Is paid a salary which remains constant and fixed and does not necessarily reflect the number of hours the executive actually worked.

NOTE: If the above conditions are met, the individual may not be subject to receive overtime pay but check with labor counsel or your local Department of Labor Office for pertinent details when in doubt.

CHECKLIST TO DETERMINE OVERTIME LIABILITY UNDER THE FAIR LABOR STANDARDS ACT
(Administrators)

Factors to govern exempt status for Administrators:

1. Is engaged in office or other non-manual work related to operations and management;

2. Often used independent judgement;

3. Supervises employees as or in an administrative function;

4. Engages in duties which require specialized skills;

5. Performs special projects independently without much specific supervision;

6. Devotes a small percentage (less than 20%) of time to work unrelated to the above; and

7. Is paid a salary which remains constant and fixed and does not necessarily reflect the number of hours the administrator actually worked.

NOTE: If the above conditions are met, the individual may not be subject to receive overtime pay but check with labor counsel or your local Department of Labor Office for pertinent details when in doubt.

HIRING RESULTS SUMMARY FORM

MONTH: _____   **YEAR:** _____

1. __ Number of job openings at beginning of month.

2. __ Number of resumes reviewed.

3. __ Number of formal interviews conducted.

4. __ Number of formal job offers.

5. __ Number of rejections.

6. __ Number of job openings at end of month.

Completed By: _____   _____
                               Name of Employee   Date

                               _____
                               Title

Reviewed By: _____   _____   _____
                               Name of Employee   Date

                               _____
                               Title

Pre-Hiring Considerations

LETTER CONFIRMATION OF JOB OFFER

Date:

Name of Applicant
Address

Dear (Name of Applicant):

We are pleased to offer you the position of (specify) at ABC Company.

Your job will commence on (specify date) and your starting salary will be (specify) per week.

Please report to (name of supervisor) on (specify) prior to your commencement of employment. You will be required to complete necessary payroll and personnel forms and your benefits package will be explained to you in detail. Additionally, we require every employee of ABC Company to complete the enclosed Confirmation of At-Will Employment Form and sign a standard Employment Agreement and Non-Competition and Confidentiality Agreement prior to your actual start date.

We look forward to your arrival at ABC Company.

If you have any questions of comments, please call me immediately.

                                                           Very truly yours,

                                                           HR Professional

Enc.

CONFIRMATION OF AT-WILL EMPLOYMENT FORM

I, (name of applicant), have received a job offer for the position of (specify) from ABC Company.

This letter confirms that no one at ABC Company has made any representations or promises that the job which I am accepting offers guaranteed employment or job security of any kind.

I understand that I have the right to leave the position at any time with or without notice and that I may be discharged at any time with or without cause or notice.

All pertinent conditions of the job offer are contained in the employment agreement I will be given and which I will sign before commencing employment with ABC Company and that all terms concerning my job will be contained in this employment agreement, which may not be modified orally.

Finally, I understand that I will be required to sign a Non-Competition and Confidentiality Agreement prior to my actual starting date as a final pre-condition of my employment.

I am returning this Confirmation immediately and have received a copy for my files:

_____
Signature of Applicant

_____
Printed Name of Applicant

Social Security Number:

Date:

SAMPLE CONFIDENTIALITY AND NON-COMPETITION AGREEMENT

In consideration of my employment or continued employment by [Name of Company] (the "Company"), together with its affiliates and subsidiaries, and any subsidiaries or affiliates which hereafter may be formed or acquired and in recognition of the fact that as an employee of the Company I will have access to the Company's customers and to confidential and valuable business information of the Company and of its parent company, [specify], together with its affiliates and subsidiaries, and any subsidiaries or affiliates which hereafter may be formed or acquired, I hereby agree as follows:

1. The Company's Business. The Company is [specify] a consulting firm. The Company is committed to quality and service in every aspect of its business. I understand that the Company looks to and expects from its employees a high level of competence, cooperation, loyalty, integrity, initiative, and resourcefulness. I understand that as an employee of the Company, I will have substantial contact with the Company's customers and potential customers.

I further understand that all business and fees including insurance, bond, risk management, self insurance, insurance consulting and other services produced or transacted through my efforts shall be the sole property of the Company, and that I shall have no right to share in any commission or fee resulting from the conduct of such business other than as compensation referred to in paragraph 3 hereof. All checks or bank drafts received by me from any customer or account shall be made payable to the Company, and all premiums, commissions or fees that I may collect shall be in the name of and on behalf of the Company.

2. Duties Of Employee. I shall comply with all Company rules, procedures and standards governing the conduct of employees and their access to and use of the Company's property, equipment and facilities. I understand that the Company will make reasonable efforts to inform me of the rules, standards and procedures which are in effect from time to time and which apply to me.

3. Compensation And Benefits. I shall receive the compensation as is mutually agreed upon, which may be adjusted from time to time, as full compensation for services performed under this Agreement. In addition, I may participate in such employee benefit plans and receive such other fringe benefits, subject to the same eligibility requirements, as are afforded other Company employees in my job classification. I understand that these employee benefit plans and fringe benefits may be amended, enlarged, or diminished by the Company from time to time, at its discretion.

4. Management Of The Company. The Company may manage and direct its business affairs as it sees fit, including, without limitation, the assignment of sales territories, notwithstanding any employee's individual interest in or expectation regarding a particular business location or customer account.

5. Termination Of Employment. My employment may be terminated by the Company or me at any time, with or without notice or cause. Upon termination of my employment, I shall be entitled to receive incentive payments in accordance with the provisions of the Company's Incentive Plan, as it may be modified by the Company from time to time, less any adjustments for amounts owed by me to the Company. I understand that I may also receive additional compensation at the discretion of the Company and in accordance with the published Company Personnel Policy on Termination Pay.

6. Agreement Not To Compete With The Company.

A. As long as I am employed by the Company, I shall not participate directly or indirectly, in any capacity, in any business or activity that is in competition with the Company.

B. In consideration of my employment rights under this Agreement and in recognition of the fact that I will have access to the confidential information of the Company and that the Company's relationships with their customers and potential customers constitute a substantial part of their good will, I agree that for One (1) year from and after termination of my employment, for any reason, unless acting with the Company's express prior written consent, I shall not, directly or indirectly, in any capacity, solicit or accept business from, provide consulting services of any kind to, or perform any of the services offered by the Company for, any of the Company's customers or prospects with whom I had business dealings in the year next preceding the termination of my employment.

7. Unauthorized Disclosure Of Confidential Information. While employed by the Company and thereafter, I shall not, directly or indirectly, disclose to anyone outside of the Company any Confidential Information or use any confidential Information (as hereinafter defined) other than pursuant to my employment by and for the benefit of the Company.

The term "Confidential Information" as used throughout this Agreement means any and all trade secrets and any and all data or information not generally known outside of the Company whether prepared or developed by or for the Company or received by the Company from any outside source. Without limiting the scope of this definition, Confidential Information includes any customer files, customer lists, any business, marketing, financial or sales record, data, plan, or survey; and any other record or information relating to the present or future business, product or service of the Company. All Confidential Information and copies thereof are the sole property of the Company.

Notwithstanding the foregoing, the term Confidential Information shall not apply to information that the Company has voluntarily disclosed to the public without restriction, or which has otherwise lawfully entered the public domain.

8. Prior Obligations. I have informed the Company in writing of any and all continuing obligations that require me not to disclose to the Company any information or that limit my opportunity or capacity to compete with any previous employer.

9. Employee's Obligation To Cooperate. At any time upon request of the Company (and at the Company's expense), I shall execute all documents and perform all lawful acts the

Company considers necessary or advisable to secure its rights hereunder and to carry out the intent of this Agreement.

10. Return Of Property. At any time upon request of the Company, and upon termination of my employment, I shall return promptly to the Company, including all copies of all Confidential Information or Developments, and all records, files, blanks, forms, materials, supplies, and any other materials furnished, used or generated by me during the course of my employment, and any copies of the foregoing, all of which I recognize to be the sole property of the Company.

11. Special Remedies. I recognize that money damages alone would not adequately compensate the Company in the event of breach by me of this Agreement, and I therefore agree that, in addition to all other remedies available to the Company at law or in equity, the Company shall be entitled to injunctive relief for the enforcement hereof. Failure by the Company to insist upon strict compliance with any of the terms, covenants, or conditions hereof shall not be deemed a waiver of such terms, covenants or conditions.

12. Miscellaneous Provisions. This Agreement contains the entire and only agreement between me and the Company respecting the subject matter hereof and supersedes all prior agreements and understandings between us as to the subject matter hereof; and no modification shall be binding upon me or the Company unless made in writing and signed by me and an authorized officer of the Company.

My obligations under this Agreement shall survive the termination of my employment with the Company regardless of the manner of or reasons for such termination, and regardless of whether such termination constitutes a breach of this Agreement or of any other agreement I may have with the Company. If any provisions of this Agreement are held or deemed unenforceable or too broad to permit enforcement of such provision to its full extent, then such provision shall be enforced to the maximum extent permitted by law. If any of the provisions of this Agreement shall be construed to be illegal or invalid, the validity of any other provision hereof shall not be affected thereby.

This Agreement shall be governed and construed according to the laws of [specify State], and shall be deemed to be effective as of the first day of my employment by the Company.

BY SIGNING THIS AGREEMENT, I ACKNOWLEDGE THAT I HAVE READ AND UNDERSTOOD ALL OF ITS PROVISIONS AND THAT I AGREE TO BE FULLY BOUND BY THE SAME.

Employee: _____ Date: _____

Accepted By: _____ Date: _____
       [Name and Title of Officer]

STANDARD EMPLOYMENT AGREEMENT

EMPLOYMENT AGREEMENT, entered into and effective as of between ("Company"), and ("Employee").

1.   Employment, Duties and Acceptance

1.1   Company hereby employs Employee for the Term (as defined in Section 2 hereof) to render exclusive and full-time services in an executive capacity to Company and to the subsidiaries of Company engaged in the business of [specify] and in connection therewith to devote his best efforts to the affairs of the Company and to perform such duties as Employee shall reasonable be directed to perform by officers of the Company.

1.2   Employee hereby accepts such employment and agrees to render such services. Employee agrees to render such services at Company's offices located in the [specify location] area, but Employee will travel on temporary trips to such other place or places as may be required from time to time to perform his duties hereunder. During the Term hereof, Employee will not render any services for others, or for Employee's own account, in the business of [specify] and will not render any services to any supplier or significant customer of Company.

2.   Term of Employment

2.1   The term of Employee's employment pursuant to this Agreement (the "Term") shall begin on the date hereof, and shall end on   , subject to the provisions of Article 4 of this Agreement providing for earlier termination of Employee's employment in certain circumstances.

3.   Compensation

3.1   As compensation for all services to be rendered pursuant to this Agreement to or at the request of Company, Company agrees to pay Employee a salary at the rate of $ per annum.

The Salary set forth hereinabove shall be payable in accordance with the regular payroll practices of the Company for executives. All payments hereunder shall be subject to the provisions of Article 4 hereof.

3.2   Company shall pay or reimburse Employee for all necessary and reasonable expenses incurred or paid by Employee in connection with the performance of services under this Agreement upon presentation of expense statements or vouchers or such other supporting information as it from time to time requests evidencing the nature of such expense, and, if appropriate, the payment thereof by Employee, and otherwise in accordance with Company procedures from time to time in effect.

3.3   During the Term, Employee shall be entitled to participate in any group insurance, qualified pension, hospitalization, medical health and accident, disability, or similar plan or program of the Company now existing or hereafter established to the extent that he is eligible under the general provisions thereof. Notwithstanding anything herein to the contrary, however, Company shall have the right to amend or terminate any such plans or programs.

4. Termination

4.1 Disability. If Employee shall be prevented from performing Employee's usual duties for a period of 3 consecutive months, or for shorter periods aggregating more than 4 months in any 12 month period by reason of physical or mental disability, total or partial, (herein referred to as "disability"), Company shall nevertheless continue to pay full salary up to and including the last day of the third consecutive month of disability, or the day on which the shorter periods of disability shall have equalled a total of 4 months, but Company may at any time or times on or after such last day (but before the termination of such disability), elect to terminate this Agreement upon written notice to employee, effective on such 1st day, without further obligation or liability to Employee, except for any compensation accrued hereunder but not yet paid. If Company does not so elect, this Agreement shall remain in full force and effect, except that Company shall not be obligated to pay any compensation set forth in Article 3 hereof to Employee during the remaining period of disability.

4.2 Death. In the event of Employee's death during the Term, this Agreement shall automatically terminate, except that (a) Employee's estate shall be entitled to receive the compensation provided for hereunder to the last day of the month in which Employee's death occurs; and (b) such termination shall not affect any amounts payable as insurance or other death benefits under any plans or arrangements then in force or effect with respect to Employee.

4.3 Specified Cause. Company may at any time during the Term, by notice, terminate the employment of Employee for malfeasance, misfeasance, or nonfeasance in connection with the performance of Employee's duties, the cause to be specified in the notice of termination. Without limiting the generality of the foregoing, the following acts during the Term shall constitute grounds for termination of employment hereunder:

4.3.1 Any willful and intentional act having the effect of injuring the reputation, business, business relationships of Company or its affiliates;

4.3.2 Conviction of or entering a plea of nolo contendere to a charge of a felony or a misdemeanor involving moral turpitude;

4.3.3 Material breach of covenants contained in this Agreement; and

4.3.4 Repeated or continuous failure, neglect, or refusal to perform Employee's duties hereunder.

5. Protection of Confidential Information

5.1 In view of the fact that Employee's work as an employee of Company will bring Employee into close contact with many confidential affairs of the Company and its affiliates, including matters of a business nature, such as information about costs, profits, markets, sales, and any other information not readily available to the public, and plans for future developments, Employee agrees:

    5.1.1 To keep secret all confidential matters of Company and its affiliates and not to disclose them to anyone outside of Company, either during or after Employee's employment with Company, except with Company's written consent; and

    5.1.2 To deliver promptly to Company on termination of Employee's employment by Company, or at any time Company may so request, all memoranda, notes, records, reports, and other documents (and all copies thereof) relating to Company's and its affiliates' businesses which Employee may then possess or have under the Employee's control.

6. Ownership of Results of Services:

6.1 Company shall own, and Employee hereby transfers and assigns to it, all rights of every kind and character throughout the work, in perpetuity, in and to any material and/or ideas written, suggested, or submitted by Employee hereunder and all other results and proceeds of Employee's services hereunder, whether the same consists of literary, dramatic, mechanical or any other form of works, themes, ideas, creations, products, or compositions. Employee agrees to execute and deliver to Company such assignments or other instruments as Company may require from time to time to evidence its ownership of the results and proceeds of Employee's services.

7. Notices:

7.1 All notices, requests, consents and other communications required or permitted to be given hereunder shall be in writing and shall be deemed to have been duly given if delivered personally or sent by prepaid telegram, or mailed first-class, postage prepaid, as follows:

If to Employee:	address
If to Company:	address
With copies to:	address

or as such other addresses as either party may specify by written notice to the other as provided in this Section 7.1.

8. General

8.1 It is acknowledged that the rights of Company under this Agreement are of a special, unique, and intellectual character which gives them a peculiar value, and that a breach of any provision of this Agreement (particularly, but not limited to, the exclusivity provisions hereof and the provisions of Article 5 hereof), will cause Company irreparable injury and damage which cannot be reasonably or adequately compensated in damages in an action at law. Accordingly, without limiting any right or remedy which Company may have in the premises, Employee specifically agrees that Company shall be entitled to seek injunctive relief to enforce and protect its rights under this Agreement.

8.2 This Agreement sets forth the entire agreement and understanding of the parties hereto, and supersedes all prior agreements, arrangements, and understandings. Nothing herein contained shall be construed so as to require the commission of any act contrary to law and wherever there is any conflict between any provision of this Agreement and any present or future statute, law, ordinance or regulation, the latter shall prevail, but in such event the provision of this Agreement affected shall be curtailed and limited only to the extent necessary to bring it within legal requirements. Without limiting the generality of the foregoing, in the event that any compensation or other monies payable hereunder shall be in excess of the amount permitted by any such statute, law, ordinance, or regulation, payment of the maximum amount allowed thereby shall constitute full compliance by Company with the payment requirements of this Agreement.

8.3 No representation, promise, or inducement has been made by either party that is not embodied in this Agreement, and neither party shall be bound by or liable for any alleged representation, promise, or inducement not so set forth. The section headings contained herein are for reference purposes only and shall not in any way affect the meaning or interpretation of this Agreement.

8.4 The provisions of this Agreement shall inure to the benefit of the parties hereto, their heirs, legal representatives, successors, and assigns. This Agreement, and Employee's rights and obligations hereunder, may not be assigned by Employee. Company may assign its rights, together with its obligations, hereunder in connection with any sale, transfer or other disposition of all or substantially all of its business and assets. Company may also assign this Agreement to any affiliate of Company; provided, however, that no such assignment shall (unless Employee shall so agree in writing) release Company of liability directly to Employee for the due performance of all of the terms, covenants, and conditions of this Agreement to be complied with and performed by Company. The term "affiliate," as used in this agreement, shall mean any corporation, firm, partnership, or other entity controlling, controlled by or under common control with Company. The term "control" (including "controlling," "controlled by," and "under common control with"), as used in the preceding sentence, shall be deemed to mean the possession, directly or indirectly, of the power to direct or cause the direction of the management and policies of such corporation, firm, partnership, or other entity, whether through ownership of voting securities or by contract or otherwise.

8.5   This Agreement may be amended, modified, superseded, cancelled, renewed or extended, and the terms or covenants hereof may be waived, only by a written instrument executed by both of the parties hereto, or in the case of a waiver, by the party waiving compliance. The failure of either party at any time or times to require performance of any provisions hereof shall in no manner affect the right at a later time to enforce the same. No waiver by either party of the breach of any term or covenant contained in this Agreement, whether by conduct or otherwise, in any one or more instances, shall be deemed to be, or construed as, a further or continuing waiver of any such breach, or a waiver of the breach of any other term or covenant contained in this Agreement.

8.6   This Agreement shall be governed by and construed according to the laws of the State of [specify state] applicable to agreements to be wholly performed therein.

IN WITNESS WHEREOF, the parties hereto have duly executed this Agreement as of the date first above written.

[Name of Company]   [Name of Employee]

By: _____   _____

Title: _____   Date: _____

Date:_____

SAMPLE EMPLOYMENT AGREEMENT—LONG VERSION
(Typically given to executives with a definite term of employment)

Employment Agreement dated as of [specify], by and between [specify Name of Company], a [specify state] corporation with its principal place of business at [specify address] (the "Company"), and [specify Name of Employee] (the "Employee").

WHEREAS, effective January 1, 1994 the Company and the Employee entered into an employment agreement, which agreement terminated December 31, 1996; and

WHEREAS, the Company desires to continue to employ the Employee, and the Employee desires to continue his employment with the Company; and

WHEREAS, the Company and the Employee wish to set forth the terms and conditions of the Employee's employment with the Company.

NOW, THEREFORE, in consideration of the mutual promises, warranties and covenants set forth below, the parties hereto, intending to be legally bound, hereby agree as follows:

1. Employment. Effective as of the commencement date described in Section 2 below, the Company employs the Employee and the Employee accepts employment by the Company upon the terms and conditions hereafter set forth.

2. Term of Employment. The employment of the Employee under this Agreement shall commence as of January 1, 1997 and terminate on December 31, 1998. Thereafter, this Agreement shall be extended automatically for successive terms of One (1) year unless (i) the Company or the Employee shall give written notice of termination to the other party hereto at least Sixty (60) days prior to the termination of the initial term of employment hereunder or any renewal term thereof, or (ii) unless earlier terminated as herein provided. The initial term of this Agreement and any renewal term thereof are hereinafter collectively referred to as the "Employment Period."

3. Scope of Duties. During the Employment Period, the Employee shall be employed as [specify] as well as such other duties and responsibilities which may be assigned to him by a Company manager or official. The Employee shall perform such service in good faith and comply with all rules, regulations and policies established or issued by the Company.

4. Extent of Service. The Employee shall devote his entire time, attention and energies to the business of the Company, and shall not during the Employment period engage in any other business activity which in the judgment of the Company conflicts with the duties of the Employee hereunder.

5. Compensation. In consideration of the services rendered by the Employee hereunder, the Company shall pay the Employee an aggregate base salary of [specify] per annum (the "Base Salary"), payable weekly. In addition to the Base Salary, the Employee shall also be paid (specify). The Employee shall also be entitled to (i) the use of an automobile provided by the Company, and (ii) medical, life insurance, disability and other such benefits which the Company may from time to time make available generally to its employees in accordance with the terms of such benefit and welfare plans.

6. Business Expenses. During the Employment period, the Company shall reimburse the Employee for all reasonable and necessary travel expenses and other disbursements incurred by him for or on behalf of the Company in the performance of his duties hereunder (hereinafter referred to as "Business Expenses") upon presentation by the Employee to the Company of appropriate expense reports.

7. Death. If the Employee dies during the Employment Period, his employment hereunder shall be deemed to terminate as of the last day of the month during which his death occurs. Upon the death of the Employee, neither the Employee nor his beneficiaries or estate shall have any further rights or claims against the Company, except the right to receive:

    A. The unpaid portion of the Base Salary, computed on a *pro rata* basis to the date of termination;
    B. Any earned, but unpaid commissions or other sales incentives;
    C. Unused personal and vacation days to which the Employee is entitled in accordance with Company policy;
    D. Reimbursement for any unpaid business expenses; and
    E. Life insurance and other post-termination benefits in accordance with the Company welfare and benefit plans.

8. Termination for Cause. Upon furnishing of notice to the Employee, the Company may terminate the employment of the Employee for cause at any time during the Employment period by reason of the Employee's (i) neglect of his duties hereunder, (ii) breach of or negligence with respect to his obligations under this Agreement, (iii) engaging in misconduct injurious to the company, or (iv) the Employee's commission of an act constituting common law fraud or a felony. If the Employee's employment is terminated by the Company for cause as herein defined, his Base Salary and his eligibility for all other benefits provided by the Company shall cease as of his termination date, after which time the Company shall have no other further liability or obligation of any kind to the Employee under this Agreement, except the Employee shall have the right to receive:

    A. The unpaid portion of the Base Salary, computed on a *pro rata* basis to the date of termination;
    B. Reimbursement for any unpaid business expenses;
    C. Any earned but unpaid commission or other sales incentives;
    D. Unused personal and vacation days to which the Employee is entitled in accordance with Company policy; and
    E. Any post-termination benefits in accordance with the Company welfare and benefit plans.

9. Employee Acknowledgments. Employee recognizes and acknowledges that in the course of Employee's employment it will be necessary for Employee to acquire information which could include, in whole or in part, information concerning the Company's sales, sales volume, sales methods, sales proposals, customers and prospective customers, suppliers and prospective suppliers, identity, practices and procedures of key purchasing and other personnel in the employ of customers and prospective customers and suppliers and prospective suppliers, amount or kind of customer's purchases from the Company, research reports, the Company's computer program, system documentation, special hardware, related software development, the Company's manuals, methods, ideas, improvements or other confidential or proprietary information belonging to the Company or relating to the Company's affairs (collectively referred to herein as "Confidential Information") and that such information is the property of the Company).

Employee further agrees that the use, misappropriation or disclosure of the Confidential Information would constitute a breach of trust and could cause irreparable injury to the Company, and it is essential to the protection of the Company's good will and to the maintenance of the Company's competitive position that the Confidential Information be kept secret and the Employee agrees not to disclose the Confidential Information to others or use the Confidential Information to Employee's own advantage or the advantage of others.

Employee further recognizes and acknowledges that it is essential for the proper protection of the business of the Company that Employee be restrained from soliciting or inducing any employee of the Company to leave the employ of the Company, or hiring or attempting to hire any employee of the Company.

10. Non-Disclosure of Confidential Information. Employee shall hold and safeguard the Confidential Information in trust for the Company, its successors and assigns and shall not, without the prior written consent of the Company, misappropriate or disclose or make available to anyone for use outside the Company organization at any time, either during his employment with the Company or subsequent to the termination of his employment with the Company for any reason, including, without limitation, termination by the Company for cause or without cause, any of the Confidential Information, whether or not developed by Employee, except as required in the performance of Employee's duties to the Company.

11. Return of Materials. Upon the termination of Employee's employment with the Company for any reason, including without limitation termination by the Company for cause or without cause, Employee shall promptly deliver to the Company all correspondence, manuals, orders, letters, notes, notebooks, reports, programs, proposals and any documents and copies concerning the Company's customers or concerning products or processes used by the Company and, without limiting the foregoing, will promptly deliver to the Company any and all other documents or material containing or constituting Confidential Information.

12. Non-Solicitation of Customers and Suppliers. Employee shall not during his time of employment with the Company, directly or indirectly, solicit the trade of, or do business with, any customer or prospective customer, or supplier or prospective supplier of the Company for any business purpose other than for the benefit of the Company. Employee further acknowledges that, in consideration of the promises contained in the Agreement and to induce the Company to enter into this Agreement, he shall not for One (1) year following the termination of his employment with the Company, including, without limitation, termination by the Company for cause or without cause, directly or indirectly, solicit the trade of, or do business with, any person or entity whatsoever who or which is or was a customer or supplier of the Company in any of the territory or territories assigned to the Employee during the Employment Period, with respect to products of the same or similar kind as those presently or in the future distributed by the Company.

13. Non-Solicitation of Employees. The Employee shall not during his employment with the Company and for One (1) year following termination of Employee's employment with the Company, including, without limitation, termination by the Company for cause or without cause, directly or indirectly, solicit or induce, or attempt to solicit or induce, any employee, current or future, of the Company to leave the Company for any reason whatsoever, or hire any current or future employee of the Company.

14. Advice of Counsel/Restrictive Covenants. The Employee has had the opportunity to consult with independent counsel and understands the nature of and the burdens imposed by the restrictive covenants contained in this Agreement. The Employee represents and acknowledges that such covenants are reasonable, enforceable, and proper in duration, scope and effect. Moreover, Employee represents and warrants that his experience and capabilities are such that the restrictive covenants set forth herein will not prevent him from earning his livelihood and that Employee will be fully able to earn an adequate livelihood for himself and his dependents if any of such provisions should be specifically enforced against Employee.

15. Authorization to Modify Restrictions. The Employee acknowledges that the remedies at law for any breach by Employee of the provisions of the restrictive covenants will be inadequate and that the Company shall be entitled to injunctive relief against the Employee in the event of any such breach, in addition to any other remedy and damage available. The Employee acknowledges that the restrictions contained herein are reasonable, but agrees that if any court of competent jurisdiction shall hold such restrictions unreasonable as to time, geographic area, activities, or otherwise, such restrictions shall be deemed to be reduced to the extent necessary in the opinion of such court to make them reasonable.

16. No Prior Agreements. Employee represents and warrants that he is not a party to or otherwise subject to or bound by the terms of any contract, agreement or understanding which in any manner would limit or otherwise affect his ability to perform his obligations hereunder, including, without limitation, any contract, agreement or understanding containing terms and provisions similar in any manner to those contained in Section 12 hereof. Employee further represents and warrants that his employment with the Company will not require the disclosure or use of any Confidential Information.

17. Covenants of the Essence. The covenants of the Employee set forth herein are of the essence of this Agreement; they shall be construed as independent of any other provision in this Agreement and the existence of any claim or cause of action of the Employee against the

Company, whether predicated on this Agreement or not, shall not constitute a defense to the enforcement by the Company of these covenants.

18. Tolling Period. If it should become desirable or necessary for the Company to seek compliance with the restrictive covenants by judicial proceedings, the period during which the Employee will not engage in the activities prohibited by Sections 12 and 13 hereof shall be extended to the first anniversary of the date of the judicial order requiring such compliance.

19. Arbitration. The parties expressly agree that all disputes or controversies arising out of this Agreement, its performance, or the alleged breach thereof, if not disposed of by agreement, shall be resolved by arbitration in accordance with this section. Either party must demand such arbitration only within Nine (9) months after the controversy arises by sending a notice of demand to arbitrate to the American Arbitration Association (the "Association"), with a copy thereof to the other party. The dispute shall then be arbitrated by a three-arbitrator panel pursuant to the Commercial Rules of the Association at the Association office in [specify state/place]. In the disposition of the dispute, the arbitrators shall be governed by the express terms of this Agreement and otherwise by the laws of the State of [specify] which shall govern the interpretation of the Agreement. The decision of the arbitrators shall be final and conclusive on the parties and shall be a bar to any suit, action or proceeding instituted in any federal, state or local court or before any administrative tribunal. Notwithstanding the foregoing, judgment on any award by the arbitrators may be entered in any court of competent jurisdiction. This arbitration provision shall survive any expiration or termination of the Agreement.

20. Notices. Any notice required or permitted to be given under this Agreement shall be sufficient if in writing, personally delivered, mailed or telecopied, if to the Employee, to the Employee's residence as contained in Company records, and if to the Company, to its principal place of business set forth in the first paragraph of this Agreement.

21. Assignment. This Agreement is personal in its nature and the Employee shall not without the prior written consent of the Company, assign or transfer this Agreement or any rights, duties or obligations hereunder.

22. Entire Agreement. This Agreement constitutes the full and complete understanding and agreement of the parties hereto with respect to any employment of the Employee by the Company and supersedes all prior agreements and understanding with respect to the subject matter hereof, whether written or oral. This Agreement may not be changed orally, but only by an agreement in writing signed by the party against whom enforcement of any waiver, change, modification or discharge is sought.

23. Governing Law. This Agreement shall be governed by, and construed in accordance with, the laws of the State of [specify].

24. Remedies. All remedies hereunder are cumulative, are in addition to any other remedies provided by law and may be exercised concurrently or separately, and the exercise of any one remedy shall not be deemed to be an election of such remedy or to preclude the exercise of any other remedy. No failure or delay in exercising any right or remedy shall operate as a waiver thereof or modify the terms of this Agreement.

IN WITNESS WHEREOF, the parties have executed this Agreement as of the date first above written.

(NAME OF COMPANY)　　　　　　　　　(NAME OF EMPLOYEE)
("The Company")　　　　　　　　　　　("The Employee")

By: _____　　　　By: _____
　　(NAME TITLE)　　　　　　　　　　　(NAME OF EMPLOYEE)

SAMPLE EMPLOYMENT AGREEMENT
ALTERNATIVE LONG VERSION
(For Executives)

The parties to this Agreement dated [specify] are [Name of Company] a [specify State and type of company] (the "Company"), and [Name of Employee] (the "Executive").

The Company wishes to employ the Executive, and the Executive wishes to accept employment with the Company, on the terms and subject to the conditions set forth in this Agreement. It is therefore agreed as follows:

1. Employment. The Company shall employ the Executive, and the Executive shall serve the Company, as a [specify] of the Company, with such duties and responsibilities as may be assigned to the Executive by the President of the Company and as are normally associated with a position of that nature. The Executive shall devote his best efforts and all of his business time to the performance of his duties under this Agreement and shall perform them faithfully, diligently and competently and in a manner consistent with the policies of the Company as determined from time to time by an officer of or President of the Company. The Executive shall report to the General Manager, [specify] Office of the Company. The Executive shall not engage in activities outside the scope of his employment if such activities would detract from or interfere with the fulfillment of his responsibilities or duties under this Agreement or require substantial time or services on the part of the Executive. The Executive shall not serve as a director (or the equivalent position) of any company or other entity and shall not receive fees or other remuneration for work performed either within or outside the scope of his employment without the prior written consent of the President of the Company. This consent shall not be unreasonably withheld.

2. Term of Employment. The Executive's employment by the Company under this Agreement shall commence on the date of this Agreement and, subject to earlier termination pursuant to section 5 or 7, shall terminate on [specify date]. This Agreement may also be extended as needed by a written amendment as discussed in section 16.

3. Compensation. As full compensation for all services rendered by the Executive to the Company under this Agreement, the Company shall pay to the Executive the compensation set forth in Schedule A attached hereto. This schedule may be amended from time to time in writing by the Company and the Executive.

4. Fringe Benefits; Expenses.

A. The Executive shall be entitled to receive all health and pension benefits, if any, provided by the Company to its employees generally and shall also be entitled to participate in all benefit plans, if any, provided by the Company to its employees generally.

B. The Company shall reimburse the Executive for all reasonable and necessary expenses incurred by him in connection with the performance of his services for the Company in accordance with the Company's policies, upon submission of appropriate expense reports and documentation in accordance with the Company's policies and procedures. The Company will reimburse the Executive for the expenses involved with his acquisition and business related use of a portable cellular telephone.

C. The Executive shall be entitled to Three (3) weeks paid vacation time annually, to be taken at times selected by him, with the prior concurrence of the General Manager to whom the Executive is to report.

5. Disability or Death.

A. If, as the result of any physical or mental disability, the Executive shall have failed or is unable to perform his duties for a period of Sixty (60) consecutive days, the Company may, by notice to the Executive subsequent thereto, terminate his employment under this Agreement as of the date of the notice without any further payment or the furnishing of any benefit by the Company under this Agreement (other than accrued and unpaid base salary and commissions and expenses and benefits which have accrued pursuant to any plan or by law).

B. The term of the Executive's employment under this Agreement shall terminate upon his death without any further payment or the furnishing of any benefit by the Company under this Agreement (other than accrued and unpaid base salary and commissions and expenses and benefits which have accrued pursuant to any plan or by law).

6. Non-Competition; Confidential Information; Inventions.

A. During the term of the Executive's employment under this Agreement, the Executive shall not, directly or indirectly, engage or be interested (as a stockholder, director, officer, employee, salesperson, agent, broker, partner, individual proprietor, lender, consultant or otherwise), either individually or in or through any person (whether a corporation, partnership, association or other entity) which engages, anywhere in the United States, in a business which is conducted by the Company on the date of termination of his employment, except that he may be employed by an affiliate of the Company and hold not more than 2% of the outstanding securities of any class of any publicly held company which is competitive with the business of the Company.

B. The Executive shall not, directly or indirectly, either during the term of the Executive's employment under this Agreement or thereafter, disclose to anyone (except in the regular course of the Company's business or as required by law), or use in any manner, any information acquired by the Executive during his employment by the Company with respect to any clients or customers of the Company or any confidential or secret aspect of the Company's operations or affairs unless such information has become public knowledge other than by reason of actions (direct or indirect) of the Executive. Information subject to the provisions of this paragraph shall include, without limitation:

(i) procedures for computer access and passwords of the Company's clients and customers, program manuals, user manuals or other documentation, run books, screen, file, or database layouts, systems flow charts, and all documentation normally related to the design or implementation of any computer programs developed by the Company relating to computer programs or systems installed either for customers or for internal use;

(ii) lists of present clients and customers and the names of individuals at each client or customer location with whom the Company deals, the type of equipment or computer software they purchase or use, and information relating to those clients and customers which has been given to the Company by them or developed by the Company, relating to computer programs or systems installed;

(iii) lists of or information about personnel seeking employment with or who are employed by the Company;

(iv) prospect lists for actual or potential clients and customers of the Company and contact persons at such actual or potential clients and customers;

(v) any other information relating to the Company's research, development, inventions, purchasing, accounting, engineering, marketing, merchandising and selling.

C. The Executive shall not, directly or indirectly, either during the term of the Executive's employment under this Agreement or for a period of One (1) year thereafter, solicit, directly or indirectly, the services of any person who was a full-time employee of the Company, its subsidiaries, divisions or affiliates, or solicit the business of any person who was a client or customer of the Company, its subsidiaries, divisions or affiliates, in each case at any time during the past year of the term of the Executive's employment under this Agreement. For purposes of this Agreement, the term "person" shall include natural persons, corporations, business trusts, associations, sole proprietorships, unincorporated organizations, partnerships, joint ventures and governments or any agencies, instrumentalities or political subdivisions thereof.

D. All memoranda, notes, records, or other documents made or composed by the Executive, or made available to him during the term of this Agreement concerning or in any way relating to the business or affairs of the Company, its subsidiaries, divisions, affiliates or clients shall be the Company's property and shall be delivered to the Company on the termination of this Agreement or at any other time at the request of the Company.

E. (i) The Executive hereby assigns and agrees to assign to the Company all of his rights to and title and interest to all Inventions, and to applications for United States and foreign patents and United States and foreign patents granted upon such Inventions and to all copyrightable material or other works related thereto.

(ii) The Executive agrees for himself and his heirs, personal representatives, successors and assigns, upon request of the Company, to at all times do such acts, such as giving testimony in support of the Executive's inventorship, and to execute and deliver promptly to the Company such papers, instruments and documents, without expense to him, as from time to time may be necessary or useful in the Company's opinion to apply for, secure, maintain, reissue, extend or defend the Company's worldwide rights in the Inventions or in any or all United States patents and in any all patents in any country foreign to the United States, so as to secure to the Company the full benefits of the Inventions or discoveries and otherwise to carry into full force and effect the text and the intent of the assignment set out in section 6E(i) above.

(iii) Notwithstanding any provision of this Agreement to the contrary, the Company shall have the royalty-free right to use in its business, and to make, have made, use and sell products, processes and services to make, have made, use and sell products, processes and services derived from any inventions, discoveries, concepts and ideas, whether or not patentable, including, but not limited to, processes, methods, formula and techniques, as well as improvements thereof and know-how related thereto, that are not inventions as defined herein, but which are made or conceived by the Executive during his employment by the Company or with the use or assistance of the Company's facilities, materials or personnel. If the Company determines that it has no present or future interest in any invention or discovery made by the Executive under this paragraph, the Company shall release such invention or discovery to the Executive within Sixty (60) days after the Executive's notice in writing is received by the Company requesting such release. If the Company determines that it does or may in the future have an interest in any such invention or discovery, such information will be communicated to the Executive within the 60-day period described above.

(iv) For purposes of this Section 6E, "Inventions" means inventions, discoveries, concepts and ideas, whether patentable or not, including, but not limited, to processes, methods, formula and techniques, as well as improvements thereof or know-how related thereto, concerning any present or prospective activities of the Company with which the Executive becomes acquainted as a result of his employment by the Company.

F. The Executive acknowledges that the agreements provided in this Section 6 were an inducement to the Company entering into this Agreement and that the remedy at law for breach of his covenants under this section 6 will be inadequate and, accordingly, in the event of any breach or threatened breach by the Executive of any provision of this Section 6, the Company shall be entitled, in addition to all other remedies, to an injunction restraining any such breach.

7. Termination. The Company shall have the right to terminate this Agreement and the Executive's employment with the Company for cause. For purposes of this Agreement, the term "cause" shall mean:

A. Any breach of the Executive's obligations under this Agreement;

B. Fraud, theft or gross malfeasance on the part of the Executive, including, without limitation, conduct of a felonious or criminal nature, conduct involving moral turpitude, embezzlement or misappropriation of assets;

C. The habitual use of drugs or intoxicants to an extent that it impairs the Executive's ability to properly perform his duties;

D. Violation by the Executive of his obligations to the Company, including, without limitation, conduct which is inconsistent with the Executive's position and which results or is reasonably likely to result (in the opinion of the President of the Company) in an adverse effect (financial or otherwise) on the business or reputation of the Company or any of its subsidiaries, divisions, or affiliates;

E. The Executive's failure, refusal or neglect to perform his duties contemplated herein within a reasonable period under the circumstances after written notice from the General Manager, or the President of the Company, describing the alleged breach and offering the Executive a reasonable opportunity to cure same;

F. Repeated violation by the Executive of any of the written work rules or written policies of the Company after written notice of violation from the General Manager or the President of the Company;

G. Breach of standards adopted by the Company governing professional independence or conflicts of interest.

If the employment of the Executive is terminated for cause, the Company shall not be obligated to make any further payment to the Executive (other than accrued and unpaid base salary and commissions and expenses to the date of termination), or continue to provide any benefit (other than benefits which have accrued pursuant to any plan or by law) to the Executive under this Agreement.

8. Miscellaneous.

A. This Agreement shall be governed by and construed in accordance with the laws of the State of [specify], applicable to agreements made and to be performed in [specify State], and shall be construed without regard to any presumption or other rule requiring construction against the party causing the Agreement to be drafted.

B. This Agreement contains a complete statement of all the arrangements between the Company and the Executive with respect to its subject matter, supersedes all previous agreements, written or oral, among them relating to its subject matter and cannot be modified, amended or terminated orally. Amendments may be made to this Agreement at any time if mutually agreed upon in writing.

C. Any amendment, notice or other communication under this Agreement shall be in writing and shall be considered given when received and shall be delivered personally or mailed by Certified Mail, Return Receipt Requested, to the parties at their respective addresses set forth below (or at such other address as a party may specify by notice to the other): [specify addresses]

D. The failure of a party to insist upon strict adherence to any term of this Agreement on any occasion shall not be considered a waiver or deprive that party of the right thereafter to insist upon strict adherence to that term or any other term of this Agreement. Any waiver must be in writing.

E. Each of the parties irrevocably submits to the exclusive jurisdiction of any court of the State of [specify] sitting in [specify] County or the Federal District Court of [specify State] over any action, suit or proceeding relating to or arising out of this Agreement and the transactions contemplated hereby. EACH OF THE PARTIES IRREVOCABLY AN UNCONDITIONALLY WAIVES THE RIGHT TO A TRIAL BY JURY IN ANY SUCH ACTION, SUIT OR PROCEEDING. Each party hereby irrevocably waives any objection, including, without limitation, any objection to the laying of venue or based on the grounds of *forum non conveniens* which such party may now or hereafter have to the bringing of any such action, suit or proceeding in any such court and irrevocably agrees that process in any such action, suit or proceeding may be served upon that party personally or by Certified or Registered Mail, Return Receipt Requested.

F. The invalidity or unenforceability of any term or provision of this Agreement shall not affect the validity or enforceability of the remaining terms or provisions of this Agreement which shall remain in full force and effect and any such invalid or unenforceable term or provision shall be given full effect as far as possible. If any term or provision of this Agreement is invalid or unenforceable in one jurisdiction, it shall not affect the validity of enforceability of that term or provision in any other jurisdiction.

G. This Agreement is not assignable by either party except that it shall inure to the benefit of and be binding upon any successor to the Company by merger or consolidation or the acquisition of all or substantially all of the Company's assets, provided such successor assumes all of the obligations of the Company, and shall inure to the benefit of the heirs and legal representatives of the Executive.

By: By:

_____   _____
[Name and Title of Employer]   [NAME OF EMPLOYEE]
[NAME OF COMPANY]   ("Executive")
("The Company")

SAMPLE SALES EMPLOYEE AGREEMENT
LONG VERSION

This EMPLOYMENT AGREEMENT ("Agreement") is made and entered into as of [specify] by and between [specify Name of Company] ("Company"), and [specify Name of Employee] ("Employee").

RECITALS

A. Company is engaged in the business of telemarketing and desires to obtain the services of Employee as a sales associate upon the terms and conditions provided herein.

B. Employee desires to be employed by Company as a sales associate upon the terms and conditions provided herein.

AGREEMENT

NOW, THEREFORE, for good and valuable consideration, the receipt and sufficiency of which are hereby acknowledged, Company and Employee agree as follows:

1. Retention Of Employee.

1.1 Engagement. Company hereby engages the services of Employee as a sales associate of Company, and Employee hereby agrees to provide such services, all upon the terms and conditions set forth in this Agreement.

1.2 No Interference. Employee hereby represents and warrants to Company that Employee is free to enter into this Agreement and has no prior or other obligations or commitments to any third party which would or might interfere with the acceptance or the full, uninhibited and faithful performance of the services to be provided hereunder.

1.3 Exclusivity. During the term of this Agreement, Employee shall not provide services in the telemarketing business or otherwise for compensation except to Company.

1.4 At-Will Employee. THE EMPLOYMENT OF EMPLOYEE BY COMPANY SHALL BE AT-WILL. SPECIFICALLY, EMPLOYEE MAY QUIT HIS OF HER EMPLOYMENT WITH COMPANY AT ANY TIME, FOR ANY REASON OR FOR NO REASON AT ALL, AND COMPANY MAY TERMINATE EMPLOYEE'S EMPLOYMENT AT ANY TIME, FOR ANY REASON OR FOR NO REASON AT ALL. It is the intent of Company and Employee in executing this Agreement that the provisions of this Section 1.4 may be amended or modified only by a writing signed by both Company and Employee which specifically refers to this Section 1.4 and which states that the provisions of this Section 1.4 are being amended or modified. This Section 1.4 may not be modified by an oral agreement, and Employee agrees that any conduct, past or future, of Company or its officers, employees or agents shall not be deemed to give rise to an implied covenant or agreement which is contrary to the provisions of this Section 1.4.

2. Duties. Employee shall diligently, faithfully and legally solicit prospective customers in an endeavor to secure sales for Company. Employee shall utilize Employee's best efforts to obtain business exclusively for Company and to exclusively promote Company's business operations.

3. Term.

3.1 Commencement. The term of this Agreement and Employee's obligation to provide services hereunder shall commence on the date entered by the parties on Exhibit "A" hereto.

3.2 Termination. Employee's obligation to provide services hereunder may be terminated at any time by one party giving written or oral notice to the other. All of the other terms and conditions of this Agreement, including the obligation of Company to pay compensation pursuant to Section 4 for services heretofore provided to Company and the obligation of Employee to maintain the confidentiality of Company's Confidential Information pursuant to Section 7, shall survive the termination of Employee's services hereunder.

4. Compensation.

4.1 Computation of Amount. In consideration of Employee's services and Employee's other agreements and covenants hereunder, Company shall periodically pay Employee compensation computed in accordance with the terms of Exhibit "B" hereto. Notwithstanding anything to the contrary contained in that Exhibit "B," Employee's compensation shall at no time be less than the minimum wage required by law.

5. Expenses. In its sole discretion, the Company may reimburse Employee for such reasonable business and travel expenses as Employee may incur in connection with Employee's services hereunder and which Company has approved in writing in advance.

6. Regulatory Compliance.

6.1 Acknowledgment. Employee acknowledges that the business of telemarketing is subject to substantial regulation and that serious and adverse consequences to Company, Company's business and Employee might result if Employee fails to strictly comply with such regulations. Accordingly, Employee agrees to act in compliance with such regulations.

6.2 Sales Presentation Policy Statement. Company has adopted a Sales Presentation Policy Statement, the most recent version of which is attached hereto as Exhibit "C." Employee agrees to strictly comply with the instructions of this Sales Presentation Policy Statement, as the same may be modified or amended from time to time.

6.3 Employee Information Sheet. Company is required to provide to various governmental entities and periodically update information about Company's business and the persons acting on Company's behalf, including Employee. Accordingly, at Company's request, Employee has completed Company's standard Employee Information Sheet, which is attached hereto as Exhibit "D." Employee represents and warrants to Company that the information contained thereon is complete and accurate. Employee agrees that Company may use such information (and any updating information) in documents which Company provides to governmental entities. Employee recognizes that it is extremely important for Company to have current information in order to make accurate filings with governmental entities. Accordingly, Employee agrees that Employee shall notify Company in writing at any time if any of the information provided on Exhibit "D" hereto changes and that Employee will, upon the request of Company, at any time, complete a new Employee Information Sheet.

6.4 Prohibition Against Misrepresentations. Company has advised Employee that the principal purpose of the governmental regulation of telemarketing is to prevent fraud upon persons solicited by telephone. Accordingly, Employee agrees that, while employed by Company, Employee will not make any misrepresentation or misleading statement to any person, including without limitation, any misrepresentation or misleading statement concerning Company's identity and location, or the price, quantity or quality of any product offered for sale, or sold or shipped by Company.

6.5 Immediate Termination for Breach. COMPANY MAY IMMEDIATELY TERMINATE EMPLOYEE'S RELATIONSHIP WITH COMPANY FOR ANY VIOLATION OF THE PROVISIONS OF THIS SECTION 6.

7. Confidential Information.

7.1 Definition. Employee acknowledges that Company's operations, techniques, forms, documents, computer printouts, invoices, methods of doing business, clients, customer lists, the identity of suppliers or goods sold by Company, the prices paid by Company for its goods, and Company's accounts receivable are trade secrets and confidential information (herein "Confidential Information").

7.2 Duty to Preserve Confidential Information. Employee may receive certain Confidential Information during the term of this Agreement. Employee agrees to preserve the confidentiality of such information, and to make every effort to ensure that the confidentiality of such information is not compromised by any action or omission of Employee. Employee specifically agrees that he will not at any time, whether during or subsequent to the term of Employee's employment by Company, in any fashion, form, or manner, unless specifically consented to in writing by Company, either directly or indirectly, use or divulge, disclose, or communicate to any person, firm, or corporation, in any manner whatsoever, any Confidential Information of any kind, nature or description.

7.3 Specific Prohibitions. Employee shall not:

7.3.1 Disclose, grant, assign, license, sell, give away, or otherwise transfer to any third party, or develop, produce, promote, or otherwise exploit any idea, proprietary information, trade secret or Confidential Information, the knowledge of which Employee obtains by reason of Employee's relationship with Company hereunder;

 7.3.2 Remove from Company's business premises any original or any copy of any Company document or form, including, without limiting the generality of the foregoing, computer printouts, or all or any portion of the Confidential Information, or

 7.3.3 Undertake planning for or organization of any business activity competitive with Company's business or combine or join with other employees, representatives, or independent contractors of Company's business for the purpose of organizing any such competitive business activity.

 7.4 Return of Confidential and Order Material. Upon the termination of Employee's employment with Company hereunder, Employee will immediately return to Company any Confidential Information in Employee's possession or control.

8. Indemnification.

 Employee shall indemnify and hold the Company harmless against any claim, demand, damage, debt, liability, account, reckoning, obligation, cost, expense, lien, action or cause of action (including the payment of attorneys' fees and costs actually incurred whether or not litigation is commenced) arising from the breach of this Agreement.

9. Additional Covenants.

 9.1 Other Business Interests. During Employee's employment with Company, Employee agrees that he will not, directly or indirectly, own an interest in, operate, join, control, or participate in, or be connected as an officer, employee, agent, independent contractor, partner, shareholder, or principal of any corporation, partnership, proprietorship, firm, association, person, or other entity producing, designing, providing, soliciting orders for, selling, distributing, or marketing products, goods, equipment, or services that directly or indirectly compete with Company's products or Company's business.

 9.2 Subsequent Activities. For Six (6) months following termination as an employee, Employee agrees not to undertake any employment or activity competitive with Company's business in which the loyal and complete fulfillment of the duties of the competitive employment or activity would call on Employee to reveal, to make judgments on, or otherwise to use any trade secrets of Company's business to which Employee had access by reason of Company's business.

 9.3 Solicitation Requirements. During the term of this Agreement, Employee agrees that he will not, directly or indirectly, either for himself or for any other person, firm, or corporation, divert or take away or attempt to divert or take away (and following termination as an employee, call on or solicit or attempt to call on or solicit) any of Company's customers or patrons, including but not limited to those on whom he called or solicited or with whom he became acquainted while engaged as an employee in Company's business.

9.4 Non-Waiver. Nothing in this Paragraph 9 shall be deemed a waiver of Employee's obligations under Paragraph 7; in the event of any conflict or inconsistency between provisions of Paragraph 9 and Paragraph 7, the provisions in Paragraph 7 shall control.

10. Miscellaneous.

10.1 Entire Agreement, Waiver and Amendment. This Agreement embodies and constitutes the entire understanding between the parties hereto with respect to the transactions contemplated herein, and all prior and contemporaneous agreements, understandings, representations, and statements, oral and written, are merged herein. No provision of this Agreement shall be waived, modified, amended, discharged or terminated, except by an instrument in writing signed by the party against which the enforcement of such waiver, modification, amendment, discharge or termination is sought and then only to the extent set forth in such written instrument.

10.2 Applicable Law. This Agreement shall be governed by and construed in accordance with the laws of the State of [specify].

10.3 Paragraph Headings. Descriptive paragraph headings are for convenience only and shall not control or affect the meaning or construction of the provisions of the Agreement.

10.4 Gender. Whenever the context herein shall so require, the singular shall include the plural, the male gender shall include the female gender and the neuter, and vice versa.

10.5 Unenforceability. In case any one or more of the provisions contained in this Agreement shall for any reason be held to be invalid, illegal or unenforceable in any respect, such invalidity, illegality or enforceability shall not affect any other provisions hereof, and this Agreement shall be construed as if such invalid, illegal or unenforceable provision had never been contained herein.

10.6 Waiver. No waiver by Company of any breach of this Agreement shall be deemed a waiver of any preceding or succeeding breach of the same or of any other provision hereof. Each and all of the several rights, remedies, and options of Company hereunder shall be construed as cumulative and no one of them is exclusive of the other or of any right, remedy or priority allowed by law or in equity.

10.7 Exhibits. All exhibits attached hereto are incorporated herein by this reference.
IN WITNESS WHEREOF, Company and Employee have executed this Standard Telemarketer Employment agreement as of the date above written.

[NAME OF COMPANY]   [NAME OF EMPLOYEE]
"Company:"   "Employee:"

By:_____

Title:_____

EXHIBIT "A"
ENGAGEMENT AND TERMINATION DATES UNDER EMPLOYMENT AGREEMENT

Date of Agreement:_____, 19___

"Company:" _____

"Employee:"_____

Date Engagement Began:_____, 19___

Initials of   Initials of
Company Officer _____   Employee _____

Date of Termination: _____, 19___

Initials of
Company Officer _____

EXHIBIT "B"
(INSERT COMPENSATION TERMS HERE)

EXHIBIT "C"
SALES PRESENTATION POLICY STATEMENT

Only those sales presentations that are specifically authorized by the Company may be used. Use of an unauthorized sales presentation is grounds for immediate termination. Any false or misleading statements made in connection with the sale, or offering for the sale, of any product is also grounds for immediate termination. Among other things, all salespersons are required to observe the following guidelines when soliciting customers:

1. Stick to the script. Any deviation from it may result in your termination.

2. You must represent yourself as calling from the Company.

3. You must state where the Company is located pursuant to the script.

4. You must not suggest or imply that a customer should withhold any information from the verification department.

5. You must accurately advise the customer of the shipping time on the product. If they are expecting it sooner than it arrives, they may fear it is not going to come and cancel their order. Our standard shipping time is [specify days/weeks] from receipt of payment for the product.

6. Avoid rude behavior. Any substantiated reports of customer harassment or verbal abuse will result in your immediate termination.

The kinds of statements, omissions or other conduct that constitute misrepresentations or deceitful conduct and will result in your immediate dismissal include:

A. Failure to properly identify the Company or misrepresenting the name or identity of the Company for whom you are calling.

B. Statements or the omission of statements made for the purpose of misleading the customer as to the nature of the product being sent to the customer.

C. Statements made to the customer that are intended to lead the customer to believe that the customer has had prior dealings with the Company when the customer has not had such dealings.

D. Misleading the customer as to the purpose of the telephone call.

7. You must make the customer realize that the Company is not selling and shipping merchandise subject to the customer's approval.

Obviously, these are only a few of the possible ways a customer can be misled, and this list is not intended to be exclusive. You may not make any statement intended or likely to

---
Pre-Hiring Considerations

mislead a customer. If you are in doubt as to whether a particular statement is misleading, ask yourself, "Is what I am saying untrue?," and, "Even if what I am saying is technically correct, is my purpose in saying it to lead the customer to believe something other than what is in fact true?" If your answer to either question is "yes" do not make the statement. Not only are you violating Company Policy, you are violating the law!

In order to further ensure that these standards will be followed by all salespeople, the Company will have a manager or assistant manager on the floor at all times monitoring your sales efforts. In addition, from time to time, "test" leads will be inserted into the group of leads that you happen to be working from. The customer will be fictitious, but you won't know that. Management evaluation of your performance will be based in part on how you interact with these fictitious customers.

AGREED AND ACCEPTED:
"Employee"

_____

_____

DATE

SAMPLE SALES EMPLOYEE AGREEMENT
SHORT VERSION

THIS EMPLOYMENT AGREEMENT (the "Agreement") made and entered into on [specify date], by and between [Name of Employee] (the "Employee"), an individual residing at [specify address] and [Name of Company] (the "Company), a [specify the state] corporation having offices at [specify address].

WITNESSETH:

WHEREAS, the Employee is willing to enter into this Agreement and employment with the Company upon the conditions and terms herein set forth;

NOW THEREFORE, for the valuable consideration set forth in this Agreement and intending to be legally bound, the Employee and the Company mutually promise and agree as follows:

1. Position and Duties. During the time this Agreement is in effect, the Company will employ the Employee and the Employee will accept such employment, in such capacities and with such powers and duties as may from time to time be determined by the President of the Company. The Employee will devote substantially all of his time and attention to, and will use his best energies and abilities in the performance of, his duties and responsibilities as prescribed in this Paragraph 1, and will not engage as a director, officer, employee, partner, shareholder, or any other capacity, in any business which competes, conflicts or interferes with the performance of his duties hereunder in any way, or solicit, canvass or accept any business or transaction for any other such competing business.

2. Compensation and Incentives.

A. For all services to be rendered by the Employee pursuant to Paragraph 1 of this Agreement, and in part of the consideration for the other obligations and promises of the Employee as set forth in this Agreement, the Company will compensate the Employee at the annual rate of [specify] ("Base Compensation") with it being intended that such Base Compensation shall be reviewed annually hereafter, with the changes in Base Compensation to be determined by the President in his sole discretion from time to time based on the performance of the Employee and the results of the Company. The Base Compensation shall be paid to the Employee in equal installments and shall be subject to applicable income tax withholding deductions required by law and other deductions authorized by the Employee. The Employee will be entitled to reasonable vacation and sick leave in accordance with Company policy.

B. In addition to his Base Compensation, the Employee will be entitled to the following performance incentives during the time he is employed by the Company:

i) A sales commission of [specify] percent of the gross amount of all sales to new customers with whom it was the Employee who made the initial contact on behalf of the Company. From time to time, the Company may also designate existing customers as accounts of the Employee, for which the Employee will earn Sales Commissions at the above rate. Sales Commissions earned will be paid upon the completion of each respective project (i.e., when all engineering work has been completed and the customer's invoices relating thereto have been fully paid).

3. Term. This Agreement for employment by and between the parties shall be an agreement for employment at will commencing on the date hereof, subject to immediate termination by either party with or without notice or cause.

Nothing contained in this Agreement shall be construed to prevent the Company from terminating the employment of the Employee hereunder at any time for cause. As used in this Agreement, "termination for cause" shall mean a termination based upon the dishonesty, gross negligence, incompetence or moral turpitude of the Employee or any failure to perform his duties hereunder or otherwise comply with and observe the covenants and agreements made by him herein.

4. Non-Competition. During the time of his employment by the Company, and for a period of One (1) year thereafter, the Employee shall not, directly or indirectly, acting alone or in conjunction with others:

A. Request any customers of any business then being conducted by the Company to curtail or cancel their business with the Company;

B. Solicit, canvass or accept any business or transaction for any other person, firm or corporation or business similar to the business of the Company, from any past or existing customers of the Company;

C. Induce, or attempt to influence, any employee of the Company to terminate employment with the Company or to enter into any employment or other business relationship with any other person (including the Employee), firm or corporation; or

D. Act or conduct himself in any manner which is contrary to the best interests of the Company.

The Employee recognizes that immediate and irreparable damage will result to the Company if the Employee breaches any of the terms and conditions of this Paragraph 4 and, accordingly, the Employee hereby consents to the entry by any court of competent jurisdiction of an injunction against him to restrain any such breach, in addition to any other remedies or claims for money or damages which the Company may seek. The Employee represents and warrants to the Company his experience and capabilities are such that he can obtain employment in business without breaching the terms and conditions of this Paragraph 4, and that his obligations under the provisions of this Paragraph 4 (and the enforcement thereof by injunction or otherwise) will not prevent him from earning a livelihood. The Employee agrees to pay any and all reasonable attorney fees sustained by the Company in connection with any breach of this Agreement.

5. Trade Secrets/Confidential Information. The Employee agrees that he will not at any time or in any manner divulge, disclose or communicate to any person, firm or corporation any trade, technical or technological secrets; any details of the Company's organization or business affairs, its manner of operation, its plans, processes, and/or other data; any names of past or present customers of the Company; or any other information relating to the business of the Company, without regard to whether all of the foregoing matters will be deemed confidential, material, or important. With respect to the foregoing, the Employee hereby stipulates and agrees that the same are confidential, material, and important, and any breach of this Paragraph 5 will adversely affect the business of the Company, its effective and successful management, and its inherent good will.

6. Assignment. The benefits of this Agreement are and shall be personal to the Employee, and none thereof shall inure to the benefit of his heirs, personal representatives, or assigns. The obligations and duties of the Employee hereunder shall be personal and not assignable or delegable by him in any manner, whatsoever. This Agreement shall be binding upon and inure to the benefit of the Company and it shall be assignable by the Company to any entity which may acquire substantially all of the business and assets of the Company, or with or into which the Company may be merged or consolidated.

7. Entire Agreement, Amendment. This Agreement constitutes the entire agreement between the parties with respect to the employment of the Employee by the Company and shall be deemed to supersede and cancel any other written agreements between the parties hereto relating to the transactions herein contemplated. No representation, inducement or condition set forth herein has been made or relied upon by any party. This Agreement may be amended, modified or waived only by an instrument in writing signed by the Employee and an authorized executive officer of the Company.

8. General. The headings of the Articles and Paragraphs of this Agreement are for the convenience of reference and not to be used to interpret or construe any provisions of this Agreement. This Agreement shall be construed and enforced in accordance with and governed by the laws of [specify state].

IN WITNESS WHEREOF, the parties have executed this Agreement on the date first above written.

[NAME OF EMPLOYEE]　　　　　　　　　　[NAME OF EMPLOYER]
("Employee")　　　　　　　　　　　　　　　("Employer")

_____　_____
Signature

　　　　　　　　　　　　　　　　　　　　　　Title: _____

SAMPLE EMPLOYMENT AGREEMENT
SHORT VERSION

THIS AGREEMENT made and entered into as of [specify], by and between [Name of Company], a [specify state] corporation (herein called the "Company") and [Name of Employer] (herein called "Employee").

WITNESSETH

1. The Company hereby employs Employee for a term commencing on the date of this Agreement [specify], and Employee hereby accepts such employment.

2. During his employment hereunder Employee shall:

A. devote such business, time and services to the affairs of the Company as may be reasonable required by the President and the Board of Directors of the Company to carry out his duties;

B. not engage in any other business or as a consultant to any other business entity or to other individuals during the term of this Agreement, without the written consent of the Company's President; and

C. perform such duties as Vice President as may be reasonably assigned to him from time to time by the President and Board of Directors of the Company.

3. For his services performed pursuant to this Agreement, the Company shall pay to the Employee:

A. During the period of his employment, annual compensation equal to the sum of: [specify formula]

B. For a period of Two (2) years commencing on (specify), the Employee will receive an additional bonus of ten percent (10%) of commission revenue received by the Company from principals listed on Exhibit A. This payment will be made quarterly commencing with the quarter ending [specify], and continuing each quarter thereafter through the quarter ending [specify].

C. For the purpose of sub-paragraph A. hereof, annual compensation shall include the cost of all fringe benefits provided to the Employee by the Company, including, without limitation, medical, hospitalization, disability and life insurance, employee paid FICA and similar taxes, travel expenses, car allowance and other related expenses.

D. For the purpose of sub-paragraph A:

i) A monthly draw against the annual compensation plan will be established at the rate of Three Thousand Dollars ($3,000.00) per month;

ii) A car allowance against the annual compensation plan will be established at the rate of Five Hundred Dollars ($500.00) per month; and

iii) Travel expenses will be reimbursed on a monthly basis.

E. The Company shall pay the Employee pursuant to subparagraph A. quarterly, based upon commission revenue received, less advances, pursuant to subparagraph D. Within ninety (90) days after the close of each calendar quarter, the Company or the Employee, as the base may be, shall pay or repay any deficiency or excess of compensation advanced.

4. Employee agrees that during the period of his employment by the Company and for a further period of One (1) year after termination of such employment or through [specify date], whichever period is the shorter, he will not directly or indirectly as an owner, stockholder, partner, employee or otherwise engage in the business of acting as a broker of products customarily sold by the Company within the States of [specify]. Employee further agrees that during such period he will not, directly or otherwise, engage in any business on behalf of any principal or customer of the Company.

5. Employee recognizes that the business of the Company involves the use of information of a confidential nature which constitutes an asset of substantial value. Accordingly, Employee hereby covenants and agrees that during the term of this Agreement and thereafter he will not, directly or indirectly, disclose to others any such confidential information or render any service to others which would in any way involve the divulging of such information. Employee further covenants and agrees that he will not remove, without the Company's written consent, any figures, calculations, letters, papers, drawings, blueprints or copies thereof.

6. Employee agrees that the Company, at its own discretion, may apply for and procure in its own name and for its own benefit life insurance and disability insurance in any amount considered advisable; and, that he shall have no right, title or interest therein; and, further agrees to submit to any medical or other examination and to execute and deliver any application or other instrument in writing, reasonably necessary to effectuate such insurance.

7. In the event of the merger or consolidation of the Company into or with another corporation or in the event of the sale or transfer of substantially all of the Company's stock or assets to another entity, the Company shall have the right to assign all of its right, title and interest under this Agreement to the successor to its business.

8. At any time the Company may, upon delivery of written notice to the Employee, discharge him for cause or for no cause. Discharge of the Employee for cause shall mean discharge because of a) dishonesty, b) breach of this Agreement or c) other misconduct which in the judgment of the President of the Company is detrimental to the best interests of the Company.

9. A. Employee's employment thereunder shall terminate (i) in the event of his death, as of the date of such death; (ii) in the event of Employee's discharge pursuant to Section 8 hereof, as of the date of such discharge; (iii) in the event of the Employee's inability to perform all or any substantial portion of the duties prescribed in or assigned pursuant to this agreement for a period of Thirty (30) consecutive days, Ten (10) days following written notice of such fact from the Company to the Employee; and, (iv) in the event Employee leaves the employment of the Company for any cause or reason (whether voluntary or involuntary on his or the Company's part).

B. Upon termination of the Employee's employment, all rights and obligations of the Company and Employee hereunder shall terminate except (i) any rights or causes of action arising out of the occurrences which constituted the cause of termination, (ii) the obligation not to disclose pursuant to Section 5 of this Agreement, (iii) the covenant not to compete set forth in Section 4 of this Agreement, (iv) the right of the Employee or his heirs to receive any salary or bonus which had been earned prior to termination, but not yet paid.

10. This Agreement shall be interpreted and its validity and effect determined under and in accordance with the laws of the State of [specify].

11. This Agreement embodies the entire agreement and understanding between the Company and Employee and supersedes all prior agreements and understandings relating to the matter of employment of Employee by the Company. This Agreement may be modified or amended only in writing signed by Employee and by an officer of the Company on behalf of the Company.

12. Until advised otherwise in writing, all notices, demands and other communications hereunder shall be in writing and shall be deemed to have been duly given if sent by registered mail to the following addresses:

If to the Company: [specify address]
If to the Employee: [specify address]

13. This Agreement may be executed in as many counterparts as desired by the parties; any one of which shall have the force and effect of an original.

IN WITNESS WHEREOF, the Company has caused this Agreement to be signed and its corporate seal to be hereunto affixed by its duly authorized officers, and Employee has hereto set his hand and seal on the date first above written.

Attest:
[NAME OF EMPLOYER]　　　　　　　　　　[NAME OF EMPLOYEE]
("the Company")　　　　　　　　　　　　　("the Employee")

By_____　　　_____
its [specify title]

SAMPLE EMPLOYMENT AGREEMENT
LETTER VERSION

Date

Name of Employee
Address
City, State, Zip

Dear [Name of Employee]:

This letter confirms that [Name of Company] ("The Company") has hired you as its [specify title]. In consideration thereto, you agree to be employed under the following terms and conditions:

1. You agree to work full-time and use your best efforts while rendering services for the Company. As our [specify title], you will be responsible for: [specify in detail]

2. You will make no representations, warranties, or commitments binding the Company without our prior consent nor do you have any authority to sign any documents or incur any indebtedness on the Company's behalf.

3. You shall assume responsibility for all samples, sales literature and other materials delivered to you and you shall return same immediately upon the direction of the Company.

4. THE COMPANY EMPLOYS YOU AT WILL AND MAY TERMINATE YOUR EMPLOYMENT AT ANY TIME, WITHOUT PRIOR NOTICE, WITH OR WITHOUT CAUSE. LIKEWISE, YOU ARE FREE TO RESIGN AS OUR SALES MANAGER AT ANY TIME, WITH OR WITHOUT NOTICE.

5. The Company shall pay you a salary of [Specify $X] per [specify] as consideration for all services to be rendered pursuant to this Agreement. In addition, the Company shall provide you with health insurance coverage for you and your family, and you will be eligible to participate in the Company pension plan. You will also receive Two (2) weeks paid vacation each year, provided you give the Company appropriate notice and the Company reserves the right to schedule your vacation(s) so as not to conflict with its normal business operations.

6. You shall also be paid for absences due to illness up to a maximum of Two (2) weeks per year, provided you submit a doctor's authorization indicating the reason for extended illness and the treatment received.

7. The Company shall also provide you time off with pay for the following holidays: [specify].

8. You agree and represent that you owe the Company the highest duty of loyalty. This means that you will never make secret profits at the Company's expense, will not accept kickbacks or special favors from Customers or Manufacturers, and will protect Company property.

9. While acting as an employee for the Company, you will not directly or indirectly, own an interest in, operate, control, or be connected as an employee, agent, independent contractor, partner, shareholder or principal in any company which markets products, goods or services which directly or indirectly compete with the business of the Company.

10. All lists and other records relating to the Customers of the Company, whether prepared by you or given to you by the Company during the term of this Agreement, are the property of the Company and shall be returned immediately upon termination or resignation of your employment.

11. You further agree that for a period of Six (6) months following the termination or resignation of your employment, you shall not work for, own an interest in, or be connected with as an employee, stockholder or partner, any company which directly or indirectly competes with the business of the Company.

12. There shall be no change, amendment or modification of this Agreement unless it is reduced to writing and signed by both parties. This Agreement cancels and supersedes all prior agreements and understandings.

13. If any provision of this Agreement is held by a court of competent jurisdiction to be invalid or unenforceable, the remainder of the Agreement shall remain in full force and shall in no way be impaired.

Your signature in the lower right corner of this Agreement will indicate the acceptance of the terms and conditions herein stated.

Sincerely yours,

By: _____
[specify Name and Title]
[NAME OF COMPANY]
("The Company")

I, [Name of Employee], the Employee stated herein, have read the above Agreement, understand and agree with its terms, and have received a copy.

_____
[NAME OF EMPLOYEE]

SAMPLE SALES EMPLOYEE AGREEMENT
LETTER VERSION

Date

Name of Employee
Address
City/State/Zip

Dear [Name of Employee]:

This will confirm your engagement as our employee, pursuant to the terms and conditions set forth herein.

1. Employment. The Company hereby employs [Name of employee] ("The Employee") to loyally render exclusive and full-time services as a sales employee for the Company.

2. Duties. The Employee shall work an eight-hour day, five days per week, excluding holidays, out of the Company's premises located at [specify], and throughout the Employee's territory as more fully described herein. The Employee shall devote his/her best efforts to the affairs of the Company and shall perform such duties as shall be directed by the supervisors and officers of the Company.

3. Acceptance. In consideration of the Company's employing or continuing to employ The Employee, The Employee hereby accepts such employment and agrees to render such services. As an exclusive and full-time employee, the Employee will not, during the term hereof, render any services for other corporations, businesses or entities directly or indirectly in competition with the Company.

4. Terms of Employment. THE COMPANY EMPLOYS THE EMPLOYEE AT WILL AND MAY TERMINATE THE EMPLOYEE AT ANY TIME WITHOUT PRIOR NOTICE WITH OR WITHOUT CAUSE.

5. Compensation. The Company agrees to pay the Employee a salary at the rate of [specify $X] per [specify] as consideration for services rendered pursuant to this Agreement. Salary increases will be at The Company's discretion and may be based, among other things, on productivity. The salary set forth hereinabove shall be payable in accordance with the regular payroll practices of the Company.

In addition, the Company shall pay The Employee a commission as listed on Exhibit A of this Agreement. Said commission shall be paid on all shipped orders paid by Customers in the Employee's designated territory. Bad debts, defined as non-payments by the Customer after a period of One Hundred and Twenty (120) days, shall be deducted from the Employee's commission for each order which remains unpaid to the extent of commission credited to the Employee for that particular order.

6. Expenses. The Company shall pay or reimburse the Employee for all necessary and reasonable expenses incurred or paid by the Employee in connection with the performance of services under this Agreement, upon presentation of expense statements or vouchers or such other supporting information as it may from time to time request, evidencing the nature of such expense, and, if appropriate, the payment thereof by the Employee, and otherwise in accordance with Company procedures from time to time in effect.

7. Additional Benefits. The Employee shall be entitled to participate in any group insurance, qualified pension, hospitalization, medical health and accident, disability or similar plan or program of the Company now existing, or hereafter established, to the extent that he is eligible under its general provisions hereof. NOTWITHSTANDING ANYTHING HEREIN TO THE CONTRARY, HOWEVER, THE COMPANY SHALL HAVE THE RIGHT TO AMEND OR TERMINATE ANY SUCH PLANS OR PROGRAMS WITHOUT PRIOR NOTICE. In addition, the Company reserves the right to schedule vacations so as to not conflict with normal business operations.

8. Maintenance of Business Automobile. The Employee shall purchase and operate an automobile to be used in connection with his selling duties. The Company shall be notified of the make and model of said vehicle in a timely fashion.

The Employee covenants that he shall maintain a valid driver's license at all times and carry automobile liability insurance for no less than One Million Dollars ($1,000,000). The Employee shall submit a certificate of insurance from his insurance carrier documenting said coverage upon the Company's request and the failure to comply with said request shall be grounds for immediate dismissal.

9. Representations And Warranties. The Employee will make no representations, warranties, or commitments binding the Company without the Company's prior consent.

10. Price And Product Changes. The Company will provide product specifications, prices, delivery schedules and discounts, and will give the Employee timely notice of any and all changes.

11. Acceptance Of Orders. All orders are subject to acceptance or rejection by the Company at its home office. The Company shall also provide the Employee with the names of all persons and companies within his/her territory requesting information.

12. Duty Of Loyalty. The Employee covenants and represents that he owes the Company the highest duty of loyalty with respect to his/her duties. This means that he/she will, among other things, maintain a constant vigil over the Company's property, never make secret profits at the Company's expense, never service customers of the Company but bill them himself, never accept kickbacks or special favors from Customers, dress in a proper fashion, not use drugs or alcohol while on the job, and maintain his/her personal automobile in good condition together with a valid driver's license.

13. Protection Of Confidential Information. In view of the fact that the Employee's work will bring him into close contact with many confidential matters such as information about costs, profits, vendors, inventory, service techniques, technical manuals, customer needs and lists, markets, sales, discounts and other information not readily available to the public, and in consideration of the Company's employing or continuing to employ the Employee, the Employee hereby covenants and agrees, as an essential condition of his/her employment or continued employment by the Company, as follows:

A. To keep secret all confidential matters of the Company and its affiliates and not to disclose them to anyone outside of the Company, either during or after the Employee's employment with the Company, except with the Company's consent;

B. To avoid discussing any matters of a confidential nature with competitors or their employees. This includes discussions regarding the Company's customers, pricing, and policies. The Employee is reminded that any such discussions may cause the Company, and the Employee personally, to have violated anti-trust laws including the Sherman and Clayton Acts. Sanctions of up to Three (3) years imprisonment and fines up to $100,000 have been imposed on individual employees who violate such laws.

C. To deliver promptly to the Company upon termination of the Employee's employment, or at any time the Company may so request, all memoranda, notes, records, reports, technical manuals and other documents (and all copies thereof) relating to the Company's and its affiliate's businesses which the Employee may then possess or have under the Employee's control.

14. Obligations After Termination. The Employee agrees that for a period of Six (6) months after the termination of his/her employment with the Company, he/she shall not work for, own an interest in, operate, join, control, participate in or be connected, either directly or indirectly, as an officer, employee, agent, independent contractor, shareholder or principal of any of the Principals of the Company, whom you sold for during the past Two (2) years while acting as our sales employee. The Employee further agrees to notify any prospective employer of the existence of this Agreement, in writing, with a copy of such notice to an officer of the Company.

If the Employee is unable to obtain employment consistent with his abilities and education solely because of the provisions of this paragraph, the Employee shall promptly notify the Company and the Company shall have the option of waiving the requirements of this paragraph or making payments to the Employee equal to [specify] of the weekly base pay at termination, provided the Employee has made and continues to make, conscientious and aggressive efforts to find other employment. Documentation of these efforts will be required on a regular and consistent basis.

15. Right To Seek Injunctive Relief. The Employee agrees that any breach of any of the covenants contained in Paragraphs 12, 13 and 14 of this Agreement constitutes substantial and irreparable harm to the Company, and that such harm could not be adequately compensated by the Company's recovery of monetary damages. Therefore, the Employee agrees that the Company may seek injunctive relief, or any other relief which it deems necessary and appropriate, in order to protect its rights under this Agreement and other common law rights, and that such injunctive proceeding shall not limit or in any way restrain the Company from seeking any other relief or damages.

16. Right To Seek Other Relief Or Damages. Notwithstanding the right to seek injunctive relief, the Company may, upon finding by it that the Employee has violated his covenant of Duty Of Loyalty as more fully defined in Paragraph 12 of the Agreement:

A. Terminate the Employee without notice and without severance pay or other benefits not previously earned; and

B. Recover all monies paid in salary, commission and other benefits to the Employee for the period of time said Duty Of Loyalty was violated.

17. Resignation Of Employee. The Employee shall give the Company written notice of his decision to resign from said employment no less than Two (2) weeks prior to the effective termination date.

Said notice shall be in writing, and sent Certified Mail or hand-delivered to the (headquarter) office of the Company.

18. Final Accounting. At the termination of the Agreement, The Company shall pay the Employee his/her final commission due, as calculated more fully on Exhibit A attached hereto. Said commission shall be earned on all accepted orders in house at the date of termination which are shipped within one (1) month after the termination date.

19. Non-Affiliate. Nothing in this Agreement shall be construed to constitute the Employee as a partner or affiliate of the Company.

20. Prior Agreement. This Agreement forms the entire understanding between the parties. It cancels and supersedes all prior agreements and understandings.

21. Modifications. There will be no change, amendment, or modification of any of the terms in this Agreement unless it is reduced to writing and signed by both parties. The Employee shall not be excused from compliance with the provisions of this Agreement by the failure of the Company to protest any changes instituted by either the Company or the Employee.

22. Enforceability. If any provision of this Agreement is held by a court of competent jurisdiction to be unenforceable, the remainder of the Agreement shall remain in full force and effect and shall in no way be impaired.

Dated this _____ day of _____

Sincerely yours,

By _____
[specify Name and Title]

NAME OF COMPANY
("The Company")

I, [Name of Employee], the Employee, have read the above letter, understand and agree with its terms, and have received a copy.

_____
[NAME OF EMPLOYEE]

SAMPLE CONSULTING AGREEMENT

This Consulting Agreement (the "Agreement") is entered into this [specify date] by and between [Name of Consultant], an individual, ("Consultant") and [Name of Company] (the "Company").

RECITALS

WHEREAS, the Company is in need of assistance in the [specify] support area; and

WHEREAS, Consultant has agreed to perform consulting work for the Company in providing [specify] support and consulting services and other related activities as directed by the Company;

NOW, THEREFORE, the parties hereby agree as follows:

1. Consultant's Services. Consultant shall be available and shall provide to the Company professional consulting services in the area of [specify] support ("Consulting services") as requested.

2. Consideration.

A. RATE. In consideration for the Consulting Services to be performed by Consultant under this Agreement, the Company will pay Consultant at the rate of [specify rate] per hour for time spent on Consulting Services. Consultant shall submit written, signed reports of the time spent performing Consulting Services, itemizing in reasonable detail the dates on which services were performed, the number of hours spent on such dates and a brief description of the services rendered. The Company shall pay Consultant the amounts due pursuant to submitted reports within 14 days after such reports are received by the Company.

B. EXPENSES. Additionally, the Company will pay Consultant for the following expenses incurred while the Agreement between Consultant and the Company exists:

- All travel expenses to and from all work sites
- Meal expenses;
- Administrative expenses;
- Lodging Expenses if work demands overnight stays; and
- Miscellaneous travel-related expenses (parking and tolls.

Consultant shall submit written documentation and receipts where available itemizing the dates on which expenses were incurred. The Company shall pay Consultant the amounts due pursuant to submitted reports within 14 days after a report is received by the Company.

3. Independent Contractor. Nothing herein shall be construed to create an employer-employee relationship between the Company and Consultant. Consultant is an independent contractor and not an employee of the Company or any of its subsidiaries or affiliates. The consideration set forth in Section 2 shall be the sole consideration due Consultant for the services rendered hereunder. It is understood that the Company will not withhold any amounts for payment of taxes from the compensation of Consultant hereunder. Consultant will not represent to be or hold herself out as an employee of the Company.

4. Confidentiality. In the course of performing Consulting Services, the parties recognize that Consultant may come in contact with or become familiar with information which the Company or its subsidiaries or affiliates may consider confidential. This information may include, but is not limited to, information pertaining to the Company [specify] systems, which information may be of value to a competitor. Consultant agrees to keep all such information confidential and not to discuss or divulge it to anyone other than appropriate Company personnel or their designees.

5. Term. This Agreement shall commence on [specify date] and shall terminate on [specify date], unless earlier terminated by either party hereto. Either party may terminate this Agreement upon Thirty (30) days prior written notice. The Company may, at its option, renew this Agreement for an additional One (1) year term on the same terms and conditions as set forth herein by giving notice to Consultant of such intent to renew on or before [specify date].

6. Notice. Any notice or communication permitted or required by this Agreement shall be deemed effective when personally delivered or deposited, postage prepaid, in the first class mail of the United States properly addressed to the appropriate party at the address set forth below:

1. Notices to Consultant: [specify address]

2. Notices to the Company: [specify address]

7. Miscellaneous.

7.1 Entire Agreement and Amendments. This Agreement constitutes the entire agreement of the parties with regard to the subject matter hereof, and replaces and supersedes all other agreements or understandings, whether written or oral. No amendment or extension of the Agreement shall be binding unless in writing and signed by both parties.

7.2 Binding Effect, Assignment. This Agreement shall be binding upon and shall inure to the benefit of Consultant and the Company and to the Company's successors and assigns. Nothing in this Agreement shall be construed to permit the assignment by Consultant of any of its rights or obligations hereunder, and such assignment is expressly prohibited without the prior written consent of the Company.

7.3 Governing Law, Severability. This Agreement shall be governed by the laws of the State of [specify]. The invalidity or unenforceability of any provision of the Agreement shall not affect the validity or enforceability of any other provision.

WHEREFORE, the parties have executed this Agreement as of the date first written above.

[COMPANY:]

By: _____

[CONSULTANT:]

By: _____
    [Date]

SAMPLE EMPLOYMENT AGREEMENT WHEN HIRING OUTSIDE CONSULTANTS AND INDEPENDENT CONTRACTORS
(Such as Investigators, Polygraphers and Physicians)

This Independent Contractor Agreement (the "Agreement") is entered into this [specify date] by and between [Name of Independent Contractor/Consultant] (the "Consultant"), a corporation located at [specify], d/b/a [specify], for itself and its heirs, executors, administrators, related entities and assigns and [Name of Company] (the "Company").

RECITALS

WHEREAS, the Company is in need of assistance in the area of (specify); and WHEREAS, Consultant has agreed to perform consulting work for the Company in (specify) services and other related activities for the Company;

NOW, THEREFORE, the parties hereby agree as follows:

1. Consultant's Services. Consultant shall be available and shall provide to the Company professional services in the area of (specify) ("Consulting Services") as needed and requested.

2. Consideration.

A. RATE. In consideration of the Services to be performed by Consultant under this Agreement the Company will pay Consultant the flat rate of (specify per job) or at the rate of (specify) per hour for time spent on Consulting Services. Consultant shall submit written, signed reports of the time spent performing Consulting Services, itemizing in reasonable detail the dates on which services were performed, the number of hours spent on such dates and a brief description of the services rendered. The Company shall pay Consultant the amounts due pursuant to submitted reports within (specify) after such reports are received by the Company.

B. EXPENSES. Additionally, the Company will pay Consultant for the following expenses (specify, such as: all travel expenses to and from all work sites; meal expenses; administrative expenses; lodging expenses if work demands overnight stays; and miscellaneous travel-related expenses including parking and tolls) incurred while this Agreement between Consultant and the Company exists.

Consultant shall submit written documentation and receipts where available itemizing the dates on which expenses are incurred. The Company shall pay Consultant the amounts due pursuant to submitted reports within (specify) after a report is received by the Company.

3. Independent Contractor. Nothing contained herein or any document executed in connection herewith, shall be construed to created an employer-employee partnership or joint venture relationship between the Company and Consultant. Consultant is an independent contractor and not an employee of the Company or any of its subsidiaries or affiliates. The consideration set forth in Section 2 shall be the sole consideration due Consultant for the services rendered hereunder. It is understood that the Company will not withhold any amounts for payment of taxes from the compensation of Consultant hereunder. Consultant will not represent to be or hold itself out as an employee of the Company and Consultant acknowledges that he/she shall not have the right or entitlement in or to any of the pension, retirement or other benefit programs now or hereafter available to the Company's regular employees. Any and all sums subject to deductions, if any, required to be withheld and/or paid under any applicable state, federal or municipal laws or union or professional guild regulations shall be Consultant's sole responsibility and Consultant shall indemnify and hold Company harmless from any and all damages, claims and expenses arising out of or resulting from any claims asserted by any taxing authority as a result of or in connection with said payments.

4. Confidentiality. In the course of performing consulting services, the parties recognize that Consultant may come in contact or become familiar with information which the Company or its subsidiaries or affiliates may consider confidential. This information may include, but is not limited to, information pertaining to (specify) which information may be of value to a competitor. Consultant agrees to keep all such information confidential and not to discuss or divulge it to anyone other than appropriate Company personnel or their designees.

5. Term. This Agreement shall commence on (specify date) and shall terminate on (specify date), unless earlier terminated by either party hereto. Either party may terminate this Agreement upon Thirty (30) days prior written notice. The Company may, at its option, renew this Agreement for an additional term of (specify) on the same terms and conditions as set forth herein by giving notice to Consultant of such intent to renew on or before (specify date).

6. Consultant's Taxpayer I.D. Number. The taxpayer I.D. number of the Consultant is (specify). The Consultant is licensed to perform the agreed upon services enumerated herein and covenants that it maintains all valid licenses, permits and registrations to perform same.

7. Insurance. The Consultant will carry general liability, automobile liability, workers' compensation and employer's liability insurance in the amount of (specify). In the event the Consultant fails to carry such insurance it shall indemnify and hold harmless Company, its agents and employees from and against any damages, claims, and expenses arising out of or resulting from work conducted by Consultant and its agents or employees.

8. Competent Work. All work will be done in a competent fashion in accordance with applicable standards of the profession and all services are subject to final approval by a representative of the Company prior to payment.

9. Representations and Warranties. The Consultant will make no representations, warranties, or commitments binding the Company without the Company's prior consent.

10. Legal Right. Consultant covenants and warrants that he/she has the unlimited legal right to enter into this Agreement and to perform in accordance with its terms without violating the rights of others or any applicable law and that he/she has not and shall not become a party to any other agreement of any kind which conflicts with this Agreement. Consultant shall indemnify and hold harmless the Company from any and all damages, claims and expenses arising out of or resulting from any claim that this Agreement violates any such agreements. Breach of this warranty shall operate to terminate this Agreement automatically without notice as specified in Paragraph 5 and to terminate all obligations of the Company to pay any amounts which remain unpaid under this Agreement.

11. The Waiver. Failure to invoke any right, condition, or covenant in this Agreement by either party shall not be deemed to imply or constitute a waiver of any rights, condition, or covenant and neither party may rely on such failure.

12. Notice. Any notice or communication permitted or required by this Agreement shall be deemed effective when personally delivered or deposited, postage prepaid, in the first class mail of the United States properly addressed to the appropriate party at the address set forth below:

1. Notices as to Consultant: (specify address)

2. Notices to the Company: (specify address)

13. Enforceability. If any provision of this Agreement is held by a court of competent jurisdiction to be unenforceable, the reminder of the Agreement shall remain in full force and effect and shall in no way be impaired

14. Miscellaneous.

    a. Entire Agreement and Amendments. This Agreement constitutes the entire agreement of the parties with regard to the subject matter hereof, and replaces and supersedes all other agreements or understandings, whether written or oral. No amendment or extension of this Agreement shall be binding unless in writing and signed by both parties.

    b. Binding Effect, Assignment. This Agreement shall be binding upon and shall inure to the benefit of Consultant and the Company and to the Company's successors and assigns. Nothing in this Agreement shall be construed to permit the assignment by Consultant of any of its rights or obligations hereunder, and such assignment is expressly prohibited without the prior written consent of the Company.

    c. Governing Law, Severability. This Agreement shall be governed by the laws of the State of (specify). The invalidity or unenforceability of any provision of this Agreement shall not affect the validity or enforceability of any other provision.

WHEREFORE, the parties have executed this Agreement as of the date written above.

COMPANY:

By:_____ Date:_____

CONSULTANT:

By:_____ Date:_____

CONSULTANT

State of _____

County of_____

    Before me, the undersigned authority on this date personally appeared _____, known to me to be person whose name is subscribed to the foregoing instrument and acknowledged to me he executed the same for the purposes and considerations therein expressed.

    Given under my hand and seal of office the ___ day of _____, 19___.

_____
Notary Public

_____
County

My Commission Expires: _____

SAMPLE INDEPENDENT SALES REPRESENTATIVE AGREEMENT
LONG VERSION

This Agreement is made in [specify State] as of [specify], between [Name of Company], a [specify State] corporation, having its principal place of business at [specify address] (hereinafter called "the Company") and [Sales Representative's Full Legal Name and D/B/A (if different from Legal Name)] having its principal place of business at [specify address] (hereinafter called "Representative").

A. The Company markets various [specify] products in the United States.

B. The Company desires to obtain the services of Representative, and Representative desires to provide services to the Company in accordance with the terms, conditions and covenants set forth in this Agreement. Accordingly, in consideration of the mutual covenants and undertakings set forth herein, the parties hereby agree as follows:

1. Appointment and Acceptance.

A. The Company hereby appoints Representative as one of the Company's independent sales representatives to solicit orders for those [specify] products marketed from time to time by the Company. Representative's appointment shall not be applicable to any other products marketed by the Company.

B. Representative shall solicit orders for Company Products in the geographic territory designated on Exhibit "A" (hereinafter called "the Territory"). Representative shall not solicit orders for Company Products in any other geographic territory. The Company shall have the right, from time to time, at its sole discretion, to change the scope of the Territory. In any such instance, the Company shall issue a new Exhibit "A" to Representative reflecting such change, which shall, as of the effective date stated thereon, supersede the prior Exhibit "A". Representative acknowledges and agrees that it neither has, nor will acquire, any vested or proprietary right or interest with respect to the Territory, any Company customers in the Territory, or any Company customer lists. Representative further acknowledges and agrees that any goodwill accruing in the Territory during the term of this Agreement with respect to the Company or Company Products shall be considered the property of the Company rather than Representative.

C. Notwithstanding anything contained herein, unless specifically authorized by the Company in writing, Representative shall not solicit orders for the Products from any O.E.M. or private label accounts, it being understood and acknowledged by Representative that the Company may solicit orders from such accounts directly (in which case they shall be considered "Reserved Factory Accounts") or may authorize other specially appointed Company sales representatives to solicit orders from such accounts. Further, the Company shall have the right, from time to time, at its sole discretion, to designate other account categories and/or specific accounts within the Territory as accounts which shall be serviced by the Company directly as Reserved Factory Accounts, or by other Company sales representatives, regardless of whether

Representative previously has serviced such account categories or accounts on the Company's behalf.

D. Representative hereby accepts its appointment hereunder.

2. Responsibilities of Representative. Representative shall satisfy the following responsibilities at all times during the term of this Agreement:

A. Representative and its staff shall conduct themselves in a manner consistent with the high image, reputation and credibility of the Company and Company Products, and shall engage in no activities which reflect adversely on the Company or the Products.

B. Representative shall use its best efforts to solicit orders for the Products, shall promote the sale of the Products in a diligent and aggressive manner, and shall forward all orders to the Company promptly.

C. Representative shall maintain an office in the Territory which shall be open and staffed adequately during normal business hours. Representative shall employ and maintain adequately trained and competent personnel in numbers sufficient to carry out and perform properly and fully all of Representative's responsibilities under this Agreement.

D. In the event that Representative becomes aware of any actual or potential claim against the Company by any person or entity, Representative shall notify the Company immediately.

E. Representative shall use its best efforts to achieve sales quotas assigned periodically by the Company to Representative. The Company shall have the right to adjust or revise any assigned sales quotas, from time to time, at its sole discretion, by written notice to Representative. Representative understands that sales volume is only one factor which will be considered by the Company in evaluating Representative's performance, and that the achievement of any sales quota(s) shall not preclude the Company from exercising its non-extension or termination rights pursuant to paragraph 14 of this Agreement.

F. Representative shall furnish the Company, on a timely basis, with sales call reports, sales forecasts, and such other information pertinent to Representative's performance hereunder, as the Company may request.

G. Representative shall attend any and all meetings and trade shows required by the Company.

H. Representative shall comply with all applicable federal, state and local laws and regulations in performing its responsibilities hereunder.

I. Representative shall assist the Company in obtaining relevant financial information concerning Company accounts and potential accounts within the Territory.

J. Representative shall keep the Company informed as to competitive and economic conditions within the Territory which may affect the marketing or sales of the Company Products therein.

K. To the extent not otherwise required herein, Representative shall provide complete cooperation to the Company in order to assist the Company in maximizing the Company's success within the Territory.

3. Relationship of the Parties. Representative acknowledges that it has its own independently established business which is separate and apart from the Company's business. Representative at all times shall be considered an independent contractor with respect to its relationship with the Company. Nothing contained in this Agreement shall be deemed to create the relationships of employer and employee, master and servant, franchisor and franchisee, partnership or joint venture between the parties.

4. Scope and Limitations of Representative's Authority.

A. Representative has authority to solicit orders only and has no authority to accept orders. All orders solicited by Representative shall be subject to acceptance or rejection by the Company, in whole or in part, at the Company's sole discretion.

B. The Company shall have the sole right to determine the accounts to whom the Products shall be sold, and Representative shall have no right or authority to obligate the Company to sell the Products to any account.

C. Prices, credit terms, sales programs and other terms and conditions of sale governing transactions between the Company and its customers shall be those adopted by the Company from time to time, at its sole discretion. Representative shall have no authority to modify any such prices, credit terms, sales programs or other terms or conditions of sale, to authorize any customer to return the Products to the Company for credit, or to obligate or bind the Company in any other manner.

D. Representative at no time shall engage in any unfair trade practices with respect to the Company or the Products, and shall make no false or misleading representations with respect to the Company or the Products. Representative shall refrain from communicating any information with respect to guarantees or warranties regarding the Products, except such as are expressly authorized by the Company or are set forth in the Company's literature or other promotional materials.

E. Except as authorized by the Company, Representative shall have no authority to make collections from customers, but shall assist the Company in collections upon the Company's request, and shall remit any collected funds to the Company immediately.

F. Representative shall not use the Company's tradenames or trademarks or any names closely resembling same as part of Representative's corporate or business name, or in any manner which the Company in its sole discretion, may consider misleading or otherwise objectionable.

G. Representative shall not attempt to fix the prices at which any account or prospective account of the Company may resell the Company Products, it being acknowledged and understood that the Company accounts are free to determine resale prices at their sole discretion.

5. Commissions.

A. The sole and exclusive compensation to be paid by the Company to Representative in consideration for all services rendered by Representative as an independent sales representative for the Company shall be commissions on sales of the Products in accordance with the commission schedule set forth on Exhibit "B" ("the Commission Schedule"), which is attached hereto and shall be considered an integral part of this Agreement. The Company shall have the right, from time to time, at its sole discretion, to modify the Commission Schedule, in whole or in part. In any such instance, the Company shall issue a new Exhibit "B" to Representative reflecting such change(s), which shall, as of the effective date stated thereon, supersede the prior Exhibit "B". Anything contained herein or on Exhibit "B" notwithstanding, the Commission Schedule shall not govern close-out sales, sales made at less than regular prices or sales involving terms different from the Company's standard terms of sale. The Company shall have the right to determine the commissions on such sales at its sole discretion, on a case by case basis, without the requirement of advance notice to Representative.

B. Commissions shall be computed on the net invoice price of the Products. The "net invoice price" shall be computed by deducting from the gross sales price, all taxes, freight, insurance charges, credits (arising from returns or other adjustments), discounts, rebates or allowances of any kind, except prompt payment discounts.

C. Subject to the final settlement procedures set forth in paragraph 6 and to the debit provisions of subparagraph E hereof, commissions shall become earned and due to Representative in accordance with the following provisions:

i) Except as otherwise provided in this Agreement, commissions on commissionable orders shall be considered earned and due to Representative on the [specify time] following the [specify time] in which the order is shipped and invoiced to the Company's customer. For example, commissions on commissionable orders shipped in [specify] shall be considered earned and due to Representative on [specify].

ii) Commissions on any shipment(s) made subsequent to any expiration or termination of this Agreement shall be considered earned and due to Representative only if the shipment relates to an order received and accepted by the Company prior to the expiration or termination date, is made within Thirty (30) days of such expiration or termination date, and otherwise becomes earned and due pursuant to the provisions of Paragraph 6 hereof.

iii) No commissions shall be considered earned and due to Representative under any circumstances with respect to:

a) Sales to any Reserved Factory Accounts or to any other accounts from which Representative is not authorized by the Company to solicit orders; or

b) Sales of parts or promotional items, sales of any products not covered by this Agreement, accommodation sales, sales made to Representative or to any of its employees, or sales to any other entity in which Representative or any principal(s) of Representative has any ownership or other financial interest; or

c) Any unfilled orders; or

d) Any shipments made more than Thirty (30) days after any expiration or termination of this Agreement, regardless of whether the order(s) in question has been submitted to the Company prior to the expiration or termination date; or

e) Any orders submitted to the Company after any expiration or termination of this Agreement; or

f) Any orders or portions thereof as to which the Company is obligated to pay the commissions to any other Company sales representative.

D. In those cases in which the Company ships an order to an account's outlets in more than one territory, or to an account's central redistribution to more than one territory, the Company, at its sole discretion, may apportion such commissions to more than one representative, in proportions deemed by the Company, in its sole judgment, to be equitable. All such determinations in any particular instance shall not be binding on the Company in subsequent instances.

E. The monthly commissions otherwise payable to Representative shall be offset by any debits issued against Representative's commission account. Debits shall be issued in accordance with the following provisions of Paragraph 6 hereof:

i) If any credits, discounts, rebates or allowances (except prompt payment discounts) are granted to an account after merchandise has been shipped and invoiced, a debit will be issued for the commissions allocable thereto.

ii) A debit will be issued for the commissions allocable to any amounts which are more than Ninety (90) days past due, and/or are written off by the Company as bad debts. Any subsequent collection of all or any portion of such amounts shall not serve to reduce, offset, or reverse the debit. In situations in which the Company engages an attorney or collection agency, the provisions of subparagraph iii) will be controlling.

iii) If the Company incurs any legal expense or pays any collection agency for the collection or attempted collection of any unpaid amounts from accounts serviced by

Representative, a debit will be issued for the commissions allocable to the entire amount sought to be collected, and the collection of all or any portion of the indebtedness shall not serve to reduce, offset, or reverse the debit.

iv) If Representative (or any other business entity in which Representative or any of its principals has any ownership or other financial interest) becomes indebted to the Company, regardless of the basis or nature of the indebtedness, the Company shall have the right to issue a debit against Representative's commission account for the full amount of such indebtedness or any portion thereof.

v) Debits shall be issued during the term of this Agreement and thereafter, until the completion of the final reconciliation, as provided in Paragraph 6 hereof. All debits issued in any particular calendar month shall serve to reduce the commissions payable to Representative in succeeding calendar months until said debits have been offset in their entirety against commissions. If the debits issued against Representative's commission account at any time exceed the commissions then due Representative, the Company may require, in lieu of offsetting said debits against future commissions, that Representative pay said excess amount to the Company. In such event, payment shall be made by Representative to the Company within Thirty (30) days after receipt of the Company's written demand therefor.

D. The Company shall furnish Representative periodically with statements reflecting the status of Representative's commission account. If Representative has objections with respect to any such statement, whether regarding its accuracy, completeness or any other matter, Representative shall make such objection(s) known to the Company in writing within thirty (30) days after the date of the statement. ANY AND ALL OBJECTIONS AS TO WHICH WRITTEN NOTICE IS NOT RECEIVED BY THE COMPANY WITHIN THE THIRTY (30) DAY PERIOD SHALL BE DEEMED WAIVED AND ABANDONED.

6. Final Settlement Procedures. Notwithstanding anything contained in Paragraph 5, any commissions otherwise becoming earned and due to Representative as of the expiration or termination date of this Agreement, or thereafter, may be withheld by the Company and shall become due, if at all, only after a final reconciliation is performed by the Company One Hundred Fifty (150) days subsequent to the expiration or termination date ("the Reconciliation Date"). In lieu of withholding the entire amount of such commissions, the Company may, at its option, withhold only that portion as the Company deems necessary for its financial protection. The Company shall debit Representative's commission account on the Reconciliation Date for the commissions allocable to any outstanding invoices applicable to customers serviced by Representative, which the Company believes are uncollectible or in jeopardy of non-payment. If the debits allocable to such invoices, together with any other debits not previously offset against commissions do not exceed the amount of any remaining commissions otherwise payable to Representative, the difference between the remaining commissions and the outstanding debits then shall be considered earned and due, and thereupon shall be paid by the Company to Representative. If all outstanding debits exceed the remaining commissions, no additional commissions shall be considered earned and due, and Representative shall be required to pay the Company the difference between such outstanding debits and the remaining commissions, upon receipt of the Company's statement therefor. After the Reconciliation Date, no additional commissions shall become earned and due to Representative, and the Company shall not be entitled to issue any additional debits against Representative's commission account.

7. Competitive Products.

A. Unless authorized by the Company in writing, neither Representative nor any other entity in which Representative or any of its principals has any ownership or other financial interest, shall act, at any time during the term of this Agreement, as a sales representative for any products or product lines which are in any way similar in design, function or intended use to Company Products, or which otherwise are competitive, in the Company's sole judgment, with the Company Products.

B. In order to ensure Representative's compliance with subparagraph A. hereof, Representative shall identify, from time to time, when requested by the Company, all products or product lines other than the Company Products, for which Representative (or any other business entity in which Representative or any of its principals has any ownership or other financial interest) is acting as a sales representative. Representative, in any event, shall notify the Company in writing, whenever Representative or any such other business entity is contemplating the commencement of representation for any additional products or product line(s).

8. Product Changes. The Company shall have the right, at its sole discretion, to modify or discontinue selling any or all of the Products at any time, without incurring any liability to Representative.

9. Purchases for Resale. In the event that the Company and Representative agree that Representative shall purchase quantities of the Company's Products for resale, any such purchases shall be at such prices and upon such other terms and conditions of sale as are determined by the Company from time to time, at its sole discretion. The Company shall have the right to cease selling the Company Products to Representative at any time.

10. Submission of Ideas to the Company. In consideration for the Company's execution of this agreement, Representative agrees that any and all business ideas, materials, procedures, policies and plans (hereinafter called collectively "the ideas") as may be submitted by Representative to the Company during the term of this Agreement and which pertain directly or indirectly to the business of the Company, shall belong to and be deemed to be the property of the Company. Unless otherwise agreed expressly in writing by an officer of the Company, the Company shall not be required to compensate Representative in any manner for the ideas, regardless of whether the Company utilizes or does not utilize the ideas, in whole or in part. Representative agrees to execute any additional documents as may be necessary to effectuate these provisions.

11. Proprietary Information. All financial, engineering, sales, marketing or other information disclosed by the Company to Representative as a consequence of Representative's relationship with the Company shall be treated by Representative as the Company's trade secrets and shall not be disclosed by Representative to any other person, firm or entity, during the term of this Agreement or thereafter, without the prior written consent of the Company, except to the extent that such information is in the public domain at the time of its disclosure to Representative or thereafter becomes in the public domain through no fault of Representative.

12. Representative's Business Expenses. Representative shall bear the entire responsibility for any and all expenses incurred in connection with its business (including, but not limited to leaseholding expenses, salaries, telephone and traveling expenses), and the Company shall not be obligated to pay any such expenses or to reimburse Representative therefore.

The Company shall have no responsibility for the payment of withholding, Social Security or unemployment taxes, or any similar taxes or other payments, with respect to commissions earned by Representative hereunder. If, notwithstanding the provisions of this paragraph, any such taxes or payments ever are assessed against the Company, Representative shall reimburse the Company promptly for all sums paid by the Company, including any interest or penalties.

13. Duration of Agreement/Termination.

A. This Agreement shall remain in effect until midnight of the last day of [specify] immediately following the date shown at the beginning of this Agreement, unless terminated sooner as provided in subparagraph B., or unless extended for an additional period. Any such extension shall be operative only if effectuated by a written instrument executed by both parties. NEITHER PARTY SHALL BE OBLIGATED TO EXTEND THE DURATION OF THIS AGREEMENT UPON THE EXPIRATION OF THE INITIAL TERM OR ANY SUCCEEDING TERM. Although either party may elect to provide the other with advance notice of any intention not to extend this Agreement upon its expiration, such notice shall not be required, it being understood that the notice provisions of subparagraph B apply solely to termination prior to expiration.

B. Either Representative or the Company may terminate this Agreement, at will, at any time during the initial term or any succeeding term, and such termination may be either with or without cause. If the termination is without cause, Thirty (30) days advance written notice must be provided by the terminating party to the other party. EACH PARTY ACKNOWLEDGES THAT SUCH THIRTY (30) DAY PERIOD IS ADEQUATE TO ALLOW IT TO TAKE ALL ACTIONS REQUIRED TO ADJUST ITS BUSINESS OPERATIONS IN ANTICIPATION OF TERMINATION. If the termination is for cause, no advance notice shall be required, but may be provided at the option of the terminating party. "Cause" for purposes of this paragraph shall include, but not necessarily be limited to, the following:

i) In the case of termination by Representative, cause shall exist if the Company materially breaches any provision of this Agreement.

ii) In the case of termination by the Company, cause shall exist:

a) If Representative fails to achieve any sales quota(s) assigned by the Company, fails to satisfy any of its other responsibilities provided in Paragraph 2 hereof, breaches Paragraph 7 of this Agreement, or breaches any other provision of this Agreement; or

b) If Representative is unable, by reason of illness or disability of any of its employees, to perform any of its responsibilities hereunder; or

c) If Representative sells its business or merges its business with another company, or if there is any other change in the management or control of Representative's business.

iii) Cause shall exist for termination by either party if the other party assigns or attempts to assign this Agreement, except as permitted hereunder, liquidates or terminates its business, is adjudicated a bankrupt, makes an assignment for the benefit of creditors, invokes the provisions of any law for the relief of debtors, or files or has filed against it any similar proceeding.

C. Upon any expiration or termination of this Agreement, Representative shall cease holding itself out in any fashion as a sales representative for the Company, and shall return to the Company, all sales literature, price lists, customer lists and any other documents, materials or tangible items pertaining to the Company's business, with the exception of any Company Product, which may have been purchased by Representative.

D. THIS AGREEMENT IS EXECUTED BY BOTH THE COMPANY AND REPRESENTATIVE WITH THE KNOWLEDGE THAT IT MAY BE TERMINATED OR NOT EXTENDED. NEITHER REPRESENTATIVE NOR THE COMPANY SHALL BE LIABLE TO THE OTHER FOR COMPENSATION, REIMBURSEMENT FOR INVESTMENTS OR EXPENSES, LOST PROFITS, INCIDENTAL OR CONSEQUENTIAL DAMAGES, OR DAMAGES OF ANY OTHER KIND OR CHARACTER, BECAUSE OF ANY EXERCISE OF ITS RIGHT TO TERMINATE THIS AGREEMENT, AS PROVIDED HEREUNDER, OR BECAUSE OF ANY ELECTION TO REFRAIN FROM EXTENDING THE DURATION OF THIS AGREEMENT UPON THE EXPIRATION OF THE INITIAL TERM OR ANY SUCCEEDING TERM.

14. Applicable Law, Forum Selection and Consent to Jurisdiction. This agreement shall be governed and construed in all respects in accordance with the laws of the state of [specify]. Any litigation instituted by Representative against the Company pertaining to any breach or termination of this Agreement, or pertaining in any other manner to this Agreement, must be filed by Representative before a court of competent jurisdiction in [specify state] and Representative hereby consents irrevocably to the jurisdiction of the [specify state] courts over its person. Service of process may be made upon Representative as provided by [specify state] law, or shall be considered effective if sent by Certified or Registered Mail, Return Receipt Requested, Postage Prepaid.

15. Miscellaneous.

A. Representative may not assign, transfer or sell all or any of its rights under this Agreement (or delegate all or any of its obligations hereunder), without the prior written consent of the Company. If a sale or other transfer of Representative's business is contemplated (whether by transfer of stock, assets or otherwise), Representative shall notify the Company in writing no less than Thirty (30) days prior to effecting such transfer, but such notice shall not obligate the Company in any manner. The Company may assign this Agreement only to a parent, subsidiary or affiliated firm or to another entity in connection with the sale or other transfer of all or substantially all of its business assets. Subject to these restrictions, the provisions of this Agreement shall be binding upon and shall inure to the benefit of the parties, their successors and permitted assigns.

B. The waiver by either party of any of its rights or any breaches of the other party under this Agreement in a particular instance shall not be construed as a waiver of the same or different rights or breaches in subsequent instances. All remedies, rights, undertakings and obligations hereunder shall be cumulative, and none shall operate as a limitation of any other remedy, right, undertaking or obligation hereunder.

C. Representative shall maintain automobile insurance, general liability insurance, and any other insurance required by applicable laws or regulations.

D. All notices and demands of any kind which either the Company or Representative may be required or desire to serve upon the other under the terms of this Agreement shall be in writing and shall be served by personal delivery or by mail, at the addresses set forth in this Agreement or at such other addresses as may be designated hereafter by the parties in writing. If by personal delivery, service shall be deemed complete upon such delivery. If by mail, service shall be deemed complete upon mailing.

E. The paragraph headings contained herein are for reference only and shall not be considered substantive provisions of this Agreement. The use of a singular or plural form shall include the other form, and the use of a masculine, feminine or neuter gender shall include the other genders.

F. In the event that any of the provisions of this Agreement or the application of any such provisions to the parties hereto with respect to their obligations hereunder shall be held by a court of competent jurisdiction to be unlawful or unenforceable, the remaining portions of this Agreement shall remain in full force and effect and shall not be invalidated or impaired in any manner.

G. This agreement supersedes any and all other agreements between the parties pertaining in any manner to the subject matter hereof, and contains all of the covenants and agreements between the parties with respect to said subject matter. Each party to this Agreement acknowledges that no written or oral representations, inducements promises or agreements have been made which are not embodied herein. IT IS THE INTENTION AND DESIRE OF THE PARTIES THAT THIS AGREEMENT NOT BE SUBJECT TO IMPLIED COVENANTS OF

ANY KIND. Except as otherwise provided in this Agreement, this Agreement may not be amended, modified or supplemented, except by a written instrument signed by both parties hereto.

    H. This Agreement has been executed in multiple counterparts, each of which shall be deemed enforceable without production of the others.

IN WITNESS WHEREOF, the parties hereto have executed this Agreement as of the date and year first hereinabove written.

ACCEPTED AND CONSENTED TO:

[Sales Representative's Full Legal Name] and
[D.B.A (if different from Legal Name)]
"The Representative"

[Name of Corporation]
"The Company"

By: _____
    Signature

By: _____
    Signature

Title: _____

Title: _____
    [Corporate officer]

EXHIBIT "A"
FOR INDEPENDENT SALES REPRESENTATIVE AGREEMENT BETWEEN [Name of Company] AND [Sales Representative's Full Legal Name and D.B.A (If Different from Legal Name)]

TERRITORY: Representative's appointment is applicable in the following geographic territory: In the state of [specify], includes the counties of [specify].

This Exhibit is effective as of [specify], and supersedes any prior Exhibits concerning the subject matter hereof.

[Sales Representative's Full Legal Name] and
[D.B.A (if different from Legal Name)]
"The Representative"

[Name of Corporation]
"The Company"

By: _____
      Signature

By: _____
      Signature

Title: _____

Title: _____
[Corporate officer (indicate office), Partner, Owner]

EXHIBIT "B"
FOR INDEPENDENT SALES REPRESENTATIVE AGREEMENT BETWEEN [Name of Company] AND [Sales Representative's Full Legal Name and D.B.A (If Different from Legal Name)]

COMMISSION SCHEDULE: The commission rate shall be [specify] percent of the net invoice price.

This Commission Schedule is subject to modification by the Company pursuant to the provisions of Paragraph 5A of the Independent Sales Representative Agreement.

This Exhibit is effective as of [specify date], and supersedes any prior Exhibits concerning the subject matter hereof.

[Sales Representative's Full Legal Name] and
[D.B.A (if different from Legal Name)]
"The Representative"

[Name of Corporation]
"The Company"

By: _____
    Signature

By:_____
    Signature

Title: _____

Title: _____
[Corporate officer (indicate office), Partner, Owner]

SAMPLE INDEPENDENT SALES REPRESENTATIVE AGREEMENT
Short Version

Name
Title
Street Address
City, State, Zip

Dear [Name of Officer],

This will confirm your engagement as an independent sales representative for [Name of Company] (hereinafter referred to as "the Company") under the following terms and conditions:

1. You will devote your best efforts for the solicitation of orders resulting in sales of our [specify product] to the [specify type of industry] located in the States of [specify], in which you shall have exclusive territorial rights.

2. You are hereby retained as an independent contractor and not as an employee of the Company. As an independent contractor, you shall be solely responsible to pay all applicable taxes arising from payments made to you by the Company, including, but not limited to, social security, self-employment taxes and disability insurance. Neither you nor your employees shall be entitled to participate in any Company plans, arrangements or distributions pertaining to any pension, stock, bonus, profit sharing or similar benefits.

3. You agree to indemnify and hold the Company harmless from any and all liability, claims, demands or requirements imposed by federal or state law upon self-employed individuals arising from payments made to you under this Agreement.

4. You agree to bear all expenses incurred in your sales endeavors except those which the Company agrees to pay for in writing.

5. You agree to make no representations, warranties or commitments binding the Company without the Company's prior consent. You will execute no agreement on behalf of the Company nor shall you hold yourself out as having such authority. In addition, you warrant and represent to the Company that you are free to enter into this Agreement and that this does not violate any agreement heretofore made by you.

6. You agree that if you or your employees shall operate a motor vehicle during the term of this Agreement, the Company is not responsible for any damage or loss sustained by the use of said automobile during the term hereof. If you or your employees shall operate a motor vehicle in the performance of your duties hereunder, you will maintain public liability insurance in limits not less than $300,000/$500,000, and shall promptly furnish the Company with documentation evidencing same upon our request.

7. The Company has the sole right to establish, alter or amend product specifications, prices, delivery schedules and discounts, and the Company will give you timely notice of any and all changes.

8. In full payment for all services to be rendered by you, the Company shall pay you a commission of [specify percentage] of all orders shipped into your exclusive territory, with the following exception:

The Company shall pay a split commission for any accepted orders taken from a customer in your territory but shipped to an affiliate, subsidiary or designee of said customer in another sales representative's territory. In addition, you shall receive a split commission for any accepted orders taken from a customer in another sales representative's territory but shipped into your territory. The Company reserves the right to allocate or split the [specify percentage] commission in a manner it deems most reasonable to best reward the sales representative who had greatest influence on the sale.

9. All orders are subject to acceptance by the Company at our home office and the Company may reject an order at any time for any reason.

10. The Company shall furnish you with copies of all invoices for shipments of our product into your territory and shall keep an accurate set of books and records regarding commissions due. Exceptions to this policy are split commissions whereby only the representative servicing the "Bill to" address will receive invoice copies. Commission statements and payments shall be sent to your offices at [specify City and State] no later than the Twentieth (20th) day of the month following the month the goods are shipped. Commission statements presented to you shall be deemed correct unless objections in writing are received by the Company within Thirty (30) days from the issuance of same.

11. You agree to assist the Company in all collection efforts from non-paying customers in your territory upon our request. Notwithstanding the foregoing, the Company shall deduct commission on credits, returns, and bad debts from your commission statement as they become due. For the purposes of this Agreement, bad debts are defined as uncollectible invoices exceeding 120 days.

12. You covenant and agree that during the term of this Agreement, you shall not sell, promote or offer for sale, directly or indirectly, any product which might in any way be deemed competitive to our [specify] line and that you presently carry no line which is competitive with said product. Notwithstanding the foregoing, you agree to notify the Company in writing of all future products with the name of the manufacturer you intend to carry, competing, or otherwise, before your representation of same. This covenant shall become a material part of this Agreement.

13. The Company hereby employs you at will and this Agreement may be terminated by either party at any time for any reason. Said termination will be effective after either party sends to the other, by Certified Mail, Return Receipt Requested, a written notice of intent to terminate at the expiration of Thirty (30) days from the date upon which such notice is mailed to the other.

Such termination will then occur at the end of the Thirty (30) day notice period. Notwithstanding the foregoing, the Company shall be able to terminate this Agreement immediately, without the sending of the aforesaid written Thirty (30) day notice, upon your death, bankruptcy, or in the event you breach any of the material terms of this Agreement.

14. In the event you send the Company written notice of your intent to terminate this Agreement pursuant to Paragraph 13, you shall continue to solicit orders for the Company during the aforesaid Thirty (30) day period. Notwithstanding the foregoing, if the Company sends you written notice of its intent to terminate this Agreement pursuant to Paragraph 13, you shall cease soliciting orders for the Company immediately on the day said notice of termination is received by you.

15. At the termination of this Agreement, a final accounting will be made between the Parties. In the event you send the Company notice of your intent to terminate this Agreement pursuant to Paragraph 13, you will receive full commission on all accepted orders shipped within your territory during the Thirty (30) day notice period prior to the effective termination date of this Agreement.

16. Notwithstanding the provisions contained in Paragraph 15, if the Company sends you written notice of its intent to terminate this Agreement pursuant to Paragraph 13, and you are not terminated for cause, the Company will pay you severance compensation as additional consideration for entering into this Agreement. The amount of severance to be paid shall be computed by calculating the average monthly commission earned by you during the preceding full year, multiplied by the following formula:

Years Representing Company	**Amount of Severance Compensation**
0 through 5 years	1 month
6 through 10 years	2 months
11 through 15 years	3 months
16 through 20 years	4 months
21 through 25 years	5 months
more than 25 years	6 months

The following example will illustrate the aforesaid: A representative is notified of termination by the Company on October 1, 1994, and the termination is without cause. The representative was employed by the Company for Four (4) years and earned $48,000 in commissions during 1993, or an average of $4,000 per month. Therefore, upon termination, the representative would receive full commission on all orders shipped into his territory during October 1994, and severance compensation of $4,000 upon termination of this Agreement.

17. The aforesaid severance compensation shall be paid in equal monthly installments with the first payment due commencing the effective termination date of this Agreement, provided you have complied with all terms and conditions of this Agreement. Said severance compensation shall represent full and final payment of all services rendered by you and benefits received by the Company from your efforts, and you shall have no claims for re-orders, territorial rights, or otherwise.

18. At the termination of this Agreement, you shall cease using any sales materials and product samples in your possession or under your control and shall return same, including all catalogs, brochures, advertising, literature and other property of the Company, immediately upon our request. Final severance compensation due, if any, shall not be paid until such property is received by us and has been returned in reasonably good condition, together with a duly executed general release.

19. Both parties acknowledge that the Company is entering into this Agreement due to the special, unique and extraordinary skills of [Name of Representative]. Accordingly, this Agreement may not be transferred, sold or assigned to any other individual, corporation, partnership or joint venture without the Company's prior approval. Notwithstanding the foregoing, the Company shall be notified in writing of your intention to cease selling the Company's product, an intention to liquidate your business, sell its assets, or sell or transfer more than 50% of the capital stock of the business, no less than Five (5) business days prior to the occurrence of same. In no event will the Company be bound to continue this Agreement under the same terms and conditions to your transferee, successor or majority stockholder, or in the event that [specify] is no longer personally and actively involved in selling the Company's products.

20. You shall notify the Company of all employees you intend to hire who shall assist you in representing the Company's products no less than Five (5) working days prior to their representation of same.

21. You hereby covenant, warrant and represent that both you and your employees will keep confidential, both during the term of this Agreement and forever after its termination, all information obtained from the Company with respect to all trade secrets, proprietary matters, business procedures, customer lists, needs of customers, manufacturing processes and all matters which are competitive and confidential in nature, and will not disclose this information to any person, firm, corporation or other entity for any purpose or reason whatsoever. The Company shall be entitled to an injunction restraining you from disclosing this information in the event of a breach or threatened breach of the provisions of this paragraph.

22. You agree that while this Agreement is in effect and for a period equal to the length of time you continue to receive severance compensation as more fully defined in Paragraph 17, that you and your employees shall not, directly or indirectly, for yourself or any other individual, partnership, corporation, or entity, solicit, represent, act on behalf of, sell or provide solicitation to any individual, partnership, corporation or entity competing against the Company. The Company agrees to pay, and you agree to receive the aforementioned severance compensation, as fair and reasonable consideration and an adequate bargained-for exchange so that a court of competent jurisdiction will enforce the provisions of this restrictive covenant as aforesaid.

23. Any claim or controversy arising among or between the parties hereto and any claim or controversy arising out of or respecting any matter contained in this Agreement or any difference as to the interpretation of any of the provisions of this Agreement shall be settled by arbitration in [specify City and State] by Three (3) arbitrators under the then prevailing rules of the American Arbitration Association.

24. In any arbitration involving this Agreement, the arbitrators shall not make any award which will alter, change, cancel or rescind any provision of the Agreement and their award shall be consistent with the provisions of this Agreement. Any such arbitration must be commenced no later than One (1) year from the date such claim or controversy arose. The award of the arbitrators shall be final and binding and judgment may be entered in any court of competent jurisdiction. In addition to the foregoing, the Company may apply to any court of appropriate jurisdiction for any of the provisional remedies it may be entitled to, including but not limited to injunction, attachment or replevin, pending the determination of any claim or controversy pursuant to the arbitration provisions of this Agreement.

25. Service of process and notice of arbitration of any and all documents and papers may be made either by Certified or Registered mail, addressed to either party at the addresses listed in the Agreement.

26. The Agreement is being made by each of the parties after each party has had an opportunity to fully review, analyze, and obtain legal counsel with respect to this Agreement and all of its terms.

27. Nothing in this Agreement shall be construed to constitute you as a partner, affiliate or employee of the Company.

28. This Agreement forms the entire understanding between the parties. It cancels and supersedes all prior agreements and understandings.

29. There shall be no change, amendment or modification of any of the terms of this Agreement unless it is reduced to writing and signed by both parties.

30. If any provision of this Agreement is held by a court of competent jurisdiction or arbitration to be unenforceable, the remainder of the Agreement shall remain in full force and effect and shall in no way be impaired.

31. This Agreement shall be governed by the laws of the State of [specify].

Your signature in the lower left-hand corner of the copy hereof will indicate the acceptance of the terms and conditions herein stated, and thereafter this letter shall constitute our whole and complete agreement concerning your engagement which may not be orally modified or extended.

Very truly yours,
[NAME OF COMPANY]
("The Company")

_____
By: [Name of Officer]
      [Title]

Consented and Agreed to:
By: [NAME OF REP OR REP FIRM]

_____
By: [NAME OF OFFICER]
      [TITLE]

[DATE]

SECTION TWO:
Day-to-Day Operations

SAMPLE CODE OF ETHICS POLICY STATEMENT

[Name of Company] maintains certain policies to guide its employees with respect to standards of conduct expected in areas where improper activities could damage the Company's reputation and otherwise result in serious adverse consequences to the Company and to employees involved. The purpose of this Policy is to affirm, in a comprehensive statement, required standards of conduct and practices with respect to certain types of payments and political contributions.

An employee's actions under this Policy are significant indications of the individual's judgement and competence. Accordingly, those actions constitute an important element in the evaluation of the employee for position assignments and promotion. Correspondingly, insensitivity to or disregard of the principles of this Policy will be grounds for appropriate management disciplinary action.

STATEMENT OF POLICY
Prohibition of Improper Payments

The Company expects all employees to use only legitimate practices in commercial operations and in promoting the Company position on issues before governmental authorities. As stated below, "kickbacks" or "bribes" intended to induce or reward favorable buying decisions and governmental actions are unacceptable and prohibited.

No employee of the Company or any Controlled Affiliate acting on the Company's behalf shall, in violation of any applicable law, offer or make directly or indirectly through any other person or firm, any payment of anything of value (in the form of compensation, gift, contribution or otherwise) to:

- any person or firm employed by or acting for or on behalf of any customer, whether private or governmental, for the purpose of inducing or rewarding any favorable action by the customer in any commercial transaction; or any governmental entity, for the purpose of inducing or rewarding action (or withholding of action) by a governmental entity in any governmental matter;

- any governmental official, political party or official of such party, or any candidate for political office, for the purpose of inducing or rewarding favorable action (or withholding of action) or the exercise of influence by such official, party or candidate in any commercial transaction or in any governmental matter.

In utilizing consultants, agents, sales representatives or others, the Company will employ only reputable, qualified individuals or firms under compensation arrangements which are reasonable in relation to the services performed. The [specify department] will issue from time to time criteria and procedures to be utilized in international transactions with respect to the selection and compensation of sales representatives. Consultants, agents or representatives retained in relation to the provision of goods or services to the federal government must agree to comply with all laws, regulations and Company policies governing employee conduct.

The provisions of this section are not intended to apply to ordinary and reasonable business entertainment or gifts not of substantial value, customary in local business relationships and not violative of law as applied in that environment. In some countries (but not in all countries—and particularly not in the United States), it may be acceptable to make such insubstantial gifts to minor government officials where customary in order to expedite or secure routine administrative action required in the orderly conduct of operations. Managers are expected to exercise sound discretion and control in authorizing such business entertainment and gifts.

When customer organizations, governmental agencies, or others have published policies intended to provide guidance with respect to acceptance of entertainment, gifts, or other business courtesies by their employees, such policies shall be respected.

Political Contributions

The Company will not make any contribution to any political party or to any candidate for political office in support of such candidacy except as provided in this Policy and as permitted by law.

In the United States, federal law strictly controls corporate involvement in the federal political process. Generally, federal law provides that no corporation may contribute anything of value to any political party or candidate in connection with any federal election.

While similar laws apply in some states and their political subdivisions, in many jurisdictions in the United States corporate contributions to candidates and political parties in connection with state and local election campaigns are lawful.

The laws governing participation by corporations in the political process of countries other than the United States vary widely. In certain countries, contributions to the political process (including contributions to political parties) are lawful and expected as a matter of good corporate citizenship.

In foreign jurisdictions and in state and local jurisdictions of the United States where corporate political contributions are lawful, contributions by the Company or by a Controlled Affiliate may be appropriate if prudent in amount and otherwise consistent with good judgment. Company contributions shall be governed by written guidelines. Contributions by a Controlled Affiliate shall also be governed by written guidelines or other form of written authority as established by the affiliate's Board of Directors. Any contribution by the Company or by a Controlled Affiliate shall comply in all respects with the provisions of local applicable law and shall be reported as part of the annual review process provided by this Policy.

This Policy is not intended to prevent the communication of Company views to legislators, governmental agencies, or to the general public with respect to existing or proposed legislation or governmental policies or practices affecting business operations. Moreover, under this Policy, reasonable costs incurred by the Company to establish or administer political action committees or activities organized to solicit voluntary political contributions from individual employees are not regarded as contributions to political parties or candidates, where such costs may lawfully be incurred by the Company.

Reports and Periodic Reviews

Any employee who is requested to make, authorize, or agree to any offer or payment which is, or may be, contrary to this Policy will promptly report such information to the employee's manager, to assigned Company legal counsel, or to the manager in the component having responsibility for financial activity.

Any employee who acquires information (for example, newspaper reports, reports from customers, or statements of individuals involved) that gives the employee reason to believe that any employee is engaged in conduct forbidden by this Policy, or that any sales representative, distributor, or other person or firm representing the Company in any transaction is engaged in the type of conduct (whether or not in connection with a transaction involving the Company or its products) which, if engaged in by an employee of the Company, would violate this Policy, will promptly report such information to the employee's manager, to assigned company legal counsel, or to the manager in the component having responsibility for financial activity.

Any manager receiving a report as cited above will promptly consult with assigned Company legal counsel and thereafter will, after appropriate investigation, take timely remedial or other action as warranted under the provisions of this Policy. Such manager will also promptly report the matter to higher management.

COMPLIANCE WITH THE ANTITRUST LAWS

For many years [Name of company] has recognized a need to single out compliance with the antitrust laws of the United States and other countries as a subject requiring a specific Company policy. The antitrust laws are relevant to many business decisions, and the consequences of violations anywhere can be seriously injurious to the Company and to the individuals involved.

Several provisions of the antitrust laws of the United States contain penal provisions under which employees who authorize or engage in acts in violation of such laws are personally subject to substantial fines and imprisonment. There are also in existence a number of antitrust decrees affecting the Company and its employees. Violation of any one of the provisions of these decrees is an offense which may subject the Company and the individuals involved to severe penalties.

Each manager must accept the challenge to have the Company excel competitively at the point of market confrontation; for, apart from legal penalties, Company growth and profitability objectives would be frustrated by arrangements with other business firms which restrict its competitive initiative.

Officers, managers and other key employees are expected to develop in employees a sense of commitment to comply with this policy. The antitrust compliance environment within such a key employee's assigned area of responsibility will be a significant factor in evaluating the quality of that individual's performance.

Statement of Policy

It is the objective of the Company:

- to comply with the antitrust laws of the United States and other countries applicable to its business operations, and

- to hold employees in management positions personally and strictly accountable for taking the measures necessary to achieve this objective within their areas of responsibility.

Compliance With Section 1 of the Sherman Act

In furtherance of this Policy and specifically in furtherance of compliance with Section 1 of the Sherman Act:

A. No employee shall enter into any understanding or agreement—whether expressed or implied, formal or informal, written or oral—with a competitor limiting or restricting any of the following aspects of the competitive strategy of either party or of the business offering of either party to any third party or parties:

prices
costs
profits
product or service offerings
terms or conditions of sale
production or sales volume
production facilities or capacity
market share
decisions to quote or not to quote
customer or supplier classification or selection
sales territories
distribution methods

B. No employee shall enter into any understanding or agreement with a purchaser or lessee of a product sold or leased by the Company which restricts the right of the purchaser or lessee to determine the price at which to resell or lease such product; nor shall any employee enter into such an agreement when the Company is the purchaser or lessee of a product.

C. The following understandings may be violative of the antitrust laws under certain circumstances and may be entered into by an employee of the Company only if the agreement has been reviewed by Company legal counsel in advance of execution and in the opinion of counsel is not in violation of law:

(1) Understandings with any customer or supplier which condition the sales or purchases of The Company on reciprocal purchases or sales by the customer/supplier;

(2) understandings with any purchaser or lessee of a product of the Company which in any way restrict the discretion of the customer to use or resell the product as the customer sees fit;

(3) understandings with anyone which restrict the discretion of either party to manufacture any product or provide any service, or to sell to, or buy from, any third party.

Discussions And Exchange Of Information With Competitors

Communication with a competitor on subjects as to which an understanding with the competitor would be illegal is, in antitrust litigation, likely to serve as important evidence of the existence of an understanding, particularly if the communication is accompanied or followed by similarity of action. The prohibitions set forth below are thus intended to avoid antitrust prosecutions which, though based on merely circumstantial evidence, may nevertheless be difficult to defend successfully.

Accordingly, no employee shall discuss with a competitor or any third party acting for a competitor, or otherwise furnish to or accept from a competitor or any third party acting for a competitor, information on any subject as to which an understanding with the competitor is prohibited by paragraph A. above on compliance with Section 1 of the Sherman Act unless, in the opinion of Company legal counsel, such discussions or transmittal of information would neither violate the antitrust laws nor furnish a reasonable basis for inferring such a violation. This paragraph does not preclude obtaining competitive information from independent third-party sources who are not acting for a competitor in transmitting the information. However, certain other legal and policy restrictions applicable to transactions with the federal government limit the competitive information that may be obtained from a third-party source.

Participation in Trade Associations and Other Meetings with Competitors

A. No employee shall attend or remain present:

(1) at any surreptitious meeting of competitors;

(2) at any meeting where there is a discussion by competitors of any subject which the Company's employee is precluded from discussing by the paragraph above on Discussions and Exchange of Information with Competitors; or

(3) at any informal meeting of competitor members of a trade association held for the purpose of discussing business matters without observing the formal procedural requirements established by such trade association for its business meetings.

B. Employees should also be aware that participation in standard development and product certification activities which impact competitors or suppliers may raise antitrust concerns. Before participating in committees or organizations which develop standards or certify products, employees should consult with Company legal counsel.

Violations of the Policy

A. Violations of the Policy are grounds for discharge or other disciplinary action, adapted to the circumstances of the particular violation and having as a primary objective furtherance of the Company's interest in preventing violations and making clear that violations are neither tolerated nor condoned.

B. Disciplinary action will be taken, not only against individuals who authorize or participate directly in a violation of the Policy, but also against:

(1) any employee who may have deliberately failed to report a violation of the Policy;

(2) any employee who may have deliberately withheld relevant and material information concerning a violation of this Policy; and

(3) the violator's managerial superiors, to the extent that the circumstances of the violation reflect inadequate leadership and lack of diligence.

C. Where an employee is accused of violating the antitrust laws, and the employee has relied in good faith on the advice of Company legal counsel after full disclosure of the material facts, no disciplinary action may be taken against the employee under this Policy; and the Company may, within the limits permitted by law, assist in the employee's defense.

Reports and Periodic Reviews

A. Any employee who is requested to engage in any activity which is or may be contrary to this Policy will promptly report such information to the manager whom the individual reports, or, if the employee was so directed by the manager, then to assigned Company legal counsel.

B. Any employee who acquires information that gives the employee reason to believe that any other employee is engaged in conduct forbidden by the Policy will promptly report such information to the manager to whom the employee reports or, if the manager is engaged in such conduct, then to the assigned Company legal counsel.

    I [name of Employee] have received and read a copy of this Sample Code of Ethics Policy Statement, understand all of its terms and agree to be bound by the provisions contained therein.

_____   _____   _____

   [Printed Name]   [Signature]   [Date]

RECEIPT OF IDEA

On this day, received from [specify employee], an idea concerning [specify] which was presented in the form of [specify: a note, letter, design, drawing, etc.]

The Company acknowledges the furnishing of this idea; however, it is specifically agreed to between the parties that no representations regarding compensation due for its use have been made to the Employee. Furthermore, the Employee agrees and understands that the Company is not obligated to pay any form of compensation to the Employee if the idea is eventually used or incorporated and that the Employee has voluntarily conveyed this idea to the Company on his/her behalf, without fraud, coercion or duress.

It is understood and agreed to by the Employee that any monies that may be paid to him/her by the Company are not enforceable by contract but are gratuitous and that any such payment(s) and amounts are solely determined at the Company's discretion with no right of protest by the Employee.

Finally, the Employee agrees to assign all of his/her rights to such inventions, ideas, etc. to the Company upon the signing of this acknowledgement and to sign all documents necessary to evidence same.

[NAME OF EMPLOYER]

By: _____

[NAME OF EMPLOYEE]

By: _____

TRADE SECRET CONCERNS CHECKLIST

1. All employers must establish policies dealing with trade secrets, confidential information, and other rules of employee conduct to protect their assets.

2. Understand what constitutes a trade secret.

3. Understand what constitutes confidential information.

4. Customer lists that can be compiled from a telephone directory or other readily available source are generally not trade secrets.

5. Create a climate of confidentiality to protect your trade secrets.

6. Advise employees of the seriousness of the problem.

7. Display posters reminding workers of their obligations to protect confidential information and publish such journals, work rules and policy manuals.

8. Distribute memos that employees must sign on an annual basis which confirms that the employee acknowledges the type of information that is confidential and agrees not to convey such information to non-essential third parties.

9. In some states, it is a crime to steal trade secrets.

10. Federal law prohibits stolen information worth more than $5,000 that is transported across state lines.

11. Be extra careful that a terminated or parting employee does not leave with any valuable or potentially valuable materials (or copies) such as business-generated reports, letters, etc.

12. Utilize restrictive covenants in employment agreements whenever practicable. Such clauses can:

    a. Restrict an ex-employee from working for a competitor of the former employer;

    b. Restrict an ex-employee from starting a business or forming a venture with others that competes against the former employer;

    c. Restrict an ex-employee from contacting or soliciting former or current customers or employees of the former employer;

    d. Restrict an ex-employee from using confidential knowledge, trade secrets, customer lists and other privileged information learned while working for the former employer; and

e. Restrict an ex-employee from any of the above both in geographic and time limitations.

13. To be enforceable, be sure the restriction is reasonable in terms of geographic scope and time limitations.

14. If you desire to impose such clauses on current employees, an offer of additional monetary benefits increases the odds that such arrangements may be enforceable.

15. Establish effective exit procedures to learn who a departing employee will be working for.

16. Act quickly if problems develop -- consult a labor lawyer immediately to determine your rights and options where applicable.

17. To increase the chances that your company will prevail in trade secret litigation, it is advisable to send a cease and desist letter immediately to the ex-employee and his new company. This may enable you to obtain a preliminary injunction to immediately stop the ex-employee from competing against your interests provided it is proved that:

    a. Trade secrets or confidential information is involved;

    b. Substantial economic harm will ensue if the injunction is not granted;

    c. Your company has a substantial chance of success at the eventual trial; and

    d. Immediate relief is necessary via the injunction to protect your business.

18. If you sit on your rights and not act quickly when a problem is uncovered, the chances of success at the injunction or trial may decrease.

SAMPLE STATEMENT ON TRADE SECRETS

The business of our Company involves valuable, confidential, and proprietary data and information of various kinds. Such data and information, called "Trade Secrets," concern:

- The names of Company customers and the nature of the Company's relationships (e.g., types and amounts of products acquired from the Company) with such customers;

- The Company's various computer systems and programs;

- Techniques, developments, improvements, inventions, and processes that are, or may be, produced in the course of the Company's operations; and

- Any other information not generally known concerning the Company or its operations, products, suppliers, markets, sales, costs, profits, customer needs and lists, or other information acquired, disclosed, or made known to Employees or agents while in the employ of the Company, which, if used or disclosed, could adversely affect the Company's business or give competitors an advantage.

Since it would harm our Company if any of our Trade Secrets were known to our competitors, it is the Company's policy that:

1. No Employee should, during or after his/her employment with the Company, use any Trade Secrets for his/her benefit, or disclose to any person, business, or corporation any Trade Secrets without the prior written consent of the Company.

2. Every Employee shall render exclusive and full-time services and devote his/her best efforts toward the performance of assigned duties and responsibilities (which may be changed at any time).

3. Every Employee should refrain from engaging directly or indirectly in any activity that may compete with, or result in a conflict of interest with the Company or that is not likely to be in the Company's best interests.

4. Every Employee should fully and completely disclose to the Company any inventions, ideas, works of authorship, and other Trade Secrets made, developed, and/or conceived by him/her alone or jointly with others, arising out of, or relating to, employment at the Company. All such inventions, ideas, works of authorship, copyrights, and other Trade Secrets shall be the sole property of the Company. The Employee agrees to execute and deliver to the Company such assignments, documents, agreements, or instruments which the Company may require from time to time to evidence its ownership of the results and proceeds of the Employee's services and creations.

5. The Employee understands that he/she owes the highest duty of loyalty with respect to his/her duties. This means that he/she will, among other things, maintain a constant vigil over Company property, never make secret profits at the Company's expense (e.g., service customers of the Company but bill them for personal benefit, or receive kickbacks or special favors from customers, etc.), dress in a proper fashion, not use drugs or alcohol while on the job, and maintain a personal or Company automobile in good condition, together with a valid driver's license.

6. Every Employee shall avoid discussing any matter of a confidential nature, or which constitutes a Trade Secret, with any competitor or its employees. This includes discussions regarding customers, pricing, and policies. The Employee is reminded that any such discussions may cause the Company and the Employee personally to have violated anti-trust laws, including the Sherman and Clayton Acts. Sanctions of up to three (3) years imprisonment and fines up to $100,000 have been imposed on those who violate such laws.

7. Upon termination of employment, or at any time the Company may request, every Employee shall promptly return to the Company all memoranda, notes, records, reports, technical manuals, and other documents (and all copies thereof) in his/her possession, custody, or control relating to Trade Secrets, all of which written materials, and other things shall be and remain the sole property of the Company. The failure to comply with this request shall be grounds for immediate dismissal. In addition, the Company shall not be obligated in any way to pay any severance upon termination to any Employee who fails to comply with the provisions of this paragraph specifically, and this memo generally.

8. Every Employee agrees to comply with the rules, regulations, policies, and procedures of the Company faithfully and to the best of his/her abilities. The Employee understands that the breach of any covenant contained herein may constitute substantial and irreparable harm to the Company, and the Company may seek injunctive relief and other relief which it deems necessary and appropriate under the circumstances to protect its rights and the Employee shall pay all reasonable attorney fees, costs, and expenses incurred by the Company in the enforcement of any such action.

I [name of Employee] have received and read a copy of this Trade Secrets and Confidential Information Policy statement, understand all of its terms and agree to be bound by the provisions contained therein.

_____   _____   _____
[Printed Name]   [Signature]   [Date]

SAMPLE EEO COMPLIANCE STATEMENT AND PLAN

A. Introduction

1. The Employer desires to practice equal opportunity with respect to all activities concerning its employees.

    a. Management has promulgated these guidelines on a strictly voluntary basis.

    b. The existence of these guidelines however should not be construed as an admission either in whole or in part that the Employer has engaged in any activity whereby minorities or women have been or are presently being underutilized, concentrated or discriminated against in any way in violation of federal, state or local fair employment practice laws.

2. In developing and implementing this policy, Employer has been guided by its established pre-existing policy of providing equal employment opportunity.

    a. All targets which the Employer has established shall not be considered rigid, inflexible quotas but rather reasonable objectives to be achieved in good faith.

    b. The use of goals and timetables by the Employer shall not discriminate against an individual or group of individuals with respect to any employment opportunity for which he, she or they are qualified on the grounds that he, she or they are not the beneficiaries of affirmative action themselves since the Employer does not sanction the discriminatory treatment of any person.

B. EEO Policy Statement.

1. It is the policy of the Employer not to make any adverse employment decisions against minorities or women with respect to recruitment, hiring, training, promotion and other terms and conditions of employment, provided the individual is qualified to perform the work available.

2. It is the policy to the Employer to comply voluntarily with the concepts and practices of affirmative action.

3. An officer of the Employer will review, supervise and evaluate the Company's affirmative action program and will monitor that program and make reports periodically and on an on-going basis to management.

4. Employment decisions shall be made after considering the principles of equal employment opportunity (EEO).

5. Promotion decisions shall be consistent with the principle of EEO; qualifications for promotion shall consist of merit and ability.

6. All personnel actions and programs including but not limited to compensation, benefits, transfers, layoffs, recalls, company-sponsored training, education, tuition assistance and social and recreational programs will be administered in a nondiscriminatory manner with respect to minorities and women, provided the individual is qualified to perform the work available.

C.   Reaffirmation of EEO Policy Statement.

    1.   The Employer:

    a.   Shall continue to provide equal employment opportunity to all qualified persons, and to continue to recruit, hire, train, promote and compensate persons in all jobs without regard to race, color, religion, sex or national origin.

    b.   Identify and analyze areas of its employment process so as to further the principles of equal employment opportunity.

    c.   Employment decisions in all areas will be made on the basis of furthering the objective of equal employment.

    d.   The recruitment, testing and hiring of all personnel will be without discrimination against any individual with regard to race, color, religion, sex, or national origin. Attempts will be made to contact known sources of minority and women potential applicants so as to maximize the participation of such applicants.

    e.   Individuals will be upgraded and promoted on the basis of their abilities, skills and experience.

    f.   Minority and women employees who are qualified, as well as those who are qualifiable through training will be considered for promotion.

    g.   Promotions will be based on valid occupational qualifications.

    h.   Management will attempt to effectuate transfers of minority and women employees whenever such transfers will increase the likelihood of greater job opportunity in areas where minority and female employees may have been or may now be underutilized.

    i.   If layoffs occur, they will be based on nondiscriminatory policies.

    j.   Personnel decisions affecting employees in areas such as compensation, benefits, transfers, layoffs, returns from layoff, Company-sponsored training, education, tuition assistance and social and recreational programs will be made and implemented without regard to race, color, religion, sex or national origin.

k. The Employer will periodically review personnel actions and collect data on a continuing basis to review all actions taken.

l. All employee benefits will be administered consistent with federal law.

m. Steps will be taken so that personnel and management are fully apprised of the Company's EEO policy which will be discussed and reviewed in supervisory and management meetings.

n. Periodic reviews will be conducted to insure the effectiveness of these goals.

o. EEO posters will be and remain placed in conspicuous locations.

p. New employees will be apprised of the Employer's equal opportunity policy at employee orientation and management training programs.

q. The EEO policy will be included in the Employee Handbook. Copies of the Employee Handbook will be distributed to all current employees and to new employees when they are hired and publicized in other printed materials where appropriate.

r. Special meetings will be conducted when appropriate and the Employer's EEO policy will be discussed in management training programs.

s. Periodic meetings may be held to re-emphasize to management and employees the Employers' commitment to EEO.

t. Equal employment opportunity policy will be posted on bulletin boards (in English and Spanish, where appropriate) and will continue to be displayed in the future.

u. When employees are featured in advertising, employee handbooks, or similar publications, both minority and non-minority men and women will appear in the pictures.

v. Employees are encouraged to bring questions, comments or complaints with respect to the Company's EEO/affirmative action policy, or the implementation and administration of that policy, to the Human Resources Department.

w. Management has communicated and will continue to publicize that it does not tolerate or permit harassment of any employee because of race, color, religion, sex or national origin.

x. All recruitment sources will be reminded of the Employer's commitment to EEO and affirmative action. All applicants will be treated without regard to race, color, religion, sex or national origin. Recruitment sources will be advised that the Employer actively seeks qualified women and minorities for employment.

y. Equal Opportunity Clauses shall be incorporated in all purchase orders, leases, contracts, etc. where practical.

z. When the Employer advertises in newspapers for prospective employees, the advertisement includes the EEO solicitation: "We are an Equal Opportunity Employer."

aa. No advertisements in newspapers will be placed in sex-segregated "Help Wanted" columns.

bb. Written notification of our EEO policy will be sent to all subcontractors, vendors and suppliers, and they will be requested to take appropriate action.

2. Actions by supervisory personnel inconsistent with this policy will not be tolerated and may lead to discharge.

3.

a. _____ (name) has been appointed Director of Equal Employment Opportunity Programs and has the primary management responsibility for ensuring full compliance with this policy.

b. _____'s (name) appointment been communicated to all management employees, and well as to the appropriate employees and his identity shall appear on all internal and external communications on the Company's equal opportunity programs.

c. The responsibilities of the Program Director include but are not necessarily limited to the following:

(i) Developing, modifying and maintaining effective policies and procedures.

(ii) Evaluating EEO progress and developing alternative approaches where necessary, including establishing goals and timetables that are reasonable, attainable and consistent with the Employer's affirmative action commitment.

(iii) Designing and implementing audit and reporting systems which will permit continuous monitoring of EEO progress and provide management with requisite data in that regard. Such systems will be used to:

(a) Measure the plan's effectiveness.

(b) Determine the degree to which the Employer's objectives and goals have been achieved.

(c) Indicate any need for additional action.

(iv) Serving as our representative in dealings with federal, state or local enforcement agencies.

(v) Serve as a liaison with minority organizations, women's organizations and community action groups concerned with the employment opportunities of minorities and women.

(vi) Continually educate management in the area of equal employment opportunity.

(vii) Resolve EEO-related charges or complaints.

(viii) Periodically audit training programs and hiring and promotion patterns so that any impediments to achieving the goals and timetables are removed.

(ix) Regularly discuss policies with local managers, supervisors and other employees, where appropriate, to ensure that the Company's policies are being implemented.

(x) Selectively review the qualifications of employees who are transferred or promoted to ensure that minorities and women are being given full opportunity with respect to such personnel actions.

(xi) Communicate with local supervisors and other local management employees to apprise them of the fact that their work performance is being evaluated in part on the basis of their EEO performance.

(xii) Assist supervisors in taking action to prevent harassment of any employees either because of their placement though affirmative action efforts or because of their race, color, sex, religion or national origin.

D. Identification of potential problem areas.

1. Particular attention should be paid to employee training and to those categories where minority groups and women may be underutilized.

2. Hiring statistics should reveal no adverse impact regarding minorities and females.

3. The selection process, including position descriptions, job titles, application forms, interview procedures, the use and administration of tests, referral procedures, and final selection process, training, transfers and promotions should be analyzed to ensure that such personnel practices are being uniformly applied without regard to race, color, religion, sex or national origin and that none of the selection procedures has an adverse impact on minorities or women, statistically or otherwise.

4. Employer's transfer and training experience reflects no adverse impact on minorities or women and all physical facilities, sponsored recreation and social events, and special programs, including educational assistance, are applied and made available on a nondiscriminatory basis.

E. Remedial action.

1. Where underutilization in any job group exists, goals and timetables have been established.

2. Application forms and related pre-employment inquiry forms have been drafted in compliance with applicable federal, state and local EEO laws.

3. Position descriptions are reviewed periodically and properly identify job-related requirements.

4. Where specific selection procedures for jobs are used, they are job-related.

5. Minorities and women are not excluded from any Company-sponsored activities or programs, and such programs are fully integrated.

6. No de facto segregation exists at the Company.

7. No artificial barriers or restrictive seniority provisions that result in overt or inadvertent discrimination exist at the Company.

8. Transportation, both public and private, is not a problem with respect to minority employment.

9. Subcontractors and suppliers the Employer uses have been advised of their EEO responsibilities.

10. Purchase orders contain the required Equal Opportunity Clause.

11. EEO posters provided by the federal government are prominently displayed in appropriate places at the Company.

12. A thorough analysis of the compensation, promotion, selection and other policies and practices of the Company indicates that no affected class exists among the Company's work force.

13. Job descriptions are periodically reviewed and revised to ensure that they are job-related and consistent for the same job from one department or unit to another.

14. Worker specifications are reviewed to ensure that they are job-related and do not screen out minorities or women.

15. With respect to sex discrimination:

a. Employment advertising does not express a sex preference and, if printed, does not appear in sex-segregated columns. Further, employees of both sexes are recruited for all jobs with Employer.

b. Our personnel policy manual and employment application forms expressly state there will be no discrimination on account of sex.

c. We recruit employees of both sexes for all positions, except where sex is a bona fide occupation qualification.

d. We do not rely upon a state "protective" law to deny women employees the right to any job they are qualified to perform.

e. We offer employees of both sexes an equal opportunity for any jobs they are qualified to perform, except when sex is a bona fide occupation qualification.

f. We do not make any distinction based upon sex with regard to employment opportunities, wages, hours or other terms and conditions of employment.

g. We do not make any distinction between married and unmarried persons of one sex that is not made between married and unmarried persons of the other sex.

h. We do not deny employment to women with young children and provide a day-care service for children of employees.

i. The Employer does not terminate employees of one sex in a particular job group when they reach a certain age, unless the same rule applies to members of the other sex.

j. Appropriate physical facilities to both sexes are provided.

k. Women who require time away from work for childbearing are not penalized.

l. The Employer's maternity policy fully complies with the 1978 Pregnancy Amendment to Title VII of the Civil Rights Act of 1964 and the Family and Medical Leave Act.

m. The wage schedules are not related to or based upon sex and conform to the Equal Pay Act.

n. The Employer does not discriminatorily restrict one sex to certain job groups or job classifications.

(i) Women are encouraged to apply for all positions in the Company for which they are qualified and to apply for all training programs which can facilitate their promotability.

(ii) We encourage minority and women employees to participate in community problems and support programs developed by organizations such as the National Alliance of Business, the Urban Coalition, and others concerned with improving the employment opportunities of minorities and women.

16. With respect to national origin discrimination:

a. The Employer is committed to providing and ensuring equal employment opportunity to all applicants and employees without regard to their religion or national origin.

b. This policy is general in nature, while placing particular emphasis on persons of Eastern, Middle and Southern European ancestry, such as Jews, Catholics, Italians, Greeks and Slavs.

17. Periodically the Employer shall review its practices to determine whether members of various religious and ethnic groups are receiving unfair consideration of job opportunities.

CONCLUSION

A. It is our policy not to discriminate against minorities or women with respect to recruitment, hiring, training, promotion and other terms and conditions of employment, provided the individual is qualified to perform the work available.

B. It is our policy to comply voluntarily with the concepts and practices of affirmative action.

C. An executive has been designated to administer the Company's affirmative action program and will monitor that program and make reports to senior management on a periodic and continuing basis.

D. All employment decisions shall be consistent with the principle of EEO.

E. All promotion decisions shall be consistent with the principle of EEO, and only valid qualifications will be required for promotion.

F. All other personnel actions or programs such as compensation, benefits, transfers, layoffs, recalls, company-sponsored training, education, tuition assistance and social and recreational programs will be administered in a nondiscriminatory manner with respect to minorities and women, provided the individual is qualified to perform the work available.

G. The use of goals and timetables in this written statement is not intended, nor is the effect of such goals and timetables intended, to discriminate against an individual or group of individuals with respect to any employment opportunity for which he, she or they are qualified on the basis that he, she or they are not the beneficiaries of affirmative action themselves.

CHECKLIST OF IMPORTANT ON-THE-JOB POLICIES TO FOLLOW

1. Establish policies dealing with trade secrets, confidential information and other rules of conduct to protect your assets.

2. Include a comprehensive trade secrets and confidential information policy in the company handbook and manual.

3. Display posters reminding workers of their obligation to protect company assets and publish such reminders on a continuing basis in company journals, work rules and policy manuals.

4. Distribute memos on an annual basis reminding key employees of their continuing obligation to protect company assets and secrets and retrieve all signed and dated forms.

5. Remind employees of their duties not to exceed authority, not to work for a competitor, and not to make secret profits.

6. Explain common anti-trust violations, particularly to your people in sales so potential problems in this area can be minimized, particularly in key areas including deceptive practices, refusal-to-deal situations, resale restrictions, tie-in and other restrictions, and price discrimination.

7. Take action to avoid violating numerous employee privacy rights. Areas to be especially careful include wiretapping and eavesdropping, interrogations, searches, and employee testing.

8. Do not retaliate against workers who assert union rights, voting rights and other rights of due process.

9. Always document problems in the employee's personnel file.

10. Prepare performance reviews and appraisals regularly; never inflate them.

11. State your performance appraisal policy in the company handbook.

12. Prepare forms correctly and train supervisors to prepare appraisals correctly.

13. Discuss all problems with higher level supervisors before discussing the performance appraisal with the employee.

14. Develop uniform policies with respect to employees who are given unsatisfactory reviews; never play favorites.

15. Always respond in writing to criticisms received by the appraised employee.

16. Keep the contents of all appraisals confidential.

17. Specify in your company's handbook or employee manual the kinds of conduct that are serious enough to justify immediate termination without a warning.

18. Prepare a system of progressive discipline suitable for your company.

19. Prepare written deficiency notices properly.

20. Give ample opportunity to hear the employee's version of the story before taking further action.

21. Instruct company supervisors to avoid confrontations at disciplinary conferences.

22. Use a supervisory pecking order effectively and consider suspensions without pay as a final recourse before firing, depending on the circumstances. Remember -- while applying disciplinary measures uniformly and consistently, there may be exceptions to company policy when considering the nature of the job and the circumstances of each particular case.

23. Take steps to insure on-the-job discrimination is avoided.

24. Never retaliate against workers who complain about on-the-job discriminations, particularly sexual harassment.

RECEIPT OF EMPLOYEE HANDBOOK FORM
(May be used with the Employment Application)
(By Applicant or Employee)

    I, (name of applicant or employee), have been given a copy of the XYZ Employer Handbook dated (specify). I have been advised and acknowledge that in the course of my employment with XYZ Employer, the Company may at any time change the policies, procedures, benefits and benefit plans contained therein with or without prior notice since nothing in the Handbook should be construed as a contract of employment or promise of continued benefits. If I have specific questions about any statement or provision in the Handbook, I will direct them to my Supervisor or to the Personnel Department.

    I acknowledge that the programs and statements outlined in the booklet are to be regarded only as <u>guidelines</u>, not <u>guarantees</u>, which the Company may, in its sole discretion, change as needed in order to manage its work force to the Company's benefit as XYZ Employer deems fit.

    Additionally, I acknowledge that no promise of job security has heretofore been given to me and that there are no such promises contained in the Handbook since I am employed <u>AT WILL</u> and may resign at any time or be fired from my job at any time, with or without notice and with or without cause.

_____
Signature of Applicant or Employee

_____
Printed Name of Applicant or Employee

Social Security Number: _____

Date: _____

Name of Witness: _____

COMPREHENSIVE CHECKLIST REGARDING DRUGS AND ALCOHOL IN THE WORKPLACE

A. **General Overview**

1. Illegal drug and alcohol use in the workplace is a major problem these days for employers.

2. At least 20 million workers use marijuana/hashish, 6 million are cocaine users and 100 million are alcohol users.

3. Studies suggest that the typical recreational drug user in the workplace is three times as late as fellow employees, has 2.5 times as many absences of eight or more days, is five times more likely to file a worker's compensation claim and is involved in accidents 3.6 times more frequently than other workers.

4. More companies are resorting to drug testing to identify drug users and reduce on-the-job accidents, especially those in high technology and security-conscious industries.

B. **Preliminary Considerations Concerning Applicant Drug and Alcohol Testing Programs**

1. Most state and local governments have passed laws permitting applicant drug and alcohol tests.

2. Such tests generally are not viewed as violating an individual's privacy rights if applicants are told in advance they must take and pass the test to get the job and all applicants must submit to such tests after a job offer as a condition of employment.

3. Check the law in your state and local municipal laws regarding the legality of such tests because some states (i.e., New York) still prohibit pre-employment drug testing in certain situations.

4. Drug and alcohol tests of job applicants are neither encouraged nor prohibited by the Americans With Disabilities Act (ADA).

5. Former drug users or alcoholics who have been rehabilitated or who are participating in a supervised rehabilitation program are protected under the ADA and generally must be considered for the job.

6. An applicant who is currently engaging in illegal drug use is not protected under federal ADA law.

Day-to-Day Operations

7. An employer may prohibit the use of illegal drugs and alcohol at the workplace and require that employees not be under the influence of illegal drugs or alcohol while at work.

C. **Strategies To Protect Employer When Testing Applicants**

1. Know the law.

2. Adopt a plan and record it in work rules, policy manuals, employment contracts and/or collective bargaining agreements.

3. Prepare employment applications to incorporate this right.

4. Get permission that the applicant authorizes drug and alcohol tests and agrees that a positive result will mean forfeiture of a job offer; make the applicant sign such a statement in the employment application.

5. To avoid discrimination lawsuits, be sure all applicants are tested, not just a particular class of applicant and that each applicant is tested the same way.

6. Handle the results of drug/alcohol tests as you would any other confidential information.

7. Unwarranted disclosure of this information may result in breach of privacy and defamation lawsuits.

8. Hire a reputable testing company, get references, be sure the company is bonded and licensed and will provide proof of current insurance and indemnification coverage.

9. If an applicant tests positive for drugs, be careful not to automatically disqualify that applicant should the person re-apply after a certain period of time (i.e., one year later).

10. Avoid inflexible drug policies with a fixed waiting period for future employment.

D. **Strategies To Protect Employers When Testing Employees**

1. Know the law.

2. Generally, employers are less able to test employees than applicants.

3. Obtain legal advice before implementing any testing policy.

4. Companies whose employees are represented by unions cannot unilaterally implement a testing program.

5. Review the requirements and conditions imposed by The Drug Free Workplace Act if your company has federal contracts.

6. Treat alcoholics differently than drug users since they may be considered possessing a disability under the ADA and cannot be fired if a "reasonable accommodation" can assist the employee perform the job.

7. Outline steps in work rules, policy manuals, employment agreements and other materials which discuss steps management will take if the company suspects an employee is impaired on-the-job.

8. Inform employees that immediate testing will be conducted if drug use is suspected.

9. Describe how the test will be administered and the consequences flowing from a positive result.

10. Apply stated rules consistently.

11. Determine the scope of the testing program's coverage, how employees will be tested, under what conditions and the selection of testing facilities.

12. Inform employees that testing for substance abuse is required under OSHA guidelines.

13. Avoid conducting random drug testing unless you receive clearance from counsel.

14. Treat the test results carefully.

15. Establish a separate employee file for testing information and results to minimize disclosure and safeguard employee privacy.

16. Choose correct specimen collection procedures which balance privacy with authenticity.

17. If possible, avoid direct observations of employee urination to reduce emotional distress lawsuits.

18. Take the temperature of the specimen immediately after it is provided since this makes substitution difficult.

19. Outline specimen identification procedures and establish a specific chain of custody to insure accuracy.

20. Understand the scientific ways a test could produce a mistake to minimize the risk of such a possibility.

E. **Special Concerns With Alcohol Use**

   1. Be especially careful before making any adverse decisions affecting an alcoholic worker and analyze each case on its particular facts.

   2. Offer counseling before discharge.

   3. If the employee refuses counseling, offer a first choice between treatment and discipline; do not take any adverse action during the period of the rehabilitation program.

   4. In case of relapse, do not automatically terminate, but some discipline short of discharge can be imposed.

   5. Before termination, determine if retention of the worker would create an undue hardship on your company.

   6. If removal is the only solution, consider leave without pay before termination.

   7. Treat alcoholism in a professional but sympathetic way since it may be considered a disability and protected under ADA.

   8. Always proceed with caution in this area to avoid substantial statutory potential damages.

RELEASE AND DISCLAIMER FROM DRUG TESTING
(May be used with the Employment Application)
(By Applicant or Employee)

I, (name of applicant or employee), hereby voluntarily agree to submit to any lawful drug test requested and conducted by XYZ Employer which XYZ Employer deems, in its sole discretion, to be reasonably necessary to provide its workers with a safe working environment.

I, (name of applicant or employee), acknowledge that in the course of my employment, and as a prerequisite of employment with XYZ Employer, may be asked to submit to a random drug test and provide a urine, blood or breath sample as part of a substance abuse screening test. I hereby consent to such tests and also agree to allow XYZ Employer the right to make lawful searches of my work area and my vehicle while on company property, and other lawful surveillance activities, in an effort to keep the workplace drug free.

I authorize that the results of any drug test be communicated and disclosed to third parties. As a consequence of any positive result obtained by said test, I understand that I may not be offered a job with XYZ Employer or may be disciplined leading up to or including immediate discharge if currently employed by XYZ Employer.

I hereby indemnify, release and forever discharge and hold XYZ Employer and its subsidiaries and affiliated companies, agents and employees harmless from any and all claims, demands, judgments and legal fees arising out of or in connection with such tests, the results, or any lawful use of the results.

_____
Signature of Applicant or Employee

_____
Printed Name of Applicant or Employee

Social Security Number: _____

Date: _____

Name of Witness: _____

SECURITY INVESTIGATION CONSENT AND RELEASE
(by Applicant or Employee)

I, (name of applicant or employee), do hereby voluntarily consent to any and all lawful security examination and investigations conducted at the request of XYZ Employer. The purpose and procedures of the investigation have been fully described to me and I completely understand the reasons and potential uses of such investigations. I agree that the results of the investigations will be given to XYZ Employer and that the results may be used to make decisions regarding my employment and can be disclosed to other third parties.

The cost of this investigation will be paid by XYZ Employer. As a consequence of any adverse information obtained about me by said investigation, I understand that I may not be offered a job with XYZ Employer or may be summarily discharged if I am currently working at XYZ Employer. Nonetheless, I hereby indemnify, release and forever discharge and hold XYZ Employer and its subsidiaries and affiliated companies, agents and employees harmless from any and all claims, demands, judgments and legal fees arising out of or in connection with this investigation, the results, or any lawful use of the results.

_____
Signature of Applicant or Employee

_____
Printed Name of Applicant or Employee

Social Security Number:_____

Date: _____

Name of Witness: _____

SECURITY INVESTIGATION CONSENT AND RELEASE
VERSION TWO

I, (name of applicant or employee), do hereby voluntarily consent to any and all lawful internal security examination and investigations conducted by XYZ Employer which XYZ Employer deems, in its sole discretion, to be reasonably necessary to protect its confidential and proprietary information and trade secrets or to investigate and uncover illegal conduct at the workplace.

I, (name of applicant or employee), acknowledge that in the course of my employment, I may be given access to confidential information including trade secrets, pending patents and other valuable materials or funds. I hereby consent to certain procedures that may be undertaken by XYZ Employer to protect said information, materials or funds including, but not limited to, lawful searches of my work area and my vehicle while on company property, and other lawful surveillance activities.

The results of any investigations may be communicated and disclosed to third parties. As a consequence of any adverse information obtained about me by said investigation, I understand that I may not be offered a job with XYZ Employer or may be disciplined leading up to or including immediate discharge if I am currently working at XYZ Employer. Nonetheless, I hereby indemnify, release and forever discharge and hold XYZ Employer and its subsidiaries and affiliated companies, agents and employees harmless from any and all claims, demands, judgments and legal fees arising out of or in connection with such investigation, the results, or any lawful use of the results.

_____
Signature of Applicant or Employee

_____
Printed Name of Applicant or Employee

Social Security Number: _____

Date: _____

Name of Witness: _____

CONSENT TO MEDICAL EXAMINATION
(By Applicant or Employee)

I, (name of applicant or employee), do voluntarily consent to a medical examination conducted at the request of XYZ Employer. The purpose and procedures of the examination have been fully described to me and I completely understand the reasons and potential uses of the examination. I agree that the results of the medical examination will be given to XYZ Employer with a copy given to me.

The cost of this examination will be paid by XYZ Employer at no cost to me and the results will be kept as confidential as possible. Although XYZ Employer may not discriminate against me in any way as a consequence of the result of the test, I nonetheless hereby indemnify, release and forever discharge XYZ Employer, the Examining Physician, and his employer if applicable, from any and all claims, demands, judgments and legal fees arising out of or in connection with the examination, diagnosis or results or the use of any diagnosis or results thereto.

_____
Signature of Applicant or Employee

_____
Printed Name of Applicant or Employee

Social Security Number:_____

Date: _____

Name of Witness: _____

INTERROGATION CONFIRMATION AND RELEASE FORM
(For Employees Only)

I, (name of employee), acknowledge that during the course of my employment on (specify date), I was asked a series of questions during normal business hours by investigators hired by XYZ Employer.

Before the examination, I received an explanation regarding its purpose and was advised that I had the right to leave the room at any time.

During the examination, I was free to leave.

I confirm that I suffered no harm as a result of the examination and that the examination was given in a reasonable manner in accordance with the procedures explained to me prior to the questioning.

I confirm that the following statements were made freely and voluntarily by me during the examination (specify):

I authorize that the results of any statements made by me be communicated and disclosed to third parties. As a consequence of any remarks made by me during the examination, I understand that I may be disciplined leading up to or including immediate discharge by XYZ Employer.

_____
Signature of Applicant or Employee

_____
Printed Name of Applicant or Employee

Social Security Number: _____

Date: _____

Name of Witness: _____

FINANCIAL DISCLOSURE FORM
(For Employees Only)

I, (name of employee), have been advised by XYZ Employer that the Company maintains the highest ethical standards of conduct and expects all employees to use only legitimate practices in commercial operations and in promoting the Company position on issues before governmental authorities.

I acknowledge that I have been advised during the course of my employment not to offer or make directly or indirectly through any person or firm, any payment of anything of value (in the form of compensation, gift, contribution or otherwise) to induce or reward any favorable action by a customer in any commercial transaction or any governmental entity for the purpose of inducing or rewarding action (or withholding of action) by same.

I further acknowledge that I will work exclusively and full-time for XYZ Employer and not own, directly or indirectly, any financial interest in suppliers or customers except for publicly held companies where my interest is less than 1%.

I further agree to report any transactions with suppliers, customers or competitors where I profited personally, and advise XYZ Employer of the value of all gifts (and outside income) received from any source during the course of my employment.

I acknowledge that if XYZ Employer discovers any inaccuracies in the above statements or if I breach any of the representations contained hereinabove, I may be disciplined leading up to or including immediate discharge by XYZ Employer.

_____
Signature of Applicant or Employee

_____
Printed Name of Applicant or Employee

Social Security Number: _____

Date: _____

Witness: _____

LIE DETECTOR DISCLAIMER AND RELEASE FORM
(For Employees Only)

I, (name of employee), have been advised by XYZ Employer that employers are generally prohibited from requesting or causing any applicant or employee to take a lie detector test.

Nonetheless, I, (name of employee), acknowledge that in the course of my employment, I requested that such a test be given to clear my name of the following serious alleged workplace impropriety: (specify). As a prerequisite of such a test, I was given the opportunity to obtain and consult with legal counsel before each phase of the test; I was provided at least 48 hours' notice of the time and place of the test; I was advised beforehand of the nature and characteristics of the test and the instruments involved; I was provided an opportunity to review all questions to be asked at the examination; and I was given a copy of the results together with a copy of the federal Polygraph Protection Act of 1988.

I authorize that the results of any polygraph test be communicated and disclosed to third parties. As a consequence of any negative result obtained from said test, I understand that I may be disciplined leading up to or including immediate discharge by XYZ Employer.

I hereby indemnify, release and forever discharge and hold XYZ Employer and its subsidiaries and affiliated companies, agents and employees harmless from any and all claims, demands, judgments and legal fees arising out of or in connection with such tests, the results, or any lawful use of the results.

_____
Signature of Employee

_____
Printed Name of Employee

Social Security Number: _____

Date: _____

Name of Witness: _____

REQUEST TO REVIEW EMPLOYEE RECORDS FORM
(By Employee)

I, (name of employee), hereby request the opportunity to review the following records contained in my employee file (specify):

I agree to inspect these records only in the presence of my supervisor or (specify other individual). I agree not to make copies of these documents but will only make independent notes of these records after my review of same.

I will not remove any contents or documents from my file without my supervisor's approval and, if said approval is given, I will report the documents removed and promptly return these documents in good condition.

I have been advised and understand that although XYZ Employer is granting this request, the Company may remove confidential information from my file before my review, including certain medical information, preemployment references, contents of privileged investigations and EEO data.

I acknowledge that if I breach any of the representations contained hereinabove, I may be disciplined leading up to or including immediate discharge by XYZ Employer.

_____
Signature of Employee

_____
Printed Name of Employee

Social Security Number: _____

Date: _____

Name of Witness: _____

EMPLOYER AUTHORIZATION
Request Approved:
Request Denied: (Specify Reason)
By: Title:
Department:
Documents Reviewed:
Date of Review:
Comments:
Employee Statements Regarding Accuracy of Information in file:

LEAVE OF ABSENCE REQUEST FORM
(By Employee)

      I, (name of employee), hereby request a leave of absence effective (specify date) for the following reason (specify): I have been advised that my leave of absence will be (with or without pay). I plan on returning by (specify date) or (state why it is impossible to predict a precise return date).

      (Optional: Due to the medical nature of my leave, I agree to comply with all XYZ Employer policies and submit timely and accurate physician statements or be available to submit to a physical examination by a doctor designated by the Company as the Company may reasonably request.)

      I have been advised and understand that if I am unable to return to work by (specify), the Company has the right in its sole discretion not to hold my job open until my return and I may either be re-employed in a different position or may lose the opportunity to continue my employment in any position if no replacement job is available or is not offered.

      No other representations or promises regarding continued employment or job security have been made to me as I am an AT WILL employee, free to resign at any time and capable of being terminated at any time with or without cause. I acknowledge that if I breach any of the representations contained hereinabove, or if my leave request is granted but the purpose or nature of the leave was misstated, XYZ Employer may discipline me up to or including immediate discharge.

_____
Signature of Employee

_____
Printed Name of Employee

Social Security Number: _____

Date: _____

Name of Witness: _____

EMPLOYER AUTHORIZATION

Request Approved:
Request Denied: (Specify Reason)
By: Title:
Department:
Comments:

VACATION REQUEST FORM
(By Employee)

I, (name of employee), hereby request a vacation leave commencing (specify date) through (specify date):

I have been advised that the total number of vacation days presently accrued total (specify).

Thank you for your attention to this matter.

_____
Signature of Employee

_____
Printed Name of Employee

Social Security Number:

Date:

Telephone number and address where I can be located during vacation:

EMPLOYER AUTHORIZATION

Request Approved:

Request Denied: (Specify Reason)

By: Title:

Department:

Comments:

DIRECT DEPOSIT CONSENT FORM

      I, (Name of Employee), hereby authorize (Name of Employer) to deposit the sum of (Specify) Dollars ($____) from my regular paycheck into (Name of Bank), account number (Specify).

      I understand that my consent can be withdrawn at any time, provided it is done so in writing.

_____
Signature of Employee

_____
Print Name of Employee

Social Security No.:

Date:

Approved By:

Date:

SAMPLE TIME REPORT

Name of Employee: _____ S.S.#: ____/____/____

Position: _____ Title: _____

Department: _____ From: __/__/__ To: __/__/__

DATE	DAY	ARRIVE	LEAVE	BREAKS	HOURS/REG	HOURS/OT

Total Regular Time: _____ x $ _____ = $

Total Overtime: _____ x $ _____ = $

TOTAL: $

Supervisor or Manager: If the employee was absent or late, state the reason and the action taken.

SAMPLE JOB LOG

Name of Employee: _____

Title of Employee: _____

Department: _____

Date: _____

START/END DUTY	TASK AND PURPOSE	TOTAL TIME

SAMPLE ATTENDANCE LOG

Name of Employee: _____ Dept: _____

Title of Employee: _____ Year: _____

D/M	JAN	FEB	MAR	APR	MAY	JUN	JUL	AUG	SEP	OCT	NOV	DEC
1												
2												
3												
4												
5												
6												
7												
8												
9												
10												
11												
12												
13												
14												
15												
16												
17												
18												
19												
20												
21												
22												
23												
24												
25												
26												
27												
28												
29												
30												
31												

Codes: A/approved leave of absence; B/bereavement; D-1/disability-work related; D-2/disability-not work-related; E/left early; H/paid holiday; J/jury duty; L/late; P/personal day; S/sick; V/vacation

BUSINESS VOUCHER RECEIPTS FORM
(TO BE USED WITH EXPENSE REPORT)

Employee's Name:_____

Social Security No.:_____

Department:_____

Period Covered:_____

DATE	AMOUNT OF ITEM	PURPOSE OF EXPENSE: Please explain the conditions, purpose, location and person with whom the expenditure was made.	SUPERVISOR ACCEPT/DENY

All business related expense must include:

1. The date, place and nature of the expense; and
2. The business purpose or justification for the expense.

Day-to-Day Operations

EXPENSE REPORT
(Attach All Receipts)

Employee's Name:_____   S.S. #:_____/_____/_____

Department:_____   From:___/___/___/ To: ___/___/

ENTERTAINMENT

DATE	LOCATION	DESCRIBE NATURE OF EXPENSE	AMOUNT

ENTERTAINMENT SUBTOTAL: $_____

TRAVEL

DATE	TYPE/LOCATION	AMOUNT	HOTELS	MEALS

TRAVEL SUBTOTAL: $_____

MISCELLANEOUS

DATE	DESCRIPTION	AMOUNT

MISCELLANEOUS SUBTOTAL: $_____

SUBTOTAL EXPENSES: $_____

ITEMS PREVIOUSLY PAID OR ADVANCED BY EMPLOYER: $_____

REFUND DUE COMPANY: $_____

REIMBURSEMENT DUE EMPLOYEE: $_____

The Complete Collection of Legal Forms for Employers

AUTHORIZATION FOR PAYROLL OR OTHER DEDUCTIONS FORM

Date:

Name of Company:

Name of Supervisor:

Address of Company:

Dear (name of supervisor):

    This letter confirms that I, (name of employee), authorize XYZ Company to deduct the sum of (specify) from my regular gross earnings each payroll period beginning on (date), for (specify nature of deductions).

    I authorize you to make this deduction automatically until (specify: until my indebtedness to name of recipient of deduction has been fully satisfied, until I revoke this authorization in writing, or until my employment with XYZ Company ceases).

    If this indebtedness remains unsatisfied upon my termination or resignation, then I agree to (specify).

    Thank you for your assistance in this regard.

Very truly yours,

(Name of Employee)
(Social Security #)

MANAGEMENT AUTHORIZATION

Request Approved:

Effective Date:

Request Denied: (Specify Reason)

By: Title:
Comments:

Date:

SALARY RECOMMENDATION FORM
(For Employee)

Date:
Name of Employee:
Social Security Number:
Position:
Title:
Department:
Date of Most Recent Performance Review:
Results of Most Recent Performance Review:
Previous Raises (if any) and Specify Dates:
Range of Salary Raises within Department
   for Similarly Situated Employees:
Justification for Salary Increase:
Specify Type of Increase (i.e. Bonus, Merit,
   Inflation, etc.):

MANAGEMENT AUTHORIZATION

Request Approved:
Effective Date:

Request Denied: (Specify Reason)
By: Title:
Department:

Comments:

Date:

EMPLOYEE STATUS OR FACT CHANGE FORM

Employee's Name: _____

Social Security No.: _____

Date of Hire: _____

Proposed Date of Change: _____

Effective Date of Change: _____

AREA OF CHANGE	FROM	TO	TYPE/REASON
SALARY/WAGE			
TITLE			
TRANSFER			
PAYROLL DEDUCTIONS			
LEAVE OF ABSENCE			
TERMS OF SEPARATION			
OTHER (SPECIFY)			

SPECIFIC FACTS OR STATEMENTS:

Submitted by:_____ Date: _____
          Manager/Supervisor

Approved by: _____ Date: _____
          Title

Approved by: _____ Date: _____
          Human Resources Department
          Title

SELF PERFORMANCE REVIEW EVALUATION FORM

Name: _____

Title: _____ Department/Location: _____

Date: _____

Please type or print your responses. If necessary, add additional pages.

I.   JOB DUTIES

1. In order of their importance, list job duties and functions you typically perform daily including the amount to time you spend on each activity.

2. In order of their importance, list job duties and functions you often perform (not on a daily basis) including the frequency of the activity and how much time you spend on it.

II. DISCRETIONARY DECISIONS

1. List the types of discretionary decisions you undertake in the performance of your job.

2. Describe how you come to these decisions.

III. INSTRUCTIONS

1. List the amount and position of all persons you supervise. State the amount of time you spend giving instruction to each person listed.

2. List the number and position of all employees to whom you report.

3. Describe the type of work you do for each person you listed for question III (2).

IV. MISTAKES

1. List the types of mistakes that may commonly be made in your position.

2. When a mistake occurs, how is it determined and by whom?

3. Describe the impact of these mistakes, if left unchecked, to the company.

V. ASSISTANCE

1. List the persons and entities you regularly contact as part of the performance of your job. Include in your answer the method of communication (i.e., phone, letter, etc.) and the purpose of that contact (i.e., to schedule a meeting, to negotiate a contract, etc.).

VI. **JOB REQUIREMENTS**

1. Regardless of your own background, abilities and education, please describe what you think the minimum skills and education should be required of someone in this position and describe why.

2. Describe what kind of professional background you would look for if you were hiring someone to fill your job.

VII. **REMARKS**

If you have any additional comments to make, please feel free to do so.

SAMPLE PERFORMANCE APPRAISAL

NAME_____ DEPARTMENT _____
POSITION _____ TIME IN POSITION _____
REVIEW PERIOD COVERED _____

STEP 1—RATING OF JOB DUTIES AND RESPONSIBILITIES

List significant duties, responsibilities, and requirements of the job. Rate employee's ability to perform these duties.

A—Technical Knowledge

B—Analytical Ability and Judgment

C—Attitude and Personal Characteristics

D—Other

E—Overall Rating and Reasons Why

Poor
Satisfactory
Good
Outstanding

STEP 2—PERFORMANCE EVALUATION

A—Identify employee's strengths and weaknesses:

B—Set goals to further utilize the employee's strengths and develop plans for improving deficiencies

Other comments by evaluator:

Comments of staff member being evaluated:

Signatures:
Evaluated Staff Member: _____   Date: _____

Evaluator: _____   Date: _____

ALTERNATIVE PERFORMANCE REVIEW

Name: _____

Title: _____ Department/Location: _____

Date: _____ Supervisor's Name: _____

Please type or print your responses. If necessary, attach additional pages.

Use the following scale to reply to each question:

A = Consistently Fulfills and Exceeds Duties
B = Fulfills and Frequently Exceeds Duties
C = Fulfills Duties
D = Sometimes Fulfills Duties
F = Rarely Fulfills Duties

For any mark of "D" or "F" given, a written explanation must accompany it.

I. **PERFORMANCE QUALITY:**

___ Regarding Volume Produced

___ Regarding Job Accuracy

COMMENTS:

II. INTERPERSONAL SKILLS:

How well does this employee get along with:

___ Subordinates   ___ Co-Workers

___ Supervisors   ___ Contacts Outside the Company

COMMENTS:

III. INDEPENDENCE:

___ Ability to work on his or her own

COMMENTS:

IV. RELIABILITY:

___ Regarding completion of projects

___ Regarding attendance

COMMENTS:

V. BACKGROUND AND JOB REQUIREMENTS:

___ Formal Education

___ Background Experience

___ Technical Skills

COMMENTS:

VI. PLEASE GIVE AN OVERALL MARK FOR EMPLOYEE AND EXPLAIN SAME BELOW:

_____ Overall Mark

OVERALL COMMENTS:

PREPARED BY: APPROVED BY:

_____   _____
Name and Title   Name and Title Of Supervisor

_____   _____
Signature   Signature Of Supervisor

_____   _____
Date   Date

NEW HIRING JOB APPRAISAL SUMMARY

Date of Appraisal:__/__/__

Employee: _____ Social Security No: _____

Title: _____ Department/location: _____

D/O/H: _____ Supervisor's N ame: _____

CATEGORY	1	2	3	4	RECOMMENDATIONS/ EVALUATIONS
INTERPERSONAL SKILLS: (1) Please consider ability to get along with: Supervisors, Subordinates, Co-Workers and outside contacts;					
(2) also consider level of emotional maturity and professionalism displayed.					
GENERAL WORK PERFORMANCE: Please consider: (1) the amount of work produced;					
(2) if projects are completed on time due; and					
(3) ability to follow and complete work as instructed.					
WORK ETHICS: Please consider: (1) promptness and attendance record; and					
(2) enthusiasm toward projects/ assignments					
JOB REQUIREMENTS: Please consider employee's technical skills					

Codes: 1 = Outstanding; 2 = Good; 3 = Fair; 4 = Poor

ADDITIONAL COMMENTS:

ORIENTATION PERIOD EMPLOYEE PERFORMANCE REVIEW

Date: _____

Employee: _____ Social Security No: _____

Title: _____ Department/Location: _____

D/O/H: _____ Supervisor's Name: _____

1. Does Employee's technical skills meet the standards required by the job? If not, please explain in detail.

2. Is Employee's performance level consistent? If not, please explain in detail.

3. Describe Employee's ability to communicate and interact with his/her Supervisor(s), co-workers and outside contacts, where applicable.

4. Describe Employee's ability to work without supervision.

5. Does Employee's, in your opinion, seem to enjoy his/her job? Please give specific examples to support your response.

6. Do you believe that the Employee's work performance is satisfactory?

7. Please make any other comments you feel should be included in this review.

I recommend:

__ that the Employee remain in our employ, in the position he/she currently holds.

__ that the Employee be moved to another position/department (Specify) within our company to better utilize the Employee's talents.

__ that the Employee be terminated.

PREPARED BY: APPROVED BY:

_____   _____
Name and Title   Name and Title Of Supervisor

_____   _____
Signature   Signature Of Supervisor

OBJECTIVE EMPLOYEE IMPROVEMENT EVALUATION

Date of Evaluation: __/__/__

Employee: _____ Social Security No.: _____

Title: _____ Department/Location: _____

D/O/H: _____ Supervisor's Name: _____

Appraisal Period: _____ to _____

Reason for Appraisal: _____

1. Describe employee's particular accomplishments or achievements.

2. Detail examples of the employee's improvements during the appraisal period.

3. List areas where employee can improve job duties.

4. Using examples, please list in detail why you feel further improvement(s) is required.

5. Is there any special training which will help this employee to improve in the problem areas? If so, please state.

6. What expectations do you have for this employee's improvement before the next appraisal?

7. FOR THE EMPLOYEE: Please feel free to comment on any statement made above.

_____ _____   _____ _____
Employee   Date   Supervisor   Date:

                                        _____ _____
                                        Personnel Manager   Date:

Day-to-Day Operations 175

NUMERICAL EMPLOYEE EVALUATION FORM

Date of Evaluation: _/_/_

Employee: _____

Title: _____   Department/Location: _____

D/O/H: _____   Supervisor's name: _____

Appraisal Period: _____ to _____

Reason for Appraisal: _____

Please type or print your responses. If necessary, attach additional pages.

Use the following scale to reply to each question:

1 = Consistently Fulfills and Exceeds Duties
2 = Fulfills and Frequently Exceeds Duties
3 = Fulfills Duties
4 = Sometimes Fulfills Duties
5 = Rarely Fulfills Duties

I.   Performance Goals from Last Appraisal Period

List the goals in the space provided and rate the improvement using the scale above.

1) ___

2) ___

3) ___

4) ___

5) ___

6) ___

The Complete Collection of Legal Forms for Employers

II.   Job Description

In the space below write out the job description. Please note any changes in the job description since the last evaluation.

III. General Evaluation

Using the codes below, please fill in the following chart.

CATEGORY	1	2	3	4	RECOMMENDATIONS/ EVALUATIONS
INTERPERSONAL SKILLS: (1) Please consider ability to get along with: supervisors, subordinates, co-Workers and outside contacts;					
(2) also consider level of emotional maturity and professionalism displayed.					
GENERAL WORK PERFORMANCE: Please consider: (1) the amount of work produced;					
(2) if projects are completed on time due; and					
(3) ability to follow and complete work as instructed.					
WORK ETHICS: Please consider: (1) promptness and attendance record; and					
(2) enthusiasm toward projects/ assignments					
JOB REQUIREMENTS: Please consider employee's technical skills					

Codes: 1 = Outstanding; 2 = Good; 3 = Fair; 4 = Poor

IV. Give an overall numerical value to this employee's performance.

_____   _____
Employee   Date   Supervisor   Date

                                 _____
                                 Personnel Manager   Date

TRANSFER/PROMOTION LOG

Name of Employee: _____

Date of Transfer/Promotion: _____

Transfer/Promotion From: _____ To: _____

Department From: _____ To: _____

Pay Increase From: _____ To: _____

Grade Increase From: _____ To: _____

PREPARED BY: APPROVED BY:

_____   _____
Name and Title   Name and Title Of Supervisor

_____   _____
Signature   Signature Of Supervisor

_____   _____
Date   Date

Day-to-Day Operations

EMPLOYEE REFERRAL POLICY AND AWARD

Date: _____

Employee: _____ Social Security No.: _____

Name of person being referred: _____

Position/Department for which this person is being referred:

_____

What is your relationship to the person being referred (i.e., friend, family member, former co-worker, etc.)?

_____

You will be notified as to the status of your referral. If the referral is hired you will receive a monetary award under our Employee Referral Award Program. Thank you for the referral!

To: Employee

From: HR Professional

Date: (Specify)

Re: (Name of Referral)

Under our Employee Referral Award Program, at the present time your referral:

1.   ___   Will Not Be Offered a Position

2.   ___   No Present Available Position

3.   ___   Is Being Considered

4.   ___   Rejected The Job

5.   ___   Accepted The Job

    If option number 5 above is checked, you will be receiving a check in the amount of $_____ less applicable taxes and deductions on (Specify Date). If any other option is checked, we will keep you notified of any change in status.

    Your participation in our Employee Referral Award Program is appreciated.

ACCIDENT/WORK INJURY REPORT
(To Be Completed By Immediate Supervisor)

Date of this report:
Date of accident:
Name of employee:
Social Security Number:
Position:
Title:
Department:
Employment Commencement Date:
Number of months in this department or position:
Describe accident in detail (specify time, place, duties of employee, etc.):

Describe nature of injuries:

Names of witnesses (if any):

Have those witnesses been interviewed? If so, by whom?

Has a written statement of all witnesses been prepared?

If so, where is the report now and who has seen it?

If not, by when?

Estimated medical consequence of accident/work injury to injured employee:

Estimated loss to Company from accident/work injury:

MANAGEMENT AUTHORIZATION

Name of Review:
Date:
Comments:
Action to be taken (specify, i.e., safety committee meeting, notify union or shop steward, replace position, etc.) and by when (specify date):

CHECKLIST TO MINIMIZE WORKPLACE ACCIDENTS

1. On the average, more than a dozen U.S. workers die each day from injuries in the workplace and another 10,000 are hurt seriously enough to lose work time or be placed on restricted duty.

2. Under OSHA, workers are allowed:

    a. To refuse to perform work in a dangerous environment (e.g., in the presence of toxic substances, fumes or radioactive materials);

    b. To strike to protest unsafe conditions;

    c. To initiate an OSHA inspection of dangerous working conditions by filing a safety complaint;

    d. To participate in OSHA inspections, pre-hearing conferences and review inspection hearings;

    e. To petition that employers provide adequate emergency exits, environmental control devices (e.g., ventilation, noise elimination devices, radiation detection tags, signs and protective equipment) and the ready availability of medical personnel;

    f. To request time off with pay to seek medical treatment during working hours;

    g. To request eating facilities in areas which have not been exposed to toxic substances; and

    h. To request investigations when they are punished for asserting their rights.

3. Place OSHA workplace posters where all employees can easily see them.

4. Record all workplace fatalities and report any serious accidents (e.g., accidents where 5 or more employees were injured seriously enough to be hospitalized) to a Federal or State OSHA Office within 48 hours of the fatality or serious accident.

5. Under OSHA, employers must maintain complete and accurate records concerning injuries and illnesses occurring on the job or as a result of conditions at the plant site.

6. Under OSHA, employers must consciously prepare and display an annual summary of workplace injuries and illnesses from February 1 to March 1.

7. If your company employs 10 or fewer employees, it may be exempt from OSHA record keeping requirements.

8. Notify your employees of the procedures to follow in case of an emergency. This information should be contained in any employee manuals and company handbooks and all emergency phone numbers should be prominently listed.

9. Maintaining a safe workplace begins with the orientation of new workers. Set the stage from the beginning be letting the new employee know that safety is a very important focus at your workplace.

10. While job descriptions and work environment will determine what specific safety training must be given an employee, all new workers should receive an overall safety orientation.

11. Management's commitment to accident and injury prevention must always be conveyed.

12. Make clear that employee participation is needed to prevent accidents.

13. Request that workers notify management without penalty, of any unsafe condition or potential hazard.

14. Constantly remind supervisors to maintain safe and productive work operations.

15. Advise workers not to undertake a task before learning the safe method of doing it and being authorized by a supervisor to proceed.

16. Remind new employees about hazard recognition and that any injury, even a slight one, must be reported and treated immediately.

17. Keep the workplace safe and train employees in safety on an ongoing basis.

18. All companies should take a preventive approach to avoiding worker injuries and to insure a clean and healthful working environment.

19. Take steps to reduce worker stress, exposure to hazardous substances, vision impairment, repetitive motion injuries and exposure to computer terminal-caused injuries from video display terminals.

20. Work closely with your employees and request regular employee suggestions to reduce potential safety violations.

21. Hire safety consultants who will visit the work site and make suggestions. Many insurance companies provide this service at no cost.

22. Since safety training is mandated by federal regulation, regular training sessions for management and supervisors should be conducted to insure that employees know company policies and abide by the law.

23. Conduct follow-up field inspections to monitor compliance.

24. Publicize specific, strict rules regarding employee safety and related matters in company handbooks.

25. Statements on safety should include a list of prohibited forms of conduct and the consequences of committing such acts as well as a stated policy reminding workers how to report accidents, seek medical attention, and so forth.

CHECKLIST FOR SEXUAL HARASSMENT INVESTIGATIONS

I. **PRELIMINARY CONSIDERATIONS**

    A.   Use two investigators, if possible.

    B.   Create a confidential file.

    C.   Conduct interviews in a private room.

II. **GATHERING THE FACTS**

    A.   Review relevant personnel files and company policies.

    B.   Interview the victim.
1. Take her complaint seriously.
2. Explain the investigation but don't promise complete confidentiality.
3. Find out what happened: GET SPECIFICS.
4. Find out the effect of the harassment on the victim.
5. Find out names of witnesses.
6. Ask the victim what she wants.
7. Assess her credibility.
8. Take a statement, if warranted.
9. Type the notes of the interview.

    C.   Interview the perpetrator.
1. Explain the purpose of the interview but state that no decision has been made on the truthfulness of the allegations.
2. Identify the victim and the specific basis of the sexual harassment complaint.
3. Ask him to respond to the charges.
4. Find out names of witnesses.
5. Assess his credibility.
6. Take a statement, if warranted.
7. Type the notes of the interview.

    D.   Interview corroboration witnesses.
1. Try to elicit identity of victim and perpetrator from the witness as opposed to identifying the victim and perpetrator to the witness at the beginning of the interview.
2. Find out what he or she knows: GET SPECIFICS.
3. Distinguish between firsthand and secondhand knowledge.
4. Assess the credibility of the witness.
5. Take a statement, if warranted.
6. Type the notes of the interview.

III. EVALUATING THE FACTS AND MAKING THE DECISION

A. Evaluate the facts from a reasonable woman's perspective.

B. Distinguish between "unwelcome" and "voluntary" sexual conduct.

C. Draft a thorough, even handed report.
   1. Make the report chronological.
   2. Describe when first learned of the complaint.
   3. Provide exact details of the complaint.
   4. Note the documents reviewed.
   5. Describe the interviews.
   6. For all witnesses, distinguish between firsthand knowledge and rumor.
   7. State conclusions as to whether sexual harassment occurred and provide specific justification.
   8. Recommend corrective action if sexual harassment occurred. The corrective action should:
      a. be reasonably calculated to prevent further harassment.
      b. not punish the victim.
      c. be consistent with the discipline imposed in the past in similar situations.

D. Submit the report to the decision-making official. That official should:
   1. not be a rubber stamp.
   2. point out deficiencies in the report.
   3. ask follow-up questions.
   4. conduct interviews him or herself if necessary.
   5. document his or her actions.

E. Follow up with the victim and perpetrator after the decision has been made.

Reprinted with permission from EMPLOYEE RELATIONS LAW JOURNAL, V18N2, Autumn 1992. © 1992 by Executive Enterprises, Inc., 22 West 21st Street, New York, NY 10010-6990. All Rights Reserved.

PERSONNEL ACTION FORM

Employee _____
              first name   last name

Instructions

Check the appropriate box and fill in the information in the blanks below. Employee signs only if he/she initiates action or payroll deduction is required. Supervisor signs in all cases.

- ☐ Payroll Increase
- ☐ Payroll Decrease
- ☐ Transfer
- ☐ Payroll Deduction
- ☐ Promotion
- ☐ Leave of Absence
- ☐ Separation
- ☐ Change of address
- ☐ Change in dependents
- ☐ Classification change

Change in Pay or Classification

From   To
Pay _____per_____   _____per_____

Classification _____
                 TO BE EFFECTIVE _____

Separation

- ☐ Laid off for lack of work
- ☐ Left work voluntarily
- ☐ Discharged for felonious conduct
- ☐ Other reason
- ☐ Discharged for repeated willful misconduct

Remarks (Final pay check, date, amount, etc.):

Eligible for rehire? ☐ Yes   ☐ No

Other (changes, deductions, etc.)

_____   _____
Employee Signature / Date   Supervisor Signature / Date

SECTION THREE:
Separation Documents

REDUCING LAWSUIT EXPOSURE:
ELEVEN THINGS YOUR COMPANY SHOULD KNOW

1. It may be illegal for an employer to fire a worker to deprive him/her of large commissions, vested pension rights, a year end bonus or other expected financial benefits.

2. It may be illegal for companies to fire workers who return to work after an illness, pregnancy or jury duty.

3. It may be illegal to fire workers who complain about a safety violation or other wrongdoing.

4. It may be illegal to fire a worker in a manner inconsistent with company handbooks, manuals, written contracts and disciplinary rules.

5. It may be illegal to fire a worker who is over 40, belongs to a protected minority, or is a female, primarily because of such personal characteristics.

6. It may be illegal to fire a worker who received a verbal promise of job security or other rights which the company failed to fulfill.

7. It may be illegal to fire a long-term worker when the punishment does not fit the crime and other workers were not similarly treated.

8. It may be illegal if an employer fails to act according to the terms of a written employment contract.

9. Avoid firing workers for "job performance" who have received excellent performance reviews and appraisals and have been given copies of such performance reviews; never inflate performance evaluations for this reason.

10. When possible, try to obtain an employee's resignation rather than be fired. When workers resign they often waive claims to unemployment and other severance benefits.

11. Confirm all severance arrangements in writing to document the final deal that has been made. Be sure a release is prepared and signed by the terminated worker to protect your company.

PRE-TERMINATION CONSIDERATION CHECKLIST

Remember: Avoid litigation through proper planning and execution. The time to defend against the termination lawsuit begins <u>before</u> you hire.

Remember: The first rule of personnel relations: "No good deed out of kindness goes unpunished."

A. BEFORE HIRING

1. Be sure that advertisements and help-wanted ads are not discriminatory.

2. Avoid asking discriminatory questions during job recruiting and selection.

3. Avoid making guaranteed earning claims you don't intend to keep.

4. Review employment applications, personnel manuals and work rules likely to be involved in a termination lawsuit.

5. Regulate statements that recruiters, interviewers and other intake personnel make to new or prospective employees.

6. Discuss all employment terms in advance.

7. Prepare an employment agreement to protect your company.

8. Remember that your position is strongest <u>before</u> the hiring so include many favorable provisions in the confirmation letter or employment agreement.

9. Consider arbitration to resolve employment disputes. Add this clause to your employment agreement.

B. WHILE WORKING

1. Establish clear written work rules which indicate that infractions can lead to discipline and discharge.

2. Carefully prepare periodic performance appraisals; never inflate them.

3. During discipline, be sure you are disciplining or terminating the worst offenders first, not on the basis of any other reason, to avoid charges of discrimination.

4. Respond promptly and properly to charges of sexual harassment, age, sex, race or disability discrimination.

5. Carefully review all termination decisions before making them considering such points as:

   a. Are there any potential statutory problems such as race, sex, age, or pregnancy discrimination, or violations of whistle blowing laws or exceptions to the employment-at-will doctrine?

   b. Have any representations been made to the employee concerning job security? If so, was the termination consistent with those representations?

   c. What does the employment contract say about firings? Were all provisions (i.e., notice of X days sent certified mail) followed?

   d. Are there any public policy concerns? For example, has the employee recently exercised a legal right (i.e., attend jury duty) that your company complained about? Or, had the employee been involved in any controversial events that may include misconduct on the company's behalf (i.e., wrongful surveillance or eavesdropping or other violations of employee rights of privacy)?

   e. Has the employee received progressive discipline before the discharge?

   f. Are there any mitigating factors that may excuse or explain the employee's poor performance or misconduct?

   g. What kind of overall record does the employee have? Remember that the longer and better the employee's record, the more reluctant the review should be to approve the termination.

   h. Consider whether termination is appropriate under all of the circumstances. Does the punishment fit the crime?

C. BEFORE AND AFTER THE FIRING

1. Be compassionate, yet firm.

2. Offer non-monetary benefits if appropriate.

3. Recover all company property before paying final severance and before the terminated employee parts.

4. Consider the signing of General Releases when appropriate. If so, prepare them properly.

5. Avoid accusations in front of third parties to avoid charges of defamation.

6. Take a conservative approach with potential employers. Remember, bad references lead to expensive lawsuits!

7. Contest unemployment claims where appropriate.

D. **PROTECTING YOUR COMPANY FORM DISLOYAL EX-EMPLOYEES**

1. Understand what constitutes a trade secret.

2. Create a climate of confidentiality.

3. Advise employees of the seriousness of the problem.

4. Include restrictive covenants in all sales related agreements but be sure the covenant is reasonable in terms of geographic scope and time limitations.

5. Understand the distinction between sales employees and independent contractors; this can affect the enforceability of the restrictive covenant.

6. Establish effective exit procedures.

7. Act quickly if problems develop.

MODEL DISCIPLINARY WARNING
(FOR INTERNAL USE ONLY)

Date of Warning: _/_/_

Employee: _____

Title: _____   Department/Location: _____

D/O/H: _____   Supervisor's Name: _____

1. State facts regarding warning.

2. State why the alleged acts violate company policy.

3. State whether or not the employee ever received a warning regarding this or prior incidents (if in writing, please attach a copy).

4. Has the incident been discussed with the employee?

5. If so, state employee's reaction.

6. State conclusion (consequences of incident and steps to be taken to correct the problem).

7. Final comments.

PREPARED BY: APPROVED BY:

_____   _____
Name and Title   Name and Title Of Supervisor

_____   _____
Signature   Signature Of Supervisor

_____   _____
Date   Date

Separation Documents

FINAL DISCIPLINARY WARNING

Date:

From: Name of Supervisor

To: Name of Employee

Re: Final Disciplinary Warning

___

Dear (Name of Employee):

On (specify date) you received an interim warning regarding (specify incident). You were specifically told (specify what) that the failure to correct this problem (or repeated incident of this kind) would lead to a final warning.

(State facts as to what occurred.)

Therefore, you are hereby advised that you are being placed on final warning and failure to immediately improve (specify conduct) may lead to your immediate dismissal (Optional: on or before specify date).

                                                            Very truly yours,

                                                      Signature of Supervisor
                                                      Name and Title of Supervisor

SAMPLE LEAVE OF ABSENCE LETTER

[DATE]

Name of Employee
Address
Apt.
City, State, Zip

Dear [Name of Employee]:

[Name of Company] is pleased to offer you a Leave of Absence. This Leave is based on your years of service and overall contribution to [specify company]. Your Leave will commence on September 1, 199 and end with your retirement on September 1, 199 .

During your Leave, your status with [Name of Company] (the "Company") will be that of an inactive employee on a Leave of Absence. The Company will pay your salary, on a semi-monthly basis based on your annual salary of [specify] per year. All salary paid to you by the Company during your Leave will be subject to applicable federal, state, city, and/or other local income taxes, social security deductions, and all other applicable withholdings and deductions. These taxes and deductions will be made whether your residence is in or out of [specify state]. During your Leave, the Company must comply with any changes in laws affecting the amount of involuntary deductions from your salary.

The Company will also provide you with the employment benefits you have selected under the Flex Benefits program with limitations as described in this letter. You will continue to be responsible for all premiums which will be deducted from salary payments made to you during your leave, and are subject to the same changes in premiums or in the benefits provided that affect active employees. In addition, while you are on Leave, you will not be eligible for any new benefits the Company will introduce.

The list of benefits available under the [specify] Benefit Program while on Leave are as follows:

- Medical and Dental Benefits
- Employee Life Insurance
- Dependent Life Insurance

[Specify Name of spending account]. If you are currently enrolled in [Name of spending account], you may file claims for expenses incurred up to the end of the year in which your Leave ends. If claims are not submitted by January 31 of the year following the year in which the claim was incurred, you will forfeit your [spending account] balance pursuant to the terms of the [spending account] plan.

During your Leave you may continue to make salary redirection deposits to your [spending account] on the same basis as you could as an active employee.

On the effective date of your Leave, your Flex benefit program will be changed as follows: You will no longer receive Flex credits currently used to select and fund your benefits. You will receive a rate sheet describing the cost of each benefit. These rates are subsidized by the Bank to offset the Flex credits you no longer will receive.

Your Savings Plan will continue with the following restrictions:

- You will retain your Savings Plan account during your Leave. However, no further allocations to your fund will be made during the Leave. While on Leave, you are eligible to transfer your funds from one investment fund to another and/or apply for a hardship withdrawal. These are the only two Savings Plan transactions you can make while on Leave. Final settlement of your Savings Plan account will be according to your election at the completion of your Leave.

- Any payment due from you with respect to loans from your Savings Plan account will continue to be due until the loan is repaid or the end of your Leave, whichever comes first. At the final distribution of your Savings Plan account, any unpaid balance must be settled before final payout is made.

Some of your current benefits will discontinue when you are transferred to the Leave, and are as follows:

- Long Term Disability
- Business Travel Accident Insurance
- Accidental Death and Dismemberment Insurance

You will not accrue vacation during your Leave period. At the beginning of your Leave, you will be paid for any unused entitled vacation time for the year in which you start your Leave.

If you die while on Leave, all salary and benefits payable to you under this Leave agreement will cease, although if you are married or legally separated at the time of your death, your spouse will receive spouse's benefits to the same extent that your spouse would have received them if you had been an active employee, contingent upon your enrollment in and entitlement under the Company's various benefits plans.

Before your Leave begins, you may choose to continue any or all of your voluntary deductions, such as Employee Stock Purchase Plan, Holiday Club, IRA's, voluntary insurance programs, Payroll Savings, and Savings Bonds.

All of your personal bank accounts, such as [spending account] privilege checking, savings accounts, mortgage, Visa/Mastercard, installment loans, and safe deposit boxes will remain available to you during your Leave on the same terms on which they are presently available to you.

If you are an Officer, you will be required to resign your Corporate title at the start of your Leave. You may not, as an inactive employee, conduct Company business during your Leave, except that you agree to cooperate with requests for reasonable assistance to cover matters or events relating to your employment with the Company. If you choose to secure employment elsewhere during your Leave, you will not forfeit any of the benefits, including the salary payments.

Approximately three to six months prior to the end of your Special Leave, the Retirement Center will contact you to discuss the various options offered.

If you have any questions, please call me at [specify].

Sincerely,

[NAME AND TITLE]

SAMPLE NOTICE OF TERMINATION

TO: [Name of Terminated Employee]
SUBJECT: Separation Arrangements

In connection with your separation, your attention is called to the following matters:

1. Your coverage under _____ will be continued for [specify] days from date of termination. Under federal law (COBRA), you may be covered under this policy for up to 18 months by paying the Company the premium amount specified below within 30 days of termination and by subsequently continuing to pay the premium in a timely fashion. Failure to pay the premium within any 30-day period will result in discontinuance of the insurance.

Your GROUP PREMIUM RATE is:_____
Your HEALTH PLAN NUMBER is:_____

Use this number in all correspondence concerning your benefits.

2. Your GROUP LIFE INSURANCE policy terminates on the last day of your employment, but it can be converted without a physical examination and at a higher individual rate within 30 days of termination. If you wish to convert, contact the [specify insurance company] within the next 30 days.

3. Your WEEKLY SICKNESS and ACCIDENT DISABILITY INSURANCE terminates on the last day of employment and is not convertible to an individual policy.

4. (if applicable.) When the next PROFIT SHARING DIVIDEND is determined, a check for your proportionate share of the dividend will be mailed to you within 60 days thereafter.
OR

5. (if applicable.) Since you have not satisfied the vesting requirements under our PENSION PLAN, you do not have any vested rights in the plan.

If you have any questions about these matters, please call.

_____
Personnel Director

SAMPLE JOB ELIMINATION NOTIFICATION

DATE: [specify]
TO: [Name of Terminated Employee]

As you know, our business is a dynamic one and change is inevitable. Reorganizations, productivity initiatives, market demands, profitability issues—any one of these situations may require organization redesign and reallocation of resources. As a business, we've had to make a very difficult but necessary decision to realign our business for improved workflow efficiencies and focus on our customers.

This decision requires us to eliminate your position located at [specify Company address]. As a consequence, unfortunately, you will be involuntarily terminated on [specify date] if you are unable to secure a position within the Company by that date. You will receive your last paycheck on [specify date] for all hours worked up to that date. Special severance related benefits will commence after [specify date].

Information regarding your eligibility for post-employment payments and benefits are in your Package enclosed. In addition to the post-employment payments and health benefits under the Plan, you are entitled to continuation of health coverage under the Consolidated Omnibus Budget Reconciliation Act of 1986 (COBRA).

Attached to this letter you will find important documents. **Please read them carefully.**

I realize that this will be a difficult time for you; however, I urge you to direct your attention and energies to your future. We want to help you understand your special payment package, assist in positioning you to source new opportunities, and ensure as smooth a transition as possible.

In this regard, feel free to contact me at [specify] if you have any questions. I thank you for your contributions to our business in the past and wish you well in your future endeavors.

                                                Sincerely,

Attachments   [NAME OF OFFICER]

SAMPLE SEPARATION AGREEMENT AND RELEASE

In consideration of the fact that I, [specify Name of Employee] ("The Employee"), have voluntarily and of my own free will, elected to accept a bonus payment ("Release Bonus") in the amount of [specify $], separation pay in the amount of [specify $], and that [specify name of Company], or its subsidiaries and affiliates (hereinafter "the Company") has agreed to pay me the above amounts, I acknowledge and agree to the following:

1. I understand that as of [specify date] my employment with the Company will cease.

2. I have been advised by the Company that I am being separated from the payroll pursuant to the terms of the Company's Reduction-in-Force Management Plan and that I am entitled to a severance payment in accordance with the following schedule:

Net Credited Service in Years	Length of Severance Pay Period in Months
Less than 2	1
2 but less than 4	1.5
4 but less than 6	2
6 but less than 8	2.5
8 but less than 10	3
10 but less than 12	4
12 but less than 14	5
14 but less than 16	6
16 but less than 18	7
18 but less than 20	8
20 and over	9

The Release Bonus is 33.3% of the Severance Pay.

3. I understand that the Release Bonus is being paid as consideration for my signing this Separation Agreement and Release and that these are benefits to which I would not have been entitled had I not signed this Separation Agreement and Release.

4. I also understand that, pursuant to the Older Workers Benefit Protection Act of 1990, I have the right to consult with an attorney before signing this Separation Agreement and Release, I have 45 days to consider the Release before signing it, and I may revoke the Release within 7 calendar days after signing it.

5. I realize that there are various State and Federal laws that govern my employment relationship with the Company and/or prohibit employment discrimination on the basis of age, color, race, gender, sexual preference/orientation, marital status, national origin, mental or physical disability, religious affiliation or veteran status and that these laws are enforced through the courts and agencies such as the Equal Employment Opportunity Commission, Department of Labor and State Human Rights Agencies. Such laws include, but are not limited to, Title VII of the Civil Rights Act of 1964, the Age Discrimination in Employment Act of 1967, as amended, the Employee Retirement Income Security Act, 29 U.S.C. 1001, et seq., 42 U.S.C. Section 1981, etc. In consideration of the Release Bonus provided for in this Agreement, I intend to give up any rights I may have under these or any other laws with respect to my employment and termination of employment at the Company and acknowledge that the Company has not discriminated against me, breached any express or implied contract with me, or otherwise acted unlawfully toward me.

6. Subject to paragraph 7 herein, on behalf of myself, my heirs, executors, administrators, successors, and assigns, I release and discharge the Company, its successors, assigns, subsidiaries, affiliates, directors, officers, representatives, agents and employees ("Releasees") from any and all claims, including claims for attorney's fees and costs, charges, actions and causes of action with respect to, or arising out of, my employment or termination of employment with the Company. This includes, but is not limited to, claims arising under federal, state, or local laws prohibiting age, color, race, gender, sexual preference/orientation, marital status, national origin, mental or physical disability, religious affiliation or veteran status or any other forms of discrimination or claims growing out of the Company's termination of its employees. With respect to any charges that have been or may be filed concerning events or actions relating to my employment or the termination of my employment and which occurred on or before the date of this Agreement, I additionally waive and release any right I may have to recover in any lawsuit or proceeding brought by me, an administrative agency, or any other person on my behalf or which includes me in any class. If I breach this paragraph, I understand that I will be liable for all expenses, including costs and reasonable attorney's fees, incurred by any Releasee in defending the lawsuit or charge of discrimination, regardless of the outcome. I agree to pay such expenses within Thirty (30) calendar days of written demand. This paragraph is not intended to limit me from instituting legal action for the sole purpose of enforcing this Agreement.

7. I understand that this Separation Agreement and Release in no way affects any rights I may have for benefits under the Company's Pension Plan or any other applicable benefit plan.

8. In accordance with my existing and continuing obligations to the Company, I have returned or will immediately return to the Company, or before my termination date, all Company property, including, but not limited to, files, records, computer access codes, computer programs, instruction manuals, business plans, and other property which I prepared or helped to prepare in connection with my employment with the Company.

9. I affirm my obligation to keep all proprietary Company information confidential and not to disclose it to any third party in the future. I understand that the term "proprietary Company information" includes, but is not necessarily limited to, technical, marketing, business, financial or other information which constitutes trade secret information or information not available to competitors of the Company, the use or disclosure of which might reasonable be construed to be contrary to the interest of the Company or its subsidiaries or affiliates.

10. The construction, interpretation and performance of this Agreement shall be governed by the laws of the state in which I am working of the date of my separation from the Company's payroll.

11. In the event that any one or more of the provisions contained in this Agreement shall for any reason be held to be unenforceable in any respect under the law of any state or of the United States of America, such unenforceability shall not affect any other provisions of this Release, but, with respect only to that jurisdiction holding the provision to be unenforceable, this Release shall then be construed as if such unenforceable provision or provisions had never been contained herein.

12. This Separation Agreement and General Release contains the entire agreement between the Company and me and fully supersedes any and all prior agreements or understandings pertaining to the subject matter hereof. I represent and acknowledge that in executing this Separation Agreement and Release I have not relied upon any representation or statement not set forth herein made by any of the Releasees or by any of the Releasee's agents, representatives, or attorneys with regard to the subject matter of this Agreement.

BY SIGNING THIS SEPARATION AGREEMENT AND RELEASE, I STATE THAT: I HAVE READ IT; I UNDERSTAND IT AND KNOW THAT I AM GIVING UP IMPORTANT RIGHTS; I AGREE WITH EVERYTHING IN IT; I AM AWARE OF MY RIGHT TO CONSULT AN ATTORNEY BEFORE SIGNING IT; AND I HAVE SIGNED IT KNOWINGLY AND VOLUNTARILY.

DATE: _____
Employee Signature

_____
[Employee Name Printed]

WITNESS: _____

DATE:

PRELIMINARY PAYMENT CALCULATION SHEET

[DATE]

NAME: SOCIAL SECURITY #:
SALARY BAND:

HIRE DATE: YEARS OF SERVICE:

NOTIFICATION DATE: OFF-PAYROLL-DATE:

BENEFITS COVERAGE THROUGH:

YOU MAY ELECT TO CONTINUE HEALTH INSURANCE COVERAGE FOR AN EXTENDED PERIOD UNDER C.O.B.R.A. FEDERAL BENEFITS CONTINUATION REGULATIONS. ENROLLMENT INFORMATION AND MATERIALS WILL BE MAILED TO YOUR HOME.

BASE SALARY:
INCENTIVE AMOUNT:
TOTAL:

WEEKLY RATE:

SEVERANCE:
POST-EMPLOYMENT PAYMENT:
POST-EMPLOYMENT SUPPLEMENT
    (IF APPLICABLE):
TOTAL:

RELEASE BONUS (IF APPLICABLE)
    (33.3% OF TOTAL SEVERANCE):

TOTAL OF SEVERANCE AND RELEASE:

*PAY FOR UNUSED VACATION DAYS, PERSONAL DAYS, AND FLOATING HOLIDAYS:

NUMBER OF UNUSED DAYS:

GRAND TOTAL:

If you feel that any of the data on this sheet is inaccurate, please contact [specify name] at [specify address and/or phone number].

SAMPLE SEPARATION AGREEMENT AND RELEASE

[DATE]

Name of Employee
Street Address
City, State, Zip
Dear [Name of Employee]:

This letter confirms your termination as [specify title] of [Name of Company] (the "Company") effective [specify date].

Our understanding and agreement with respect to your separation is as follows:

1. Your total and final compensation from the Company shall be provided to you as follows:

    A. You will receive a lump sum payment of [specify amount] (less statutory deductions) in the form of a Company check to be sent to you Seven (7) days following the execution of this letter.

    B. You will continue to be covered under the Company's group medical, dental, vision and life insurance programs until [specify date], which expense shall be covered by the Company and you at the same proportionate rates as are being paid on the date of separation. Thereafter, you may continue to be covered under the Company's group health insurance program, at your expense, for a period of 18 months (or such longer period as may be required by law) or until you become covered by any other group health plan, whichever occurs first. This continued coverage will be subject to and in accordance with the terms of the documents governing the program.

    C. A check in the amount of [specify amount], representing all accrued but unused vacation (less statutory deductions), will be mailed to you on [specify day and date].

    D. The Company agrees to provide you with a letter of reference attached hereto.

    E. Other than as set forth herein, you will not receive any compensation or benefits of any kind from the Company and you expressly acknowledge and agree that you are not entitled to any such payment or benefit, with the exception of any vested benefit to which you have or will become entitled under the [specify company] Pension Plan.

2. You understand and agree that the compensation and benefits provided for herein are being provided to you in consideration for the covenants undertaken and the releases contained in this Agreement.

3. A. You agree to accept the compensation and benefits provided for herein in full resolution and satisfaction of, and hereby IRREVOCABLY AND UNCONDITIONALLY

RELEASE, REMISE AND FOREVER DISCHARGE the Company from any and all liabilities, actions, causes of action, contracts, agreements, promises, claims and demands of any kind whatsoever, in law or equity, whether known or unknown, suspected or unsuspected, fixed or contingent, apparent or concealed, which you, your heirs, executors, administrators, successors or assigns ever had, now have or hereafter can, shall or may have for, upon, or by reason of any matter, cause or thing whatsoever, from the beginning of the world to the day of the date of this Agreement and Release, including, without limitation, any and all claims arising out of or relating to your employment, compensation and benefits with the Company and/or the termination thereof including, without limitation, contract claims, benefit claims, tort claims, harassment, defamation and other personal injury claims, fraud claims, whistleblower claims, unjust, wrongful or constructive dismissal claims and any claims under any municipal, state or federal wage payment, discrimination or fair employment practices law, statute or regulation, and claims for costs, expenses and attorneys' fees with respect thereto.

 B. By signing this Agreement and Release and by acceptance of the compensation and benefits provided for herein, you hereby WAIVE, RELEASE AND COVENANT NOT TO SUE the Company with respect to any matter relating to or arising out of your employment, compensation and benefits with the Company and/or the termination thereof, and you agree that neither you nor any person organization or entity acting on your behalf will (i) file or participate or join in, encourage, assist, facilitate or permit the bringing or maintenance of any claim or cause of action against the Company, whether in the form of a federal, state or municipal court lawsuit or administrative agency action or otherwise, on the basis of any claim arising out of or relating to your employment, compensation, and benefits with the Company and/or the termination thereof or (ii) seek reinstatement, reemployment or any other relief from the Company, however that relief might be called, whether back pay, compensatory damages, punitive damages, claims for pain and suffering, claims for attorneys' fees, reimbursement of expenses or otherwise, on the basis of any such claim, except for claims for a breach of this Agreement and Release.

 4. Nothing contained herein shall be deemed to constitute an admission or evidence of any wrongdoing or liability on the part of the Company.

 5. Any breach of any provision of this Agreement and Release by you shall constitute a forfeiture of all compensation and benefits set forth herein and, if any such compensation and benefits have already been conveyed as of the time of your breach, you agree to return and/or repay the same to the Company.

 6. You agree that you will not provide consulting advice or counsel to or otherwise cooperate with or assist employees, agents or independent contractors, or former employees, agents or independent contractors of the Company to pursue legal actions against the Company or its owners, stockholders, agents, directors, officers, employees, representatives, attorneys, divisions, parents, subsidiaries, trustees, predecessors, successors or assigns (together, "the Releasees") on or in connection with any matters relating to their employment or the termination thereof. You further agree that you will not participate, directly or indirectly, as a party, witness or otherwise, in any action at law, proceeding in equity, or in any administrative proceeding in which Releasees or Releasees' personnel are parties or attempt to offer into evidence against

Releasees or Releasees' personnel any fact of or concerning any act or motion of Releasees or Releasees' personnel prior to the date of this Agreement, unless compelled to do so by force of law.

7. Should you commence or prosecute any action or proceeding contrary to the provisions of this Agreement, you agree to indemnify Releasees and/or Releasees' affected personnel for all court costs and attorney's fees incurred by Releasees' personnel in the defense of such action or in establishing or maintaining the application or validity of this Agreement or provisions thereof.

8. You will not issue any communication, written or otherwise, that disparages, criticizes or otherwise reflects adversely or encourages any adverse action against the individuals or entities that are the Releasees except if testifying truthfully under oath pursuant to subpoena or otherwise.

9. You acknowledge that by reason of your position with the Company you have been given access to lists of subscribers, prices, plans, and similar confidential or proprietary materials or information respecting the Company's business affairs. You represent that you have held all such information confidential and will continue to do so, and that, unless you first secure the Company's written consent, you shall not directly or indirectly publish, market or otherwise disclose, advise, counsel or otherwise procure any other person or entity, directly or indirectly, to publish, disclose, market or use, any such secret, confidential or proprietary information or relationships of the Company ("Trade Secrets"), of which you became aware or informed during your employment with the Company, unless the Company shall have first given its express written consent to such publication, disclosure, marketing or use, except to the extent that such Trade Secrets a) were known to you at the time of their receipt, b) were in or have become part of the public domain (otherwise than through you), c) were known to the recipient prior to the disclosure, or d) are required to be disclosed by a court or governmental agency. Such Trade Secrets are and shall continue to be the exclusive proprietary property of the Company whether or not they were disclosed to or developed in whole or in part by you.
Such "Trade Secrets" include, without limitation, subscriber lists, marketing plans and programs, studies, and strategies of or about the Company or its business, customers or suppliers, which derives independent economic value, actual or potential, from not being generally known to, and not being readily ascertainable by proper means by, other persons who can obtain economic value from its disclosure.

10. You represent you have returned to the Company any and all files, calendars, distribution lists and any other information and records in your possession or under your control containing confidential or proprietary information concerning the Company or its operations. You also represent that you have no such information and records in your possession or under your control at this time. You further represent that you have returned all keys or other Company property in your possession.

11. It is expressly understood and agreed that this Agreement and Release shall act as a complete bar to any claim, demand or action of any kind whatsoever brought by you against the Company including, without limitation, any claim, demand or action under, or relating to your employment, compensation and benefits with the Company and/or the termination thereof, except for claims for breach of this Agreement and Release.

12. This Agreement and Release may not be changed orally, and no modification, amendment or waiver of any of the provisions contained in this Agreement and Release nor any future representation, promise or condition in connection with the subject matter of this Agreement and Release, shall be binding upon any party hereto unless made in writing and signed by such party.

13. This Agreement and Release shall be subject to, governed by and interpreted in accordance with the laws of the State of [specify].

14. This Agreement and Release and the terms hereof shall be kept confidential.

15. This Agreement and Release contains the entire agreement between the parties with respect to the subject matter hereof and supersedes and terminates any and all previous agreements of any kind whatsoever between the parties, whether written or oral, relating to your employment, compensation and benefits with the Company and/or the termination thereof. This is an integrated document.

16. The parties agree that this Agreement and Release may be specifically enforced in court and may be used as evidence in a subsequent proceeding in which any of the parties allege a breach of this Agreement and Release. In the event of litigation in connection with or concerning the subject matter of this Agreement and Release, the prevailing party shall recover all the party's costs, expenses and attorneys' fees incurred in each and every such action, suit or other proceeding, including any and all appeals or petitions therefrom.

17. In the event that any provision of this Agreement and Release should be held to be void, voidable, unlawful or, for any reason, unenforceable, the remaining portions hereof shall remain in full force and effect.

18. If this Agreement and Release is acceptable to you, please indicate your agreement by signing and dating the enclosed copy of this Agreement and Release in the space provided below and returning it to me on or before [specify date]. YOU WILL THEN BE PERMITTED TO REVOKE THIS AGREEMENT AND RELEASE AT ANY TIME DURING THE PERIOD OF SEVEN DAYS FOLLOWING THE EXECUTION HEREOF, AND THIS AGREEMENT AND RELEASE WILL NOT BE EFFECTIVE OR ENFORCEABLE AND NO PAYMENTS WILL BE MADE HEREUNDER UNTIL THE SEVEN-DAY REVOCATION PERIOD HAS EXPIRED. In the event you elect to revoke this Agreement and Release, this Agreement and Release will be of no further force or effect, and neither you nor the Company will have any further rights or obligations hereunder.

19. You shall have Seven (7) calendar days following the execution of this Agreement in which to revoke said Agreement. This Agreement may be revoked only in writing and only during the seven (7) day period stated in this paragraph. To be effective, written revocation must, within the Seven (7) day period, be hand-delivered or telecopied to [specify]. This Agreement shall not become effective or enforceable until the expiration of the revocation period.

20. THIS IS A LEGAL DOCUMENT. YOU SHOULD CONSULT WITH AN ATTORNEY PRIOR TO SIGNING THIS AGREEMENT AND RELEASE AND THE ATTACHMENTS HERETO. BY SIGNING THIS AGREEMENT AND RELEASE YOU ACKNOWLEDGE AND AFFIRM THAT YOU ARE COMPETENT, THAT YOU HAVE BEEN AFFORDED A TIME PERIOD OF 21 DAYS TO REVIEW AND CONSIDER THIS AGREEMENT AND RELEASE WITH AN ATTORNEY OF YOUR CHOICE, THAT SUCH TIME PERIOD IS A REASONABLE AND SUFFICIENT TIME FOR SUCH REVIEW, THAT YOU HAVE READ AND UNDERSTAND AND ACCEPT THIS DOCUMENT AS FULLY AND FINALLY WAIVING ANY AND ALL CLAIMS, DEMANDS AND DISPUTES AND DIFFERENCES OF ANY KIND WHATSOEVER WHICH YOU MAY HAVE AGAINST THE COMPANY (AS DEFINED IN PARAGRAPH 3 ABOVE), *INCLUDING ANY AND ALL CLAIMS UNDER THE AGE DISCRIMINATION AND EMPLOYMENT ACT,* THAT NO PROMISES OR INDUCEMENTS HAVE BEEN MADE TO YOU EXCEPT AS SET FORTH IN THIS AGREEMENT AND RELEASE, AND THAT YOU HAVE SIGNED THIS DOCUMENT FREELY AND VOLUNTARILY, INTENDING TO BE LEGALLY BOUND BY ITS TERMS.

[NAME OF EMPLOYER]
By: [Name of Employer]
[Title]

Accepted and Agreed:
[NAME OF EMPLOYEE]

On [specify date], before me personally came [Name of Employee], to me known and known to me to be the individual described in and who executed the foregoing Agreement and Release, and he duly acknowledged to me that he executed the same.

_____
Notary Public

GENERAL RELEASE
VERSION ONE

FOR GOOD AND VALUABLE CONSIDERATION, the adequacy of which is hereby acknowledged, in the form of payment to [Name of Employee] of a severance benefit in the amount of [specify] salary less withholding for federal and state taxes, FICA and any other amounts required to be withheld, Employee agrees that he/she, or any person acting by, through or under Employee, RELEASES AND FOREVER DISCHARGES [Name of Employer], and its parent company and its subsidiaries, affiliates, predecessors, successors, and assigns, as well as the officers, employees, representatives, agents and fiduciaries, *de facto* or *de jure* (hereinafter collectively referred to as "Released Parties"), and covenants and agrees not to institute any action or actions, causes or causes of action (in law unknown) in state or federal court, based upon or arising by reason of any damage, loss, or in any way related to Employee's employment with any of the Released Parties or the termination of said employment. The foregoing includes, but not by way of limitation, all claims which could have been raised under common law, including retaliatory discharge and breach of contract, or statute, including, without limitation, the Age Discrimination in Employment Act of 1967, 42 U.S.C. Sections 621-634, as amended by the Older Workers Benefit Protection Act of 1990, Title VII of the Civil Rights Act of 1964, 42 U.S.C. Sections 2000e *et. seq.* and the Employee Retirement Income Security Act of 1974, 29 U.S.C. Sections 1001 *et. seq.* or any other Federal or State Law; except that this General Release is not intended to cover any claim arising from computational or clerical errors in the calculation of the severance benefit provided to Employee, or retirement benefit to which Employee may be entitled from any plan or other benefits to which Employee may be entitled under any plan maintained by any of the Released Parties.

Employee covenants and agrees to forever refrain from instituting, pursuing, or in any way whatsoever aiding any claim, demand, action or cause of action or other matter released and discharged herein by Employee arising out of or in any way related to Employee's employment with any of the Released Parties and the rights to recovery for any damages or compensation awarded as a result of any lawsuit brought by any third party or governmental agency on Employee's behalf.

Employee further agrees to indemnify all Released Parties from any and all loss, liability, damages, claims, suits, judgments, attorneys' fees and other costs and expenses of whatsoever kind or individually, they may sustain or incur as a result of or in connection with the matters hereinabove released and discharged by Employee. Employee warrants that he/she has not filed any lawsuits, charges, complaints, petitions, or accusatory pleadings against any of the Released Parties with any governmental agency or in any court, based upon, arising out of or related in any way to any event or events occurring prior to the signing of this General Release, including, without limitation, his/her employment with any of the Released Parties or the termination thereof.

Employee acknowledges, understands and affirms that:

A. This General Release is a binding legal document;

B. (i) Released Parties advised him/her to consult with an attorney before signing this General Release, (ii) he/she had the right to consult with an attorney about and before signing this General Release, (iii) he/she was given a period of at least 21 calendar days in which to consider this General Release prior to signing, and (iv) he/she voluntarily signs and enters into this General Release without reservation after having given the matter full and careful consideration; and

C. (i) Employee has a period of seven days after signing this General Release in which he/she may revoke this General Release, (ii) this General Release does not become effective or enforceable and no payment shall be made hereunder until this seven-day-revocation period has elapsed, and (iii) any revocation must be in writing by Employee and delivered to the Vice-President, Human Resources within the seven-day-revocation period.

IN WITNESS WHEREOF, the Employee signs this General Release this [specify date].

[EMPLOYEE'S NAME]
(please print)

WITNESS:
[Name of Witness] Signature:_____

[DATE]

GENERAL RELEASE
VERSION TWO

KNOW ALL MEN BY THESE PRESENTS THAT I, [Name of Employee], for and in consideration of the payment to me of [specify amount], do for myself, my heirs, executors, administrators, successors and assigns, in addition to all the promises made herein, hereby release and forever discharge [Name of Employer] and its parents, divisions, successors, predecessors, subsidiaries, affiliates, assigns, and the directors, officers, servants, agents and employees of each of them, and each of their heirs, executors and administrators, and all of them (hereinafter collectively "Releasees") from any and all actions and causes of action, claims and demands, suits, damages, costs, attorneys' fees, expenses, debts due, contracts, agreements, and claims for any compensation or benefits whatsoever, in law or in equity, which I or anyone claiming by, through or under me in any way might have or could have against Employer and Releases, including, but not *limited to,* any claims whatsoever which arose out of, or which could be claimed to have arisen out of, my employment with, or the separation of my employment from, Employer that I ever had or now have against Employer or Releasees from the beginning of the world to the date of this Release.

This Release includes, but is not limited to, claims under the Age Discrimination In Employment Act of 1967, as amended ("ADEA").

I expressly acknowledge that I have read this Release and have had at least Twenty-one (21) days to discuss it with legal counsel of my choice before signing and that I realize and understand that it applies to and covers all claims, demands, and causes of action, including those under ADEA, against Employer or Releasees or any of them, whether or not I know or suspect them to exist at the present time. I further understand that this Release will not be accepted by Employer if I sign it prior to the expiration of 21 days from the date I received it.

I further acknowledge that this Release is not part of a program being offered to a group or class of employees and that my execution of this Release is made voluntarily without coercion in any way.

I understand that I shall have a period of Seven (7) days from the date I sign this Release to revoke it. If I decide to revoke this Release, the revocation must be in writing signed by me and received by Employer before the expiration of the Seventh (7th) calendar day following the date I sign this Release. Consequently, this Release shall have no force and effect until the expiration of Seven (7) calendar days following the day on which I sign it, and Employer shall likewise have no obligation hereunder until after that time.

I understand that nothing herein waives any rights or claims I may have arising under ADEA after the date on which I sign this Release.

I will not apply for or otherwise seek re-employment with Employer at any time.

I will keep the terms, amount and fact of this Release and the payment hereunder confidential and will not hereafter state the facts or terms of this Release to anyone (except my attorney and wife), including, but not limited to, any past, present or prospective employee or applicant for employment with Employer.

Nothing herein nor the payment hereunder shall be construed as an admission of any liability on the part of anyone for any matter, all liability being denied.

I have not relied on any representation, expressed or implied, made by Employer or any of its representatives.

This Release constitutes the entire understanding between myself and Employer and cannot be modified except in writing signed by both myself and [Employer].

I intend that this Release shall not be subject to any claim of fraud, duress, deception, or mistake of fact, and that it expresses a full and complete settlement of any claims whatsoever I ever had or may have against Employer or any Releasee.

I will not file any complaint, suit, claim or charge against Employee or any Releasee with any local, state or federal agency or court. If any agency or court assumes jurisdiction of any complaint, suit, claim or charge against Employer or any Releasee on my behalf, I will request such agency or court to dismiss the matter.

I understand this Release is contractual and based on my representation that I will comply with the terms set forth herein. Should I breach any of the terms of this Release, I shall repay to Employer all sums paid to me hereunder, plus reasonable attorneys' fees incurred in connection with the enforcement of the terms of this Release, in addition to any other damages caused by my breach of any of the terms of this Release. Nothing herein shall be construed to limit any other remedies Employer or Releasees may have under law or in equity.

I, intending to be legally bound, hereby apply my signature voluntarily with full understanding of the contents of this Release.

_____
Employee's Name

_____
Employee's Signature

[WITNESS]
[DATE]

I, [Name of Attorney], am an attorney licensed to practice law in the State of [specify]. I represent [Name of Client], I have explained to him the consequences of signing this Release and he has indicated to me an understanding thereof and that he is signing this Release of his own free will.

COVER LETTER AND RELEASE
(Specifically waiving an age discrimination claim)

TO: Severed Employee
FROM: The Company ("The Employer")
RE: Older Workers Benefit Protection Act

This communication apprises you of your rights under the Older Workers Benefit Protection Act ("OWBPA") which amends the Age Discrimination in Employment Act ("ADEA"), that Congress passed. The OWBPA establishes certain standards as regards waivers that the Employer obtains from its Employees.

The OWBPA amends the ADEA by adding a new section which establishes standards for a "knowing and voluntary" waiver. The OWBPA sets forth seven basic requirements for a knowing and voluntary waiver:

(1) The waiver has to be part of an agreement between the Employee and the Employer and it has to be written in understandable English;

(2) The waiver must refer specifically to rights or claims arising under the ADEA;

(3) The waiver cannot cover rights or claims that may arise after the date on which it is signed;

(4) The waiver must be exchanged for consideration, and the consideration must be in addition to anything of value to which the employee is already entitled;

(5) The Employee must be advised in writing to consult with an attorney before signing the agreement;

(6) The Employee has to be given a period of at least 21 days to decide whether to sign the waiver; and

(7) The Employee is entitled to revoke the waiver within seven days after signing it, and the waiver does not become effective or enforceable until the revocation period has expired.

GENERAL RELEASE

FOR GOOD AND VALUABLE CONSIDERATION, the adequacy of which is hereby acknowledged, in the form of payment to Employee of a severance benefit in the amount of ($XX)_____ salary less withholding for federal and state taxes, FICA and any other amounts required to be withheld, Employee agrees that he/she, or any person acting by, through or under Employee, RELEASES AND FOREVER DISCHARGES [Name of Employer], and its parent company and its subsidiaries, affiliates, predecessors, successors, and assigns, as well as the officers, employees, representatives, agents and fiduciaries, *de facto* or *de jure* (hereinafter collectively referred to as "Released Parties"), and covenants and agrees not to institute any action or actions, causes or causes of action (in law unknown) in state or federal court, based upon or arising by reason of any damage, loss, or in any way related to Employee's employment with any of the Released Parties or the termination of said employment. The foregoing includes, but not by way of limitation, all claims which could have been raised under common law, including retaliatory discharge and breach of contract, or statute, including, without limitation, the Age Discrimination in Employment Act of 1967, 42 U.S.C. Sections 621-634, as amended by the Older Workers Benefit Protection Act of 1990, Title VII of the Civil Rights Act of 1964, 42 U.S.C. Sections 2000e *et. seq.* and the Employee Retirement Income Security Act of 1974, 29 U.S.C. Sections 1001 *et. seq.* or any other Federal or State Law; except that this General Release is not intended to cover any claim arising from computational or clerical errors in the calculation of the severance benefit provided to Employee, or retirement benefit to which Employee may be entitled from any plan or other benefits to which Employee may be entitled under any plan maintained by any of the Released Parties.

Employee covenants and agrees to forever refrain from instituting, pursuing, or in any way whatsoever aiding any claim, demand, action or cause of action or other matter released and discharged herein by Employee arising out of or in any way related to Employee's employment with any of the Released Parties and the rights to recovery for any damages or compensation awarded as a result of any lawsuit brought by any third party or governmental agency on Employee's behalf.

Employee further agrees to indemnify all Released Parties from any and all loss, liability, damages, claims, suits, judgments, attorneys' fees and other costs and expenses of whatsoever kind or individually, Employee may sustain or incur as a result of or in connection with the matters hereinabove released and discharged by Employee. Employee warrants that he/she has not filed any lawsuits, charges, complaints, petitions, or accusatory pleadings against any of the Released Parties with any governmental agency or in any court, based upon, arising out of or related in any way to any event or events occurring prior to the signing of this General Release, including, without limitation, his/her employment with any of the Released Parties or the termination thereof.

Employee acknowledges, understands and affirms that: (a) This General Release is a binding legal document; (b) Released Parties advised him/her to consult with an attorney before signing this General Release, (ii) he/she had the right to consult with an attorney about and before signing this General Release, (iii) he/she was given a period of at least 21 calendar days in which to consider this General Release prior to signing, and (iv) he/she voluntarily signs and enters into this General Release without reservation after having given the matter full and careful consideration; and (c) (i) Employee has a period of seven days after signing this General Release in which he/she may revoke this General Release, (ii) this General Release does not become effective or enforceable and no payment shall be made hereunder until this seven-day-revocation period has elapsed, and (iii) any revocation must be in writing by Employee and delivered to (specify), Human Resources within the seven-day-revocation period.

IN WITNESS WHEREOF, the Employee signs this General Release this _____ day of _____, 199 .

_____
Employee's Name (please print)

WITNESS:

_____
Signature

Date:_____

ACKNOWLEDGMENT

I HEREBY ACKNOWLEDGE that [Name of Employer] in accordance with the Age Discrimination in Employment Act, as amended by the Older Workers Benefit Protection Act, informed me in writing: 1) to consult with an attorney before signing this General Release; 2) to review this General Release for a period of 21 days prior to signing; 3) that for a period of seven days following the signing of this General Release, I may revoke this General Release, and this General Release, will not become effective or enforceable until the seven-day-revocation period has elapsed; and 4) that no payment shall be made until the seven-day-revocation period has elapsed.

I HEREBY FURTHER ACKNOWLEDGE receipt of this General Release for my review on the __ day of _____, 199 .

Witness: Employee:_____
                    (Print or Type Name)

_____
Signature of Employee

TERMINATION LOG SUMMARY

Name of Employee: _____

Department: _____

Date of Termination: _____

Final Date of Employment: _____

Last Rate of Pay: _____

Last Grade: _____

Reason For Termination: _____

Additional Comments:

PREPARED BY: APPROVED BY:

_____   _____
Name and Title   Name and Title Of Supervisor

_____   _____
Signature   Signature Of Supervisor

_____   _____
Date   Date

SAMPLE EXIT INTERVIEW FORM

Date: _____

Employee: _____   Social Security No.: _____

Title: _____   Department/Location: _____

D/O/H: _____   Supervisor's Name: _____

1. What did you like about your job here?

2. What did you not like about you job here?

3. Specify the most satisfying part of your job.

4. Specify the least satisfying part of your job.

5. Specify your relationship with your direct supervisor.

6. What made you decide to leave the company?

7. Are you accepting another position? If so, with whom, when, and where?

8. Indicate your thoughts concerning the company's compensation policies.

9. In the space below, please indicate your comments on how the company can improve your job function or provide your comments on any other matter that should be brought to our attention.

_____ _____
Employee   Date

_____ _____
Interviewer   Date

FOR PERSONNEL DEPARTMENT ONLY

Interviewer's comments:

REVIEWED BY:

_____ _____
Immediate Supervisor   Date

_____ _____
Department Head   Date

_____ _____
President of Personnel Dept.   Date

CHECKLIST OF EMPLOYEE TERMINATION ACTION

Date: _____

Employee: _____   Social Security No.: _____

Title: _____   Department/Location: _____

D/O/H: _____   Supervisor's Name: _____

1. **Voluntary Resignation:**

    ___ Resignation Ltr. Received   ___ Adequate Notice Given—If Not, State Circumstances Why

2. **Involuntary Resignation/Termination:**

    A. **Signed and Attached:**

    ___ Management Approval Attached   ___ Separation Agreement & General Release Signed

    B. **Property Returned:**

    ___ Computer Diskettes   ___ Company Handbook(s)

    ___ Computer Books   ___ Pertinent Business Documents And All Copies

    ___ Computer Keys   ___ Office Keys

    ___ Company Car   ___ All Company Credit Cards

    ___ Company Car Keys   ___ All Company Equipment

    ___ Employee Identification Card(s)

    C. **Final Accounting:**

    ___ Prior Expenses Submitted   ___ Advances/Loans Repaid

    ___ COBRA Benefit Forms Completed   ___ 401(k)/Pension Forms Completed

    ___ Accrued Vacation Pay Calculated & Paid   ___ Final Paycheck Issued

CHECKLIST OF EMPLOYEE TERMINATION ACTION
(PAGE TWO)

D. Exit Interview Conducted:

___ Yes   ___ No

E.   Other:

Prepared By:

_____   _____
Department Head   Personnel Department

_____   _____
Title/Date   Title/Date

FINAL SUPERVISOR'S APPROVAL FOR TERMINATION CHECKLIST

Employee: _____ Social Security No.: _____

Title: _____ Department/Location: _____

D/O/H: _____ Supervisor's Name: _____

CHECK IF COMPLETED:

1. Has the matter been investigated? ___

2. Have all incidents leading up to the termination been considered and documented? ___

3. Have I reviewed the employee's file to check for his/her record of attendance, performance reviews and past disciplinary action? ___

4. Is the decision to terminate the employee based on objective or subjective standards? ___

5. Has the employee been adequately informed of his/her job requirements and the company's policies? If so, is there a written record supporting this? ___

6. Has the employee received at least one written warning? ___

7. Has the employee been given a reasonable opportunity to correct the problem? ___

8. Have I considered a lesser form of disciplinary action? ___

9. Would the termination of this employee be consistent with the termination of other similarly situated employees in the past? ___

10. Can the Company justify the termination of this employee if he/she brought a charge of discrimination or lawsuit against it? ___

11. Has the decision to terminate the employee been cleared by my supervisors and the Personnel Department? ___

12. Can I terminate the employee in a tactful and professional manner? ___

13. Have I scheduled the termination interview at a time when I can terminate the employee privately and when I can minimize the terminated employee's contact with other employees? ___

14. Have I made arrangements for the preparation of the employee's last paycheck, severance pay, accrued unused vacation pay, and paperwork regarding COBRA and other benefit programs, for review and completion at the exit interview? ___

15. Do I know what Company property the employee has and must return? ___

16. Have I considered who will handle the reference for the terminated employee when prospective employers call, and what will be said to them? ___

17. Has a decision been made as to what management will tell other employees regarding the terminated employee? ___

VOLUNTARY RESIGNATION BY EMPLOYEE FORM

Date: _____

Employee: _____   Social Security No.: _____

Title: _____   Department/Location: _____

D/O/H: _____   Supervisor's Name: _____

===

    I, the undersigned, am voluntarily resigning from my position as (Title) with (Company Name). My last day of employment with (Company Name) will be (Specify Date).

    I am resigning my position because:

You may contact me at the following telephone number and address:

After (Specify Date) you can reach me at:

Thank you for your attention in this matter.

                                                  _____   _____
                                                  Employee Signature   Date

                                                  _____   _____
                                                  Received by:(Name/Title)   Date

CONFIDENTIAL SETTLEMENT AGREEMENT, MUTUAL RELEASE, AND COVENANT NOT TO SUE

This Confidential Settlement Agreement, Mutual Release and Covenant Not to Sue ("Agreement") is entered into this [specify date] by and among [specify company] ("the Company"), on the one hand, and [specify company] ("Sales Rep") on the other hand.

I. RECITALS

A. WHEREAS, on or about ____, 19_, Sales Rep entered into a sales representative contract with [specify] (the "Sales Representative Contract");

B. WHEREAS, after the Sales Representative Contract was executed, the Company acquired certain of the assets of [specify];

C. WHEREAS, by letter dated ____, 19_, the Company confirmed that the Sales Representative Contract had already been terminated and outlined a superseding commission and finder's fee schedule (the "____, 19_ letter");

D. WHEREAS, Sales Rep claims an entitlement to a commission or other monetary consideration in connection with an order placed by [specify], and the Company denies Sales Rep's entitlement to same;

E. WHEREAS, the parties desire to settle, pursuant to the terms and conditions set forth herein below, all claims between them in any way related to the Sales Representative Contract, the ____, 19_ letter, the relationship between the parties, any claim to commissions, finder's fees or other monetary consideration and wish to terminate any relationship which may have existed.

II. AGREEMENT

NOW, THEREFORE, the parties mutually agree as follows:

1. Consideration. The Company shall:

A. Execute and deliver to counsel for Sales Rep a check in the amount of Fifty Thousand ($50,000.00), made payable to the Law Offices of Steven Mitchell Sack, which sum is being paid collectively to Sales Rep and its counsel and which sum they are to divide between themselves as they see fit;

B. Execute and deliver to counsel for Sales Rep a signed original of this Agreement.

2. Consideration. Sales Rep shall:

A. Execute and deliver to counsel for the Company a signed original of this Agreement, thereby fully and forever releasing the Company on the terms described in this Agreement;

B. Accept the single sum of $50,000.00 as the sole monetary consideration for the execution of this Agreement and the release herein.

3. Mutual Release of Claims.

A. Conditioned upon receipt of the consideration set forth in Section 1 hereof, Sales Rep, on behalf of itself and on behalf of its affiliates, subsidiaries, officers, directors, employees, sales personnel, agents, attorneys, accountants, insurers, representatives, successors and assigns, hereby releases and forever discharges the Company and past and present affiliates, subsidiaries, officers, directors, partners, principals, employees, attorneys, insurers, agents, servants, successors, heirs and assigns("the Released Parties"), from any and all claims, demands, obligations, losses, causes of action, costs, expenses, attorneys' fees and liabilities of any nature whatsoever, whether based on contract, tort, statutory or other legal or equitable theory of recovery, whether known or unknown, which Sales Rep has, had or claims to have against any or all of the Released Parties, including but not limited to any and all claims which relate to, arise from, or are in any manner connected to i) the Sales Representative Contract, ii) the _____, 19_ Letter and/or iii) any claimed commissions, "finder's fees" or other monetary consideration, whether accrued or not.

B. Conditioned upon payment of the consideration set forth in Section 1 hereof, the Company, on behalf of itself and its past and present partners, principals, employees, agents, servants, attorneys, insurers, representatives, affiliates, successors, heirs and assigns, hereby releases and forever discharges Sales Rep and its respective agents, attorneys, accountants, insurers, successors and assigns, from any and all claims, demands, obligations, losses, causes of action, costs, expenses, attorneys' fees and liabilities of any nature whatsoever, whether based on contract, tort, statutory or other legal or equitable theory of recovery, whether known or unknown, which the Company has, had, claims or could claim to have against Sales Rep, including but not limited to any and all claims which relate to, arise from, or are in any manner connected to A. the Sales Representative Contract, B. the _____, 19_ Letter and/or C. any claimed commissions, "finder's fees" or other monetary consideration, whether accrued or not.

4. Termination of Agreements. The parties hereto agree and confirm that, except for this Settlement Agreement, any and all agreements, written or oral, including but not limited to the Sales Representative Agreement and/or the _____, 19_ letter, have already been and are terminated and are of no further force and effect. All parties hereto agree that none of the terms, conditions or obligations, if any, have survived termination, and that this Agreement supersedes any of the terms of such agreements. All parties expressly release each other from any continuing rights, duties and/or obligations under any agreements, and Sales Rep shall make no further claim for any compensation even if such allegedly entitling sale was disclosed pursuant to the _____, 19_ letter or otherwise falls within the terms of the agreements.

5. Waiver of California Civil Code §1542 and New York counterpart, if any. Each party knowingly and intentionally waives any protection afforded to them by California Civil Code §1542, which provides:

> A general release does not extend to claims which the creditor does not know or suspect to exist in his favor at the time of executing the release, which if known by him must have materially affected his settlement with the debtor.

Each party further waives any protection under any New York counterpart to California Civil Code §1542. Each party agrees that this Agreement is intended to cover all claims or possible claims arising out of or related to those matters referenced or impliedly covered in the general release referenced above, whether the same are known, unknown or hereafter discovered or ascertained, and the provisions of §1542 of the California Civil Code and the New York counterpart (if any) are hereby expressly waived. The parties hereto expressly acknowledge that they have been advised by their counsel of the contents and effect of such provisions, and with such knowledge they hereby expressly waive whatever benefits they may have pursuant to such provisions.

6. Covenants.

A. Sales Rep covenants and agrees that it will not, at any time hereafter, either directly or indirectly, initiate, assign, maintain or prosecute, or in any way knowingly aid or assist in the initiation, maintenance or prosecution of any claim, demand or cause of action at law or otherwise, against the Released Parties, or any of them, for damages, loss or injury of any kind arising from, related to, or in any way connected to any activity with respect to which a release has been given pursuant to Section 3 of this Agreement.

B. The terms of this Agreement, and the very existence of this Agreement itself, shall remain strictly confidential. Each signatory to this Agreement individually covenants not to disclose any of the terms of this Agreement, whether generally or specifically, to any third party, except as may be required by a party's accountants or insurers, or by order of a court of competent jurisdiction. Each signatory further covenants that he or it will be personally liable for any and all damages that may be caused to any other party by his unauthorized disclosure of any of the terms of this Agreement.

7. Agreement Not an Admission of Liability. The parties hereto agree and acknowledge that this Agreement is a compromise settlement of each party's disputed claims, and that the sums and covenants given in consideration of this Agreement, as well as the execution of this Agreement, shall not be construed to be an admission of liability on the part of any party with respect to the disputed matters set forth above.

8. Parties to Bear Own Costs and Attorneys' Fees. Each party to this Agreement will bear its own costs, expenses, and claims to interest and attorneys' fees, whether taxable or otherwise, incurred in or arising out of, or in any way connected with the matters which are referenced or covered in the mutual releases referenced above or which were otherwise related to the subject of this Agreement.

9. Entire Agreement. This Agreement represents and contains the entire agreement and understanding among the parties hereto with respect to the subject matter of this Agreement, and supersedes any and all prior oral and written agreements and understandings. No representation, warranty, condition, understanding or agreement of any kind with respect to the subject matter shall be relied upon by the parties except those contained herein. This Agreement may not be amended or modified except by an agreement signed by the party against whom enforcement of any modification or amendment is sought.

10. Advice of Counsel. In entering into this Agreement, the parties each acknowledge and represent that they have sought and obtained the legal advice of their attorneys, who are the attorneys of their own choice. They further represent that the terms of this Agreement have been completely read by them, and that those terms are fully understood and voluntarily accepted by them.

11. Counterparts. This Agreement may be executed in any number of counterparts, each of which shall be deemed an original, and all of which together shall be deemed one and the same instrument.

12. Attorneys' Fees. In the event litigation is necessary to enforce a provision or provisions of this Agreement, all costs, expenses and attorneys' fees, whether taxable or not, shall be paid by the non-prevailing party or parties to the prevailing party or parties.

13. No Assignment. The parties each represent and warrant to one another that they have not sold, assigned, transferred, conveyed or otherwise disposed of any claim or demand covered by this Agreement.

14. Heirs, Successors and Assigns. This Agreement shall be binding upon and inure to the benefit of the parties' respective legal heirs, successors and assigns.

15. Severability. Should any portion (word, clause, phrase, sentence, paragraph or section) of this Agreement be declared void or unenforceable, such portion shall be considered independent and severable from the remainder, the validity of which shall remain unaffected.

Dated:
[NAME OF SALES REP]
("Sales Rep")

Dated:
[NAME OF COMPANY]
("The Company")

By: [Name and Title]
Its: [specify]

By [Name and Title]

SETTLEMENT AGREEMENT AND MUTUAL RELEASE

THIS SETTLEMENT AGREEMENT AND MUTUAL RELEASE (the [specify] "Settlement Agreement") is entered into between ABC [specify company], a Wisconsin corporation, on the one hand, and [specify sales representative] doing business as XYZ [specify D/B/A] on the other hand (collectively, the "Parties") on the _____ [specify date].

WHEREAS, the Parties entered into an agreement dated _____, 19_ entitled "Sales Representative Agreement" (the "Rep Agreement"), which is attached as Exhibit "1" to this Settlement Agreement;

WHEREAS, ABC terminated the Rep Agreement on _____, 19_;

WHEREAS, XYZ has made claims against ABC as to commissions previously owed and allegedly owing in the future; and

WHEREAS, the Parties have, between themselves, negotiated a complete resolution of any and all disputes, claims or potential claims arising between them and the subject matter of the Rep Agreement and intend, by the terms of this Settlement Agreement, to memorialize the resolution of all disputes, claims or potential claims between the Parties arising during their relationship.

NOW, THEREFORE, in consideration of the recitals stated above, which all Parties agree are accurate and complete, the agreements, promises and warranties set forth below and other good and valuable consideration, receipt of which is hereby acknowledged, the Parties agree as follows:

1. The above recitals are hereby made a part of this Settlement Agreement.

2. The Parties acknowledge that the Rep Agreement and any other contractual agreements between the Parties, whether oral or written, are terminated. XYZ shall have the unrestricted right to sell to any of its customers and shall be entitled to represent any and all manufacturers of product, including, without limitation, products similar to those manufactured by ABC.

3. Immediately upon the Parties' execution of this Settlement Agreement, ABC shall deliver to counsel for XYZ, The Law Offices of Steven Mitchell Sack ("Counsel for XYZ"), the following: (a) a corporate check drawn on the account of ABC in the amount of Thirty Thousand Dollars ($30,000.00) made payable to "Steven M. Sack, Attorney For XYZ;" (b) an executed $168,000.00 promissory note in the form of the promissory note attached hereto as Exhibit "2" ("Note"); and (c) an executed Affidavit for Judgment by Confession attached hereto as Exhibit "3" ("Affidavit"). All installment payments due under the Note are to be made payable to "Steven Mitchell Sack, Attorney For XYZ" and are to be mailed via overnight mail directly to the law offices of Steven Mitchell Sack, Esq., [specify address].

4. If and only if (a) ABC fails to make a payment required by the Note and (b) ABC thereafter fails to make said payment pursuant to the ten-day Notice of Non- Payment provisions of numbered Paragraph 2 of the Note ("Ten-Day Notice Provisions") and (c) XYZ files a declaration under penalty of perjury with the above-entitled court, after first giving a three-day Notice of intention to do so, that states that ABC failed to make a payment required by the Note and that ABC failed to make such payment pursuant to the Ten-Day Notice Provisions, then ABC authorizes XYZ to file the Affidavit and have judgment entered against ABC in the total amount of $168,000.00 (less any payments on the Note already received by XYZ from ABC (the"Judgment"), in the form of the Judgment attached as Exhibit "B" to the Affidavit. XYZ's total recovery for XYZ's claims shall consist of (1) the Judgment, (2) interest on the Judgment at the rate of Sixteen Percent (16%) per annum or the maximum legal interest rate, whichever is greater, until the Judgment is paid in full and (3) reasonable attorneys fees and costs incurred in filing, enforcing and collecting the Judgment.

5. The Parties acknowledge that they understand and agree that, upon the final payment by ABC required by the capitalized Note, or payment by ABC pursuant to the Ten-Day Notice Provision in numbered Paragraph 2 of the Note,, whichever is later, each of the Parties releases and forever discharges the other and its respective agents, servants, employees, proprietors, partners, officers, directors, shareholders,, subsidiaries, attorneys,, predecessors, successors, assigns, heirs, survivors and personal representatives of and from any and all known or unknown claims, debts, liabilities, demands, obligations, damages, losses, costs, expenses, attorney's fees, actions and causes of action, from the beginning of time to the effective date of this Settlement Agreement. From the date of this Settlement Agreement until the date of the final payment by ABC required by the Note or the date of payment by ABC pursuant to the Ten-Day Notice Provision in numbered paragraph 2 of the Note, each party agrees that it will not initiate any complaint, suit, or action of any kind against the other party, in law or equity, before a state court, federal court, foreign court, or administrative body, except as provided in paragraph 4 of this Settlement Agreement; provided, however, that if a court enters a final judgment, not reversed on appeal, pursuant to paragraph 4 of this Settlement Agreement, the Parties' agreement not to initiate complaint, suit, or action shall no longer apply.

6. Nothing in this Settlement Agreement shall constitute or be construed as an admission on behalf of any of the Parties as to the validity of any claims, defenses or allegations asserted hereto and XYZ agrees to keep confidential and not disclose the terms of this Settlement Agreement to any third parties with the exception of her attorney, accountant and immediate family.

7. Each of the Parties hereby represents and warrants to the other that it has not heretofore assigned or transferred, or purported to assign or transfer, to any person or entity any claims, debts, liabilities, demands, obligations, damages, losses, costs, expenses, attorneys' fees, actions or causes of action released herein. Each of the Parties agrees to indemnify, hold harmless and defend (including the payment of actual attorneys' fees, costs and expenses) the other of and from any claims, debts, liabilities, demands, obligations, damages, losses, costs, expenses, attorneys' fees, actions or causes of action that are in any way based on or arise out of any such assignment or transfer.

8. The Parties acknowledge that for the purpose of enforcing the terms of this Settlement Agreement or entering judgment appropriate jurisdiction and venue shall lie with the Circuit Court of [specify], County of [specify].

9. Each of the Parties represents and warrants that it has been represented by separate legal counsel of its own choice throughout all of the negotiations that preceded the execution of this Settlement Agreement and in connection with the preparation and execution of this Settlement Agreement; that it has carefully and thoroughly reviewed this Settlement Agreement in its entirety with that counsel; that its counsel has approved it as to form; and that it understands the terms used herein.

10. Each party has had the opportunity to investigate this matter, determine the advisability of entering into this Settlement Agreement and has entered into this Settlement Agreement freely and voluntarily. Each of the Parties acknowledges that in executing this Settlement Agreement they rely solely on their own judgment, belief and knowledge and on such advice as they may have received from their own counsel and that they have not been influenced by any representation or statements made by the other party or its counsel. No provision in this Settlement Agreement is to be interpreted for or against any of the Parties because that Party or its counsel drafted such provision.

11. This Settlement Agreement and its Exhibits 1 and 2, embody the entire understanding and agreement of the Parties concerning the resolution of all disputes, claims or potential claims between them that arose during their working relationship and as such, it fully supersedes any other oral or written understandings, agreements, representations and warranties between them relating thereto.

12. The terms and conditions contained in this Settlement Agreement shall inure to the benefit of, and be binding upon, the successors, assigns, heirs, survivors and personal representatives of each of the Parties.

13. The Parties, and each of them, agree to execute such other documents and take such other immediate action as may reasonably be necessary to accomplish the purpose of this Settlement Agreement.

14. In the event that any condition, covenant or other provision of this Settlement Agreement is held to be invalid or void by any court of competent jurisdiction, it shall be deemed severable from the remainder of this Settlement Agreement and shall in no way affect any other condition, covenant or other provision of this Settlement Agreement. If such condition, covenant or other provision is held to be invalid due to its scope or breadth, it is agreed that it shall be deemed to remain valid to the extent permitted by law.

15. No breach of any provision of this Settlement Agreement shall be deemed waived unless it is waived in writing. Waiver of any one breach shall not be deemed a waiver of any other breach of the same or any other provision of this Settlement Agreement.

16. This Settlement Agreement can only be amended or modified by a written agreement duly executed by all of the Parties.

17. Any corporation signing this Settlement Agreement represents and warrants that such execution is in compliance with any required resolution of its Board of Directors, duly adopted at a meeting of such Board of Directors. Any individual signing this Settlement Agreement on behalf of another individual, a corporation or a partnership represents and warrants that he or she has full authority to do so.

18. This Settlement Agreement shall be governed by and construed and enforced under the laws of the State of [specify state].

19. In the event either party commences any action in a court of law to enforce this Settlement Agreement or obtain damages for the breach of this Settlement Agreement, the prevailing Party shall be entitled to an award of its actual attorneys' fees and costs incurred in such action.

20. This Settlement Agreement may be executed in counterparts, and each counterpart shall be considered an original. This Settlement Agreement shall not be effective in any way as to any of the Parties until fully executed by all parties and until counsel for each of the Parties has been delivered a fully executed counterpart thereof.

Dated:

                      ("ABC")
                      By:

                                                  President

Dated:

                      "XYZ"
                      By:

NEGOTIABLE PROMISSORY NOTE

$168,000.00   New York, N.Y.
                                    [specify date]

THIS PROMISSORY NOTE (the "Note") is effective as of the date it is executed by ABC, a [specify state] corporation with its principal offices located at [specify address] ("Maker"), for the purpose of evidencing an obligation from Maker to XYZ ("Payee").

1.   Promise to Pay. For value received, Maker promises to pay Payee or order at the law offices of Steven Mitchell Sack, Esq., 60 East 42nd Street, 46th floor, New York, N.Y. 10165, or at such other place as may be designated in writing by the holder of this Note, the total sum of One Hundred Sixty Eight Thousand Dollars ($168,000.00) with no additional interest, costs or fees (in the event of timely payment) to be paid in the following 24 installments. The checks for all installment payments are to be made payable to "Steven Mitchell Sack, Attorney For XYZ" and are to be mailed directly to the law offices of Steven Mitchell Sack, Esq. via overnight mail. An installment payment shall be deemed paid on the date that Maker mails the installment payment to Steven Mitchell Sack, Esq., via overnight mail. All installment payments may be by corporate check drawn on the bank account of Maker. The 24 installment payments shall be made as follows:

(1) Seven Thousand ($7,000.00) Dollars on or before
(2) Seven Thousand ($7,000.00) Dollars on or before
(3) Seven Thousand ($7,000.00) Dollars on or before
(4) Seven Thousand ($7,000.00) Dollars on or before
(5) Seven Thousand ($7,000.00) Dollars on or before
(6) Seven Thousand ($7,000.00) Dollars on or before
(7) Seven Thousand ($7,000.00) Dollars on or before
(8) Seven Thousand ($7,000.00) Dollars on or before
(9) Seven Thousand ($7,000.00) Dollars on or before
(10) Seven Thousand ($7,000.00) Dollars on or before
(11) Seven Thousand ($7,000.00) Dollars on or before
(12) Seven Thousand ($7,000.00) Dollars on or before
(13) Seven Thousand ($7,000.00) Dollars on or before
(14) Seven Thousand ($7,000.00) Dollars on or before
(15) Seven Thousand ($7,000.00) Dollars on or before
(16) Seven Thousand ($7,000.00) Dollars on or before
(17) Seven Thousand ($7,000.00) Dollars on or before
(18) Seven Thousand ($7,000.00) Dollars on or before
(19) Seven Thousand ($7,000.00) Dollars on or before
(20) Seven Thousand ($7,000.00) Dollars on or before
(21) Seven Thousand ($7,000.00) Dollars on or before
(22) Seven Thousand ($7,000.00) Dollars on or before
(23) Seven Thousand ($7,000.00) Dollars on or before
(24) Seven Thousand ($7,000.00) Dollars on or before

2. **Notice of Non-Payment.** If Maker fails to make a payment set forth above on its due date, Payee shall give Maker written notice of such nonpayment. The date of such notice shall be deemed to be the date that Payee transmits such notice by facsimile to the number set forth in paragraph 3 below, so long as such facsimile is confirmed in writing via first-class mail as provided in Paragraph 3. Payee shall have Ten (10) days from the date of such notice to make said payment. The date that a payment is made pursuant to such notice shall be deemed to be the date that ABC mails such payment via overnight mail to Steven Mitchell Sack, Esq.

3. **Notice.** Any notice to be provided to Maker pursuant to the preceding paragraph or any other notice to be given by Maker or Payee shall be given in writing, by facsimile and first class mail, as follows:

[specify fax number, address, and contact names for both parties.]

4. **No Offsets.** Maker agrees to pay this Note free from any offset, deduction or counterclaim.

5. **Prepayment.** This Note may be prepaid in whole or in part at any time.

6. **Default and Acceleration.** Maker shall be immediately in default upon the occurrence of any of the following events: (a) Maker fails to pay any amount due hereunder in full when due and Maker fails to make such payment pursuant to the ten-day notice provisions of numbered Paragraph 2 above; (b) Maker violates or otherwise fails to perform or observe any term,, covenant, or agreement contained in this Note; (c) the winding up, liquidation or dissolution of Maker; (d) sale or transfer of substantially all of Maker's assets; (e) a receiver is appointed for all or any part of Maker's property; (f) Maker makes an assignment for the benefit of its creditors; or (g) Maker files or has filed against it any petition under any existing or future bankruptcy law. In the event that Maker defaults under this Note, then, at the option of the holder of this Note, the entire unpaid balance of principal shall become immediately due and payable.

7. **Waivers.** Maker waives presentment, protest and demand, notice of protest, dishonor and nonpayment of this Note and expressly agrees that this Note, or any payment hereunder, may be extended from time to time at the written consent of the holder, all without in any way affecting the liability of Maker.

8. **Attorneys' Fees and Interest.** If an event of default has occurred and the holder of this Note refers it to any attorney for collection, Maker agrees to pay all costs and reasonable attorneys' fees incurred by the holder of this Note in connection therewith. Interest shall accrue from the date of default at the rate of Sixteen Percent (16%) per annum or the maximum legal interest rate, whichever is greater.

9. **Construction.** This Note shall be governed by and construed and enforced under the laws of the State of [specify].

10. Successors. The terms and conditions of this Note shall inure to the benefit of and be binding jointly and severally upon the successors, assigns, heirs, survivors and personal representatives of Maker and shall inure to the benefit of any holder, its legal representatives, successors and assigns.

11. No Breach. No breach of any provision of this Note shall be deemed waived unless it is waived in writing. Waiver of any one breach shall not be deemed a waiver of any other breach of the same or any other provision of this Note.

12. Amendments. This Note may only be amended or modified by written agreement duly executed by Maker and Payee or the holder of this Note.

13. No Default. If the due date of any payment under this Note falls on a Saturday, Sunday or public holiday, such payment may be made on the next business day without constituting a default in payment under this Note.

14. Dishonored Checks. In the event that any payment on this Note is made by a check that is dishonored by the drawee bank, for any reason whatsoever, there shall be added to the amount owing under this Note, the sum of Fifty Dollars ($50.00) to cover the banking charges and expenses related to such dishonored check.

"Maker"
XYZ, a [specify state] corporation

Dated: By: _____

           Its:

PERSONAL GUARANTY

FOR VALUE RECEIVED, the undersigned jointly and severally hereby forever waives presentment, demand, protest, notice of protest, and notice of dishonor of the aforesaid Note and personally guarantees payment of said each and every installment due thereunder together with interest, attorneys' fees and costs of collection and consents without further notice to any and all extensions of time, or terms of payment made by the Payee or Holder of said Note.

_____
GUARANTOR

Dated:

Witnessed and Sworn To Before Me this ____ day of [specify month], 199 .

_____
NOTARY PUBLIC

Separation Documents

CIRCUIT COURT OF THE STATE OF [specify]
COUNTY OF [specify]
- -x

XYZ - d/b/a [specify d/b/a]

       Plaintiff

   against

ABC, Inc.

       DEFENDANT.
- -x

STATE OF [specify]
) ss.,:
COUNTY OF [specify]

INDEX NO.

AFFIDAVIT FOR JUDGMENT BY CONFESSION

[specify name], being duly sworn, deposes and says:

1. I am the President of Defendant [specify company] whose corporate address is [specify address].

UNDERLYING FACTS

2. This Affidavit for Judgment by Confession ("Affidavit") is given for a debt due to Plaintiff ("XYZ"), arising out of the following facts: ABC and XYZ entered into an agreement dated ____, 19 entitled "Sales Representative Agreement" ("Rep Agreement"). ABC terminated the Rep Agreement on ____, 19_.

3. XYZ has made claims against ABC as to commissions allegedly owing to XYZ for orders placed prior to the termination.

4. In settlement of all claims, ABC delivered to counsel for XYZ, Law Offices of Steven Mitchell Sack, all three of the following: (1) an executed Settlement Agreement and Mutual Release; (2) this Affidavit; and (3) a $168,000.00 promissory note, an unsigned copy of which is attached as Exhibit" A" to this Affidavit ("Note").

Confession of Judgment

5. If and only if (a) ABC, Inc. fails to make a payment required by the Note and (b) ABC, INC. fails to make said payment pursuant to the ten-day Notice of Non-Payment provisions of Numbered Paragraph 2 of the Note ("Ten-Day Notice Provisions") and (c) XYZ files a declaration under penalty of perjury with the above-entitled court after first giving a three-day Notice of intention to do so that ABC, Inc. failed to make a payment required by the note and that ABC, Inc. thereafter failed to make such payment pursuant to the Ten-Day Notice Provisions, then ABC, Inc. authorizes XYZ to file this Affidavit and have judgment entered against ABC, INC. in the total amount of $168,000.00 (less any payments on the Note already received by XYZ) ("the Judgment"), in the form of the Judgment attached as Exhibit "B". Such

judgment may be entered in the Circuit Court of [specify] County or such other court or jurisdiction that may be necessary or convenient to the plaintiff.

6. XYZ's total recovery for its claims for all services previously provided to ABC, INC. shall consist of (1) the Judgment, (2) interest on the Judgment at the rate of Sixteen Percent (16%) per annum or the maximum legal rate, whichever is greater, and (3) reasonable attorneys fees incurred in filing, enforcing and collecting the Judgment.

7. In the event ABC, Inc. is unable to pay any portion of the judgment, I, [specify name], personally guarantee to pay and satisfy any default therein and authorize this Court to enter the Judgment against myself personally, jointly and severally pursuant to the Personal Guaranty which I have signed and which is annexed to and made a part of the Note.

8. This Affidavit for Judgment by Confession is not for the purpose of securing ABC, Inc. against a contingent liability and is not an installment loan.

9. I, [specify name], am an authorized agent of ABC, Inc. and I am duly authorized to bind ABC, Inc., and to enter into this Affidavit on behalf of ABC, Inc.

By:

President

Sworn to before me this

day of February, 199

NOTARY PUBLIC

CIRCUIT COURT OF THE STATE OF [specify]
COUNTY OF [specify]
----------------------x
XYZ - d/b/a [specify d/b/a]

      Plaintiff

against

ABC, Inc.

      DEFENDANT.
----------------------x

INDEX NO.

JUDGMENT PURSUANT TO AFFIDAVIT FOR JUDGMENT BY CONFESSION

Pursuant to the Affidavit for Judgment by Confession ("Affidavit") executed by ABC, Inc. that has been filed with this Court, and the concurrently filed declaration under penalty of perjury of XYZ that states that ABC failed to make a payment required by the Note that is referenced in the Affidavit and that ABC, Inc. thereafter failed to make said payment pursuant to the Ten-day Notice of Non-Payment provisions of Numbered Paragraph 2 of the Note after first receiving a three-day Notice of intention to do so, judgment is entered in favor of XYZ and against ABC, Inc. in the amount of $168,000.00 less any payments already received by XYZ from ABC, Inc. on the Note ("the Judgment"). The Judgment shall include additional amounts for interest, costs and reasonable attorneys' fees. XYZ shall also be awarded interest on the amount of the Judgment, after Judgment is entered and until the Judgment is paid in full, at the rate of Sixteen Percent (16%) per annum or the maximum legal rate, whichever is greater. Furthermore, XYZ shall be entitled to reasonable attorneys fees and costs incurred in filing, enforcing and collecting the Judgment.

      Principal amount   _____
      ($168,000.00 less
      any payments already
      received by XYZ from
      ABC on the Note)

      Pre-judgment Interest   _____

      Interest   _____

      Pre-judgment
      Attorneys Fees   _____

Attorneys Fees   _____

Costs   _____

TOTAL JUDGMENT   _____

Judge of the Circuit Court of the
State of [specify], County of [specify]

SALES REP PROTECTION STATUTES

State	Time Limit	Non-Compliance Penalty	Written Contract	Legal Reference
Alabama	Within 7 working days after termination if no written agreement	Triple damages plus reasonable attorney fees and costs	Required	Code of Alabama 1975, Vol. 6, §§8-24-1 through 8-24-5
Arizona	Within 30 days after termination of contract	Damages sustained by the sales representative plus cost of suit including reasonable attorney fees	Required	§1. Title 44, Chap. 11, Arizona Rev. Statutes, Art. 15, §§ 44-1798 through 44-1798.03
Arkansas	Within 30 working days after termination of contract	Liable in civil action for three times damages sustained by sales rep plus attorney fees and costs	Required	Arkansas Code, §§ 4-70-301 through 4-70-306
California	Within 72 hours after termination if no written agreement	Liable in civil action for triple damages	No	California Statutes 1937, c.90 p.197,§202;1963, c. 1088, p.2549, §§ 1,2
Florida	Within 14 days of termination	Commission amount plus exemplary damages up to twice commissions owed, plus reasonable attorney fees	Required	Official Florida Statues, §686.201
Georgia	Within 14 days after terminaton if no contract	Commission amount plus exemplary damages up to twice commissions owed, plus reasonable attorney fees	Required	Official Code of Georgia Annotated, Article 24, §§10-1-700 through 10-1-704
Iowa	Within 30 days after commission earned; upon termination, within 30 days	Commission plus liquidated damages (5% of commission due times number of days past due), including court costs and attorney fees	No	Code of Iowa, Vol. 1, 1989, Chap. 91A, §§91A.1 through 91A.13
Kansas	Within 30 days after commission earned	The commission amount	No	Kansas Statutes Annotated, 1987 cumulative Supplement, chap. 44, Art. 3, §§44-341 through 44-347

Kentucky	Within 30 working days after effective date of termination	Commission plus exemplary damages not to exceed two times commission due plus attorney fees and court costs; if a sales rep action found frivolous, principal will be awarded attorney fees and court costs	No	Kentucky Rev. Statutes, chap. 371, §§371.370-371.375 and 371.380-371.385
Louisiana	Within 30 working days after termination if no contract; otherwise as in written agreement	Triple damages plus attorney fees and costs	No	Louisiana Rev. Statutes (West 1988), Title 51, R.S. 51:441 through 445
Illinois	Within 13 days of termination or when commission earned	Up to three times commission amount plus reasonable attorney fees and court costs	No	Illinois Rev. Statutes, chap. 48, para. 2251, 2252, 2253
Indiana	Within 14 days after payment would have been due under contract	Exemplary damages up to three times commission, plus reasonable attorney fees and costs	No	Indiana Code, 1988 Ed., §§24-4-7-1 through 24-4-7-6
Maryland	Within 45 days after payment would have been due if contract not terminated	Exemplary damages not to exceed three times commission plus court costs, provided principal furnished written notice 10 days prior of intent to file civil action for exemplary damages	No	Annotated Code Maryland, Art. 100, §§127 through 131
Massachusetts	Within 7 days after termination	The commission amount	Required	Massachusetts Gen. Laws Annotated (West, 1988), Chap. 104, §§7 through 9
Minnesota	Within 3 working days of salesperson's last day of work	Commission plus 1/15th of commission for every day of nonpayment	No	Minnesota Statutes 1988, Chap. 181.13m 181.14, 181.145
Mississippi	Within 21 days after effective date of termination	Up to triple commission due plus reasonable attorney fees and costs	No	1988 Mississippi Gen. Laws, Chap. 588, §§75-87-1, 75-87-3, 75-87-5, and Notes
New Hampshire	Within 45 days after date of termination of contract	In civil action, damages, exemplary damages, plus reasonable attorney fees and costs	Required	Amendments to RSA 339-E:1 through 339-E:4 to SB 16, New Hampshire

Separation Documents

New Jersey	Within 30 days after payment would have been due under contract if contract had not been terminated	Commissions plus exemplary damages not to exceed two times the amount of the commissions due plus reasonable attorney fees and court costs	Required	New Jersey Act concerning sales representatives supplementing Title 56 of the Rev. Statutes
New York	Within 5 business days after termination, or when commission earned	Two times commission, plus reasonable attorney fees, court costs, and disbursements	Required	Labor Law Book No. 30, chap. 451, §§191-a, 191-b, 191-c
North Carolina	Within 45 days after effective date of contract termination	In civil action, amounts due plus exemplary damages not to exceed amount of commissions, plus reasonable attorney fees and court costs	Required	§1. chapter 66, Art. 27, §§66-190 through 66-193 Illinois Rev. Statutes, chap. 48, para. 2251, 2252, 2253
Ohio	All commissions must be paid within 13 days of when due, or as specified by contract	Liable in civil action for triple damages plus reasonable attorney fees and costs	No, but strongly recommended	Ohio Rev. Code 1988, § 1355.1
Oklahoma	If contract, within 14 calendar days; without contract, according to past practice or industry custom and usage	Commissions plus reasonable attorney fees and court costs	No	Oklahoma Statutes, Title 15 §§675 through 680
Pennsylvania	Within 14 days after payment due if contract not terminated	In civil action, commissions plus exemplary damages not to exceed two times commission plus reasonable attorney fees and court costs	Required	Pennsylvania Laws of 1988, Act 184
South Carolina	As required by contract or upon termination if there is no contract	In civil action, all amounts due plus punitive damages not to exceed three times commissions plus attorney fees and court costs	Required	Cumulative Suppl. of Code of Laws of South Carolina, Vol 13A, Chap. 65, pp. 59, 60, §§39-65-1-, through 39-65-80
Tennessee	Within 14 days of salesperson's termination	Up to three times commission, plus reasonable attorney fees and court costs	No	Tennessee Code Annotated, §47-50-114Labor Law Book No. 30, chap. 451, §§191-a, 191-b, 191-c

| Texas | Within 30 working days after termination date, or as specified in contract | In civil action, triple damages plus reasonable attorney fees and costs | Required | Texas Business & Commerce Code Annotated (Vernon, 1987), §§35.81 through 35.86 |

SECTION FOUR:
Business Formation

SAMPLE PARTNERSHIP AGREEMENT

THIS PARTNERSHIP AGREEMENT is made this ___ day of _____ 199_, by and between John Doe ("Doe") and Mark Smith ("Smith").

Explanatory Statement

The parties hereto desire to enter into the business of purchasing, acquiring, operating, leasing, owning and selling [specify], including but not limited to that certain parcel of land, and all improvements constructed thereon, described as [specify address] and engaging in any other lawful phase or aspect of [specify]. In order to accomplish their aforesaid desires, the parties hereto desire to join together in a general partnership under and pursuant to the Uniform Partnership Act, amended from time to time (the "Act").

NOW THEREFORE, in consideration of their mutual promises, covenants, and agreements, and the Explanatory Statement, which Explanatory Statement is incorporated by reference herein and made a substantive part of this Partnership Agreement, the parties hereto do hereby promise, covenant and agree as follows:

Definitions

Throughout this Partnership Agreement, and unless the context otherwise requires, the word or words set forth below within the quotation marks shall be deemed to mean the words which follow them:

A. **"Agreement"**—This Partnership Agreement.

B. **"Bankruptcy"**—The filing by a Partner of a petition commencing a voluntary case under the Bankruptcy Code; a general assignment by a Party for the benefit of creditors; an admission in writing by a Partner of his inability to pay his debts as they become due; the filing by a Partner of any petition or answer in any proceeding seeking for himself or consenting to, or acquiescing in, any insolvency, receivership, composition, readjustment, liquidation, dissolution, or similar relief under any present or future statute, law or regulation, or the filing by a Partner of an answer or other pleading admitting or failing to deny, or to contest, the material allegations of the petition filed against him in any such proceeding; the seeking or consenting to, or acquiescence by a Partner in, the appointment of any trustee, receiver, or liquidator of him, or any part of his property; and the commencement against a Partner of an involuntary case under the Bankruptcy Code, or a proceeding under any receivership, composition, readjustment, liquidation, insolvency, dissolution or like law or statute, which case or proceeding is not dismissed or vacated within 60 days.

C. **"Partner"**—Each of the persons signatory hereto and any other person or persons who may subsequently be designated as a general partner of this partnership pursuant to the further terms of this Agreement.

D. "Partnership"—This general partnership.

E. "Partnership Interest"—The share of profits and surplus of a Partner.

F. "Partnership Rights"—The property rights of a Partner, which are comprised of a Partner's: (1) right in specific partnership property, (2) interest in the Partnership and (3) right to participate in the management thereof.

G. "Persons"—Individuals, partnership, corporations, unincorporated associations, trusts, estates and any other type of entity.

H. "Retirement"—The decision or determination of a Partner to no longer continue as a Partner, upon written notice to all of the other Partners.

Section 1. Name

The name of the Partnership shall be [specify name].

Section 2. Principal Place of Business

The principal office and place of business of the Partnership (the "Office") shall be located at [specify address]. The Partnership shall have such other or additional offices as the Partners may, from time to time, determine in accordance with Section 8 of this Agreement.

Section 3. Business and Purpose

3.1. The business and purposes of the Partnership are to acquire, hold, manage, operate, develop, sell and lease real property (the "Property"), or interest therein, including but not limited to that certain parcel of land, and all improvements constructed thereon, described on Exhibit A hereto and incorporated herein by reference, and to engage in any other phase or aspect of the real estate business, and such other businesses and purposes as the Partners may from time to time determine in accordance with Section 8 of this Agreement.

3.2. The Partnership may also do and engage in any and all other things and activities and have all powers incident to the said acquisition, holding, management, operation, development, sale and leasing of the Property, or any part or parts thereof, including, by way of illustration and not by way of limitation, arranging for and delivering contracts of sale, deeds, leases, deeds of trust, ground leases, mortgages, notes and other evidence of indebtedness, security agreements, and other security instruments; entering into agreements for the construction, design and management of improvements; and doing all things reasonably incident to the development, management, leasing and sale of the Property.

Section 4. Term

The Partnership shall commence upon the date of this Agreement, as set forth above. Unless sooner terminated pursuant to the further provisions of this

Agreement, the Partnership shall continue until the close of business on [specify], or until renewed.

Section 5. Capital Contribution

5.1. The original capital contributions to the Partnership of each of the Partners shall be made concurrently with their respective execution, acknowledgement, sealing and delivery of this Agreement in the following dollar amounts set forth after their respective names:

        Doe $20,000.00
        Smith $20,000.00

5.2. An individual capital account shall be maintained for each Partner. The capital account of each Partner shall consist of his or her original capital contribution, increased by (a) additional capital contributions made by him or her, (b) his or her share of Partnership profits, and decreased by (i) distributions of such profits and capital to him or her, and (ii) his or her share of Partnership losses.

5.3. Except as specifically provided in this Agreement, or as otherwise provided by and in accordance with law to the extent such law is not inconsistent with this Agreement, no Partner shall have the right to withdraw or reduce his or her contributions to the capital of the Partnership.

Section 6. Profit and Loss

6.1 The percentages of Partnership Rights and Partnership Interest of each of the Partners shall be as follows:

        Doe   50 %
        Smith   50 %

6.2. Except as provided in Section 7.3. of this Agreement, for purposes of Sections 702 and 704 of the Internal Revenue Code of 1954, or the corresponding provisions of any future federal internal revenue law, or any similar tax law of any state or jurisdiction, the determination of each Partner's distributive share of all items of income, gain, loss, deduction, credit or allowance of the Partnership for any period or year shall be made in accordance with, and in proportion to, such Partner's percentage of Partnership Interest as it may then exist.

Section 7. Distribution of Profits

7.1. The net cash from operations of the Partnership shall be distributed at such times as may be determined by the Partners in accordance with Section 8 of this Agreement among the Partners in proportion to their respective percentages of Partnership Interest, provided, however, that no amount of net cash from operations shall be distributed during any fiscal year of the Partnership until after the Partnership has paid any required installment of the aggregate Purchase Price or Special Aggregate Purchase Price, as the case may be, provided in Section 19 hereof.

7.2. As used in this Section 7, the term "net cash from operations" shall mean:

7.2.1. The taxable income of the Partnership for federal income tax purposes as shown on the books of the Partnership, increased by (a) the amount of depreciation and amortization deductions taken in computing such taxable income and (b) any non-taxable income or receipts of the Partnership, and reduced by (i) payments upon the principal of any installment obligations, mortgages or deeds of trust respecting Partnership assets or of other Partnership debts, and (ii) such expenditures for capital improvements or replacements, such reserves for said improvements and replacements and such reserves for repairs and to meet anticipated expenses and for working capital as the Partners, in accordance with Section 8 of this Agreement, shall deem to be reasonably necessary in the efficient conduct of the business; plus

7.2.2. Any excess funds resulting from the placement, or excess of refinancing of, any mortgages or deeds of trust on Partnership Property or the encumbrancing or financing of such Property in any other manner; plus

7.2.3. Any other funds (including amounts previously set aside for reserves by the Partners, in accordance with Section 8 of this Agreement, to the extent the Partner, in accordance with Section 8 of this Agreement, no longer regards such reserves as reasonably necessary in the efficient conduct of the Partnership business) deemed available for the distribution by the Partners, in accordance with Section 8 of this Agreement.

7.2.4. In determining the amount of net cash from operations any negative balances in any category described in Section 7.2.1., 7.2.2. and 7.2.3. shall be netted against the positive balances in the other such categories. Cumulative negative or positive balances shall be carried forward.

7.3. In addition to the distributions pursuant to Section 7.1. of this Agreement, upon any sale, transfer or other disposition of any capital asset of the Partnership (hereinafter referred to as a "Disposition"), the proceeds of such Disposition shall first be applied to the payment or repayment of any selling or other expenses incurred in connection with the Disposition and to the payment of any indebtedness secured by the asset subject to the Disposition immediately prior thereto; all proceeds remaining thereafter (the "Net Proceeds") shall be retained by the Partnership or be distributed, at such time or times as shall be determined by the Partners in accordance with Section 8 of this Agreement to the Partners in proportion to their respective percentages of Partnership Interest; provided, however, that for purposes of Sections 702 and 704 of the Internal Revenue Code of 1954, or the corresponding provisions of any future federal internal revenue law, or any similar tax law of any state or jurisdiction, each Partner's distributive share of all items of income, gain, loss, deduction, credit or allowance in respect of any such Disposition shall be made and based upon such Partner's basis in such capital asset.

Section 8. Management of the Partnership Business

8.1. All decisions respecting the management, operation and control of the Partnership business and determination made in accordance with the provisions of this Agreement shall be made only by the unanimous vote or consent of all of the Partners.

8.2. Nothing herein contained shall be construed to constitute any Partner or the agent of another Partner, except as expressly provided herein, or in any manner to limit the Partnership to the carrying on of their own respective businesses or activities. Any of the Partners, or any agent, servant or employee of any of the Partners, may engage in and possess any interest in other businesses or ventures of every nature and description, independently or with other persons, whether or not, directly or indirectly, in competition with the business or purpose of the Partnership, and neither the Partnership nor any of the Partners shall have any rights, by virtue of this Agreement or otherwise, in and to such independent ventures or the income or profits derived therefrom, or any rights, duties or obligations in respect thereof.

8.3. The Partners shall devote to the conduct of the Partnership business so much of their respective time as may be reasonably necessary for the efficient operation of the Partnership business.

Section 9. Salaries

Unless otherwise agreed by the Partners in accordance with Section 8 of this Agreement, no Partner shall receive any salary for services rendered to or for the Partnership.

Section 10. Legal Title to Partnership Property

Legal title to the property of the Partnership shall be held in the name of or in such other name or manner as the Partners shall determine to be in the best interest of the Partnership. Without limiting the foregoing grant of authority, the Partners may arrange to have title taken and held in their own names or in the names of trustees, nominees or straw parties for the Partnership. It is expressly understood and agreed that the manner of holding title to property (or any part thereof) of the Partnership is solely for the convenience of the Partnership, and that all such property shall be treated as Partnership property subject to the terms of this Agreement.

Section 11. Banking

All revenue of the Partnership shall be deposited regularly in the Partnership savings and checking accounts at such bank or banks as shall be selected by the Partners in accordance with Section 8 of this Agreement, and the signatures of such Partners as shall be determined in accordance with Section 8 of this Agreement shall be honored for banking purposes, other than the extension of credit to, or the borrowing of money by or on behalf of, the Partnership.

Section 12. Fiscal Year, Audits

Accurate and complete books of account shall be kept by the Partners and entries promptly made therein of all of the transactions of the Partnership, and such books of account shall be open at all times to the inspection and examination of the Partners. The books shall be kept on the basis of accounting selected by the accountant regularly servicing the Partnership and the fiscal year of the Partnership shall be the calendar year. A compilation, review or audit of the Partnership, as shall be determined by the Partners in accordance with Section 8 of this Agreement, shall be made as of the closing of each fiscal year of the Partnership by the accountants who shall then be engaged by the Partnership.

Section 13. Transfer of Partnership Interest and Partnership Rights

Except as otherwise provided in Sections 14, 15 and 16 hereof, no Partner (hereinafter referred to as the "Offering Partner") shall, during the term of the Partnership, sell, hypothecate, pledge, assign or otherwise transfer with or without consideration (hereinafter collectively referred to as a "Transfer") any part or all of his Partnership Interest or Partnership Rights in the Partnership to any other person (a "Transferee"), without first offering (hereinafter referred to as the "Offer") that portion of his Partnership Interest and Partnership Rights in the Partnership subject to the contemplated transfer (hereinafter referred to as the "Offered Interest") first to the Partnership, and secondly, to the other Partners, at a purchase price (hereinafter referred to as the "Transfer Purchase Price") and in a manner as follows:

13.1. The Transfer Purchase Price shall be the Appraised Value (as defined in Section 18.1.)

13.1.1. The Offer shall be made by the Offering Partner first to the Partnership by written notice (hereinafter referred to as the "Offering Notice). Within twenty (20) days (hereinafter referred to as the "Partnership Notice"), whether or not the Partnership shall accept the Offer and shall purchase all but not less than all of the Offered Interest. If the Partnership accepts the Offer to purchase the Offered Interest, the Partnership Notice shall fix a closing date not more than twenty-five (25) days (hereinafter referred to as the "Partnership Closing Date") after the expiration of the Partnership Offer Period.

13.1.2. In the event the Partnership decides not to accept the Offer, the Offering Partner or the Partnership, at his or its election, shall, by written notice (hereinafter referred to as the "Remaining Partner Notice") given within that period (hereinafter referred to as the "Partner Offer Period") terminating ten (10) days after the expiration of the Partnership Offer Period, make the Offer of the Offered Interest to the other Partners, each of whom shall then have a period of twenty-five (25) days (the "Partner Acceptance Period") after the expiration of the Partner Offer Period within which to notify in writing the Offering Partner whether or not he intends to purchase all but not less than all of the Offered Interest. If two (2) or more Partners of the Partnership desire to accept the Offer to purchase the Offered Interest, then, in the absence of an agreement between them, such Partners shall have the right to purchase the Offered Interest in the proportion which their respective percentage of Partnership Interest in the Partnership bears to the percentage of Partnership Interest of all of the Partners who desire to accept the Offer. If the other Partners intend to accept the Offer and purchase the Offered Interest, the written notice required to be given by them shall fix a closing date not more than ten (10) days after the expiration of the Partner Acceptance Period (hereinafter referred to as the "Partner Closing Date").

13.2. The aggregate dollar amount of the Transfer Purchase Price shall be payable in cash on the Partnership closing date or on the Partner Closing date, as the case may be, unless the Partnership or the purchasing Partners shall elect prior to or on the Partnership Closing Date or the Partner Closing Date, as the case may be, to purchase such Offered Interest in installments pursuant to the provisions of Section 19 hereof.

13.3. If the Partnership or the other Partners fail to accept the Offer or, if the Offer is accepted by the Partnership or the other Partners and the Partnership or the other Partners fail to purchase all of the Offered Interest at the Transfer Purchase Price within the time and in the manner specified in this Section 13, then the Offering Partner shall be free, for a period (hereinafter referred to as the "Free Transfer Period") of sixty (60) days from the occurrence of such failure, to transfer the Offered Interest to a Transferee; subject only to any additional restrictions on such Transfer that may be imposed by this Agreement or any other agreement. Any such Transferee, upon acquiring the Offered Interest, shall automatically be bound by the terms of this Agreement and shall be required to join in, execute, acknowledge, seal and deliver a copy of this Agreement as a result of which he shall become an additional party hereto. If the Offering Partner shall not transfer the Offered Interest within the Free Transfer Period, his right to transfer the Offered Interest free of the foregoing restrictions shall thereupon cease and terminate.

13.4. No transfer made pursuant to this Section 13 shall dissolve or terminate the Partnership or cause the Partnership to be wound-up, but instead, the business of the Partnership shall be continued as if such Transfer had not occurred.

Section 14. Buy Sell Agreement

The parties agree to enter into a buy/sell agreement to effect purchase of the deceased partner's share upon such partner's death, to be funded by life insurance policies.

Section 15. Purchase Upon Bankruptcy or Retirement.

15.1. Upon the Bankruptcy or Retirement from the Partnership of any Partner (the "Withdrawing Partner"), the Partnership shall neither be terminated nor wound-up, but, instead, the business of the Partnership shall be continued as if such Bankruptcy or Retirement, as the case may be, had not occurred, and the Partnership shall purchase and the Withdrawing Partner shall sell all of the Partnership Interest and Partnership Rights (the "Withdrawing Partner's Interest") owned by the Withdrawing Partner in the Partnership on the date of such Bankruptcy or retirement (the "Withdrawal Date"). The Partnership shall, by written notice addressed to the

Withdrawing Partner or to the legal representative of a bankrupt Partner, fix a closing date for such purchase which shall be not less than seventy-five (75) days after the Withdrawal Date. The Withdrawing Partner's Interest shall be purchased by the Partnership on such closing date at a price (the "Withdrawing Purchase Price") which shall be the Appraised Value (as defined in Section 18.1 of this Agreement.)

15.2. The aggregate dollar amount of the Withdrawing Purchase Price shall be payable in cash on the closing date, unless the Partnership shall elect prior to or on the closing date to purchase the Withdrawing Partner's Interest in installments as provided in Section 19 of this Agreement.

Section 16. Certain Further Events Giving Rights to Purchase Option.

16.1. In the event that any Partner (the "Defaulting Partner"):

16.1.1. Shall have filed against him any tax lien respecting all or substantially all of his property and such tax lien shall not be discharged, removed or bonded within sixty (60) days of the date on which it was filed; or

16.1.2. Shall subject his Partnership Interest or Partnership Rights or any part thereof or interest therein to a charging order entered by any court of competent jurisdiction; then, immediately upon the occurrence of either of said events (the "Occurrence Date"), the Partnership shall have the right and option, exercisable by written notice to the Defaulting Partner, within thirty (30) days of the Occurrence Date, to purchase from the Defaulting Partner, who shall sell to the Partnership, all of the Partnership Interest and Partnership Rights (the "Defaulting Partner's Interest) owned by the Defaulting Partner in the Partnership on the Occurrence Date. The Partnership shall, by written notice delivered to the Defaulting Partner or his successors, fix a closing date for such purchase which shall be not less than forty (40) days after the Occurrence Date, but in no event longer than seventy-five (75) days after the Occurrence Date. The Defaulting Partner's Interest shall be purchased by the Partnership on such closing date at a price (the "Defaulting Partner's Purchase Price") which shall be the Appraised Value (as defined in Section 18.1 of this Agreement).

16.2. The aggregate dollar amount of the Defaulting Partner's Purchase Price shall be payable in cash on the closing date, unless the Partnership shall elect prior to or on the closing date to purchase the Defaulting Partner's Interest in installments as provided in Section 19 of this Agreement.

Section 17. Certain Tax Aspects Incident to Transactions Contemplated by this Agreement.

It is the intention of the parties that the Transfer Purchase Price, the Decedent Purchase Price, the Withdrawing Purchase Price and the Defaulting Partner's Purchase Price shall constitute and be considered as made in exchange for the interest of the retired Partner in partnership property, including good will, within the meaning of Section 736(b) of the Internal Revenue Code of 1954, as amended.

Section 18. The Appraised Value.

18.1. The term "Appraised Value" as used in this Agreement shall be the dollar amount equal to the product obtained by multiplying (a) the percentage of Partnership Interest and Partnership Rights owned by a Partner by (b) the Fair Market Value of the Partnership's assets, as determined in accordance with Section 18.2.

18.2. The Fair Market Value of the Partnership's assets shall be determined in the following manner:

18.2.1. Within thirty (30) days of the date of the Offering Notice, date of the death of a Decedent, the Withdrawal Date or the Occurrence Date, as the case may be, the remaining Partners shall select an appraiser (the "Partnership Appraiser") to determine the Fair Market Value of the Partnership's assets, and the Partnership Appraiser shall submit his determination thereof within thirty (30) days after the date of his selection (the "Appraisal Due Date").

18.2.2. If the appraisal made by Partnership Appraiser is unsatisfactory to the Offering Partner, the personal representatives of the Decedent or Heir, the Withdrawing Partner or the Defaulting Partner, as the case may be, then within fifteen (15) days after the date of the Appraisal Due Date, the Offering Partner, the personal representatives of the Decedent or Heir, the Withdrawing Partner or the Defaulting Partner, as the case may be, shall select an appraiser (the "Partner's Appraiser") to determine the Fair Market Value of the Partnership's assets, and such appraiser shall submit his determination thereof within thirty (30) days after the date of his selection.

18.2.3. If the appraisal made by the Partner's Appraiser is unsatisfactory to the remaining Partners, then the Partnership Appraiser and the Partner's Appraiser shall select a third appraiser (the "Appraiser") to determine the Fair Market Value of the Partnership's assets and such Appraiser shall submit his determination thereof within thirty (30) days after the date of his selection. The Appraiser's determination thereof shall be binding upon the Partnership, the remaining Partners and the Offering Partner, the personal representatives of the Decedent or Heir, the Withdrawing Partner or the Defaulting Partner, as the case may be.

18.3. Any and all appraisers selected in accordance with the provisions of this Section 18 shall be [specify city] area appraisers, who shall conduct appraisals provided for in this Section 18 in accordance with generally accepted appraising standards. Any and all costs incurred in connection with any of the appraisals provided for in this Section 18 shall be borne equally by the remaining Partners, and the Offering partner, the personal representatives of the Decedent or Heir, the Withdrawing or the Defaulting Partner, as the case may be.

Section 19. Installment Payments.

19.1. In the event that there shall be an election pursuant to the provisions of Sections 13.2, 14.2, 15.2 or 16.2 hereof to purchase (the Partner or the Partnership so purchasing shall be hereinafter, where appropriate, referred to as the "purchasing person", the Offering Partner's interest, the Decedent's Interest, the Withdrawing Partner's Interest or the Defaulting Partner's Interest, as the case may be (hereinafter where appropriate, referred to as the "Interest"), on an installment basis, then the terms and conditions of such installment purchase shall be as set forth in Section 19.1.1 and Section 19.1.2 in the case of an election pursuant to Section 13.2 or Section 14.2 and as set forth in Section 19.1.2 and Section 19.1.3 in the case of an election pursuant to Section 15.2 or Section 16.2 hereof.

    19.1.1. Twenty-nine percent (29%) of the aggregate purchase price due for such Interest (hereinafter, where appropriate, referred to as the "Aggregate Purchase Price') shall be paid on the closing date; and

    19.1.2. The remainder of the Aggregate Purchase Price shall be paid in three (3) equal consecutive annual installments on each anniversary of the closing date over a period, beginning with the year following the calendar year in which the sale occurred (hereinafter referred to as the "Installment Payment Period").

    19.1.3. Twenty-nine percent (29%) of the aggregate purchase price due for such Interest (hereinafter, where appropriate, referred to as the "Special Aggregate Purchase Price") shall be paid on the closing date; and

    19.1.4. The remainder of the Special Aggregate Purchase Price shall be paid in three (3) equal consecutive annual installments on each anniversary of the closing date over a period, beginning with the year following the calendar year in which the date occurred (hereinafter referred to as the "Special Installment Payment Period").

    19.1.5. Anything contained in this Section 19 to the contrary notwithstanding, the entire unpaid balance of the Aggregate Purchase Price and Special Aggregate Purchase Price shall become immediately due and payable upon the sale, exchange, transfer or other disposition of all or substantially all of the Property or assets of the Partnership.

    19.1.6. The purchasing person shall pay simple interest at a rate shall be equal to the prime rate of interest then being charged by CitiBank, N.A., New York City, New York, to its highest credit-rated corporate borrowers on short term unsecured commercial borrowings on the unpaid balance of the Aggregate Purchase Price of Special Aggregate Purchase Price on each anniversary of the closing date during the Installment Payment Period or Special Installment Payment Period, as the case may be.

    19.2. So long as any part of the Aggregate Purchase Price or Special Aggregate Purchase Price remains unpaid, the Partners shall permit the Offering Partner, the personal representatives of the Decedent or the Heir, the Withdrawing Partner (or the legal representative of the Withdrawing Partner in the event of the bankruptcy of the Withdrawing Partner) or the Defaulting Partner, as the case may be, and the attorneys and accountants of each of the foregoing persons, to examine the books and records of the Partnership and its business following the event that shall have given rise to the election referred to in Section 19.1 hereof during regular business hours from time to time upon reasonable prior notice and to receive copies of the annual accounting reports and tax returns of the Partnership.

Section 20. Delivery of Evidence of Interest

On the closing date, upon payment of the Aggregate Purchase Price for the purchase of the Interest hereunder or, if payment is to be made in installments pursuant to the provisions of Section 19 hereof, upon the first payment, the Offering Partner, the Withdrawing Partner, the personal representative of the Withdrawing Partner (in the event of the bankruptcy of the Withdrawing Partner) or the Defaulting Partner, as the case may be, shall execute, acknowledge, seal and deliver to the purchasing person such instrument or instruments of transfer to evidence the purchase of the Interest (the "Instrument of Transfer") that shall be reasonably requested by counsel to the purchasing person in form and substance; reasonably satisfactory to such counsel. If a tender of the Aggregate Purchase Price or Special Aggregate Purchase Price or, if payment is to be made in installments pursuant to the provisions of Section 19.1 hereof, the tender of the first payment thereof, shall be refused, or if the Instrument of Transfer shall not be delivered contemporaneously with the tender of the Aggregate Purchase Price or Special Aggregate Purchase Price or of the first payment thereof, as aforesaid, then the purchasing person shall be appointed, and the same is hereby irrevocably constituted and appointed the attorney-in-fact with full power and authority to execute, acknowledge, seal and deliver the Instrument of Transfer.

Section 21. Family Members.

For purposes of this Agreement, members of the "immediate family" of a Partner are hereby defined to be such person's spouse or children.

Section 22. Notices.

Any and all notices, offers, acceptances, requests, certifications and consents provided for in this Agreement shall be in writing and shall be given and be deemed to have been given when personally delivered against a signed receipt or mailed by registered or certified mail, return receipt requested, to the last address which the addressee has given to the Partnership. The address of each partner is set under his signature at the end of this Agreement, and each partner agrees to notify the Partnership of any change of address. The address of the Partnership shall be its principal office.

Section 23. Governing Law.

It is the intent of the parties hereto that all questions with respect to the construction of this Agreement and the rights, duties, obligations and liabilities of the parties shall be determined in accordance with the applicable provisions of the laws of the State of [specify].

Section 24. Miscellaneous Provisions.

24.1. This Agreement shall be binding upon, and inure to the benefit of, all parties hereto, their personal and legal representatives, guardians, successors, and their assigns to the extent, but only to the extent, that assignment is provided for in accordance with, and permitted by, the provisions of this Agreement.

24.2. Nothing herein contained shall be construed to limit in any manner the Partners, or their respective agents, servants, and employees, in carrying on their own respective businesses or activities.

24.3. The Partners agree that they and each of them will take whatever action or actions as are deemed by counsel to the Partnership to be reasonably necessary or desirable from time to time to effectuate the provisions of intent of this Agreement, and to that end, the Partners agree that they will execute, acknowledge, seal and deliver any further instruments or documents which may be necessary to give force and effect to this Agreement or any of the provisions hereof, or to carry out the intent of this Agreement, or any of the provisions hereof.

24.4. Throughout this Agreement, where such meanings would be appropriate: (a) the masculine gender shall be deemed to include the feminine and the neuter and vice-versa, and (b) the singular shall be deemed to include the plural, and vice-versa. The headings herein are inserted only as a matter of convenience and reference, and in no way define, limit or describe the scope of this Agreement, or the intent of any provisions thereof.

24.5. This Agreement and exhibits attached hereto set forth all (and are intended by all parties hereto to be an integration of all) of the promises, agreements, conditions, understandings, warranties and representations, oral or written, express or implied, among them other than as set forth herein.

24.6. Nothing contained in this Agreement shall be construed as requiring the commission of any act contrary to law. In the event there is any conflict between any provision of this Agreement and any statute, law, ordinance or regulation contrary to which the Partners have no legal right to contract, the later shall prevail, but in such event the provisions of this Agreement thus affected shall be curtailed and limited only to the extent necessary to conform with said requirement of law. In the event that any part, article, section, paragraph or clause of this Agreement shall be held to be indefinite, invalid or otherwise unenforceable, the entire Agreement shall not fail on account thereof, and the balance of this Agreement shall continue in full force and effect.

24.7. Each married party to this Agreement agrees to obtain the consent and approval of his or her spouse, to all the terms and provisions of this Agreement; provided, however, that such execution shall be for the sole purpose of acknowledging such spousal consent and approval, as aforesaid, and nothing contained in this Section 24.7 shall be deemed to have constituted any such spouse a Partner in the Partnership.

24.8. Each partner agrees to insert in his Will or to execute a Codicil thereto directing and authorizing his personal representatives to fulfill and comply with the provisions hereof and to sell and transfer his percentage of Partnership Interest and Partnership Rights in accordance herewith.

24.9. The Partnership shall have the right to make application for, take out and maintain in effect such policies of life insurance on the lives of any or all of the Partners, whenever and in such amounts as the Partners shall determine in accordance with Section 8 of this Agreement.

Each Partner shall exert his best efforts and fully assist and cooperate with the Partnership in obtaining any such policies of life insurance.

    IN WITNESS WHEREOF, the parties hereunto set their hands and seals and acknowledged this Agreement as of the date first above written.

WITNESS:_____   Percentage of Partnership
                                                                               Interest and Partnership
Rights
NAME OF PARTNER:_____

DATE:_____

WITNESS:_____   Percentage of Partnership
                                                                               Interest and Partnership
Rights
NAME OF PARTNER:_____

DATE:_____

SAMPLE SHAREHOLDER AGREEMENT

AGREEMENT made and entered into as of the ____ day of ____, 199 , by and among John Doe, residing at [specify address] (hereinafter "Doe"), and Mark Smith, residing at [specify address] (hereinafter "Smith"), and XYZ, Inc. ("the Corporation").

W I T N E S S E T H:

WHEREAS, all of the issued shares and outstanding stock of the Corporation are owned in the following percentages:

      Doe   50%
      Smith   50%

WHEREAS, the Shareholders hereto deem it to be in the best interest of the Corporation to act together concerning the management of the Corporation as well as to make provision for the contingency of the death or disability of any Shareholder and to set forth the manner and method by which a Shareholder may sell his stock during his lifetime.

NOW, THEREFORE, IT IS MUTUALLY AGREED AS FOLLOWS;

FIRST: <u>MANAGEMENT AND OPERATION OF THE CORPORATION</u>

A. 1. <u>Directors and Officers</u>. For the duration and term of this Agreement, the Shareholders will elect and continue in office as Directors of the Corporation the following:

      Smith
      Doe

The Officers of the Corporation shall be:

      Smith - President; Treasurer
      Doe - Vice President; Secretary

B. <u>Voting</u>. All decisions within the ordinary course of business shall be made by the unanimous consent of both the President and the Vice President, who shall have equal say in the management of the ordinary course of business of the Corporation. In addition, for the purposes of selling, terminating, liquidating, entering loans or changing the basic purposes of the Corporation, the quorum and voting requirements shall be 100 percent of all shareholders and/or directors. Simultaneously herewith the Certificate of Incorporation is being amended to provide for the terms of this section.

C. <u>Checks.</u> All cash, checks and instruments for the payment of monies are to be deposited in the Corporation's bank account. All checks drawn upon such account are to be signed jointly by the President and Vice President and/or their nominees.

D. <u>Salaries.</u> The President and Vice President agree to draw equal salaries, as voted upon by the Board of Directors of the Corporation.

E. <u>Employment.</u> The President and Vice President agree to work full-time and exclusively for the Corporation. Neither party shall be permitted to own an interest in, operate, join, control, participate in directly or indirectly, or be connected as an officer, employee, agent, independent contractor, partner, stockholder or principal of or in any corporation, partnership, firm, association, person or other entity soliciting orders for, selling, distributing or otherwise marketing products, goods, equipment and/or services which directly or indirectly compete with the business of the Corporation, without the express written consent of the other, which consent shall not be unreasonably withheld.

Both parties shall provide such services to the operation of the Corporation and Corporate business as shall be deemed proper and necessary, including keeping each other informed of all letters, accounts, writings and other information which shall come to their attention concerning the business of the Corporation.

Both parties shall keep or cause to be kept full records of each transaction of the Corporation and shall maintain such records at the principal office of the Corporation at [specify address], or at the principal office of the Corporation's accountant. Said records shall be open for inspection and examination by each of them, or their duly authorized representative, at all reasonable times.

Notwithstanding the foregoing, each of the Executive officers above named agree to be employed by the Corporation and the Corporation agrees to employ them under the following terms and conditions:

1. The employment of each such Officer shall continue so long as he is a Shareholder of the Corporation.

2. Each Executive Officer devotes all of his working time, energy and attention solely and exclusively to the business of the Corporation, and none of his working time to any other firm or business without the written consent of the other.

3. In the event any Executive Officer terminates his employment with the Corporation or it is determined by arbitration as hereinafter provided that such Officer has breached the terms of his employment hereunder, by committing acts constituting just cause to terminate such employment as determined by the arbitrators, or by failing to render exclusive time and attention to the business of the Corporation, or by participating, either directly or indirectly, in another business competitive with the business of the Corporation, then either of any such occurrences shall be deemed an offer to sell all of the shares that such Officer owns in the Corporation at the price, terms and conditions set forth in this Agreement.

F. <u>Disability</u>. In the event either Shareholder is unable to perform the normal duties of his employment due to physical or mental disability, then the following shall apply:

1. During the first three hundred sixty five (365) consecutive days of such disability the Corporation shall pay to the disabled Shareholder such weekly salary and compensation as was then being paid to the disabled Shareholder prior to the onset of disability.

2. After three hundred sixty five (365) consecutive days of disability, no further compensation or salary shall be paid to the disabled Shareholder.

3. After three hundred sixty five (365) days of such disability, the Corporation and the remaining shareholder shall, at any time thereafter and prior to the resumption of the normal duties of employment have the right to purchase all shares of stock of the disabled Shareholder as if the disabled Shareholder offered to sell all of his shares in the Corporation at the same price, terms and conditions set forth in the Article of this Agreement entitled Lifetime Sale of Shares.

4. There shall be deducted from any salary paid to a disabled Shareholder all payments received by the disabled Shareholder from any private or public disability insurance, the premiums of which were paid for by the Corporation.

G. <u>Indemnity</u>. In the event any Shareholder is held personally liable for any liability of the Corporation, then the other Shareholder shall indemnify him against fifty percent (50%) of any such personal liability.

H. <u>Death Of A Shareholder</u>. In the event of the death of a Shareholder, the legal representative of his Estate shall be required to sell all of decedent's shares of stock of the Corporation and he shall be deemed to have offered all of said shares to the Corporation and surviving Shareholder.

1. <u>Acceptance.</u> The Corporation shall be deemed to have accepted the offer to purchase as many shares as it may legally purchase. In the event the Corporation is unable to legally purchase all of such shares, the surviving Shareholder shall purchase those shares which the Corporation cannot legally purchase.

2. <u>Closing</u>. Closing shall be held at the office of the attorney for the Corporation, [specify attorney], on a date and time to be mutually agreed upon but no later than ten (10) days after either the determination of the purchase price or appointment of a legal representative for the decedent's estate, whichever is later. The article of this Agreement entitled Manner Of Payment, sets forth the documents and papers to be executed and/or delivered at closing.

3. <u>Purchase Price.</u> The purchase price of a deceased Shareholder's stock shall be determined by the Shareholders in writing every six (6) months. If no such written determination has been agreed upon within six (6) months from date of death, then the price shall be fixed at the gross commission income received by the Corporation during the preceding full fiscal year.

4. The Corporation may obtain life insurance policies on the lives of each of the Shareholders. In the event such life insurance policies are so obtained, then the Corporation shall collect the proceeds thereof, hold same as trustee and turn same immediately over to the legal representative of the deceased Shareholder as payment on account for decedent's share of stock. In the event said insurance proceeds exceed the amount of the purchase price as hereinabove provided, then the legal representative of the decedent shall retain the amount of said proceeds as payment in full for decedent's stock. In the event the purchase price of decedent's stock as hereinabove provided exceeds the proceeds of insurance, then the balance of the purchase price shall be paid pursuant to the article of this Agreement entitled <u>Deferred Payment</u>. The amount of the insurance collected by the Corporation on decedent's life shall in all events constitute the minimum purchase price to be paid by the Corporation for the shares of the decedent.

5. If one of the two (2) Shareholders should die, and if the remaining Shareholder should die within ninety (90) days after the death of the first Shareholder, then, notwithstanding any agreement to the contrary, neither the Corporation nor the Estate of the second deceased Shareholder shall be obligated to purchase, nor shall the Estate of the first deceased Shareholder be obligated to sell the stock held by said Estate. In such event, the proceeds of the life insurance on the lives of both Shareholders shall be delivered to the Corporation and shall belong exclusively to the Corporation, which shall be immediately liquidated and dissolved, and the proceeds of liquidation, after payment in full of the liabilities of the Corporation shall be paid to the Estates of the deceased Shareholders, proportionately to the stock interest of the deceased Shareholders in the Corporation.

6. In the event the Corporation is not legally able to purchase all or part of said shares and the surviving Shareholder fails or refuses to purchase all or the balance of such shares as hereinabove provided, and such failure or refusal continues for a period of ten (10) days after written notice by the personal representative of the deceased Shareholder to the Corporation and surviving Shareholder, the parties do hereby agree that the Corporation shall and will be liquidated and dissolved forthwith and all salaries of all Officers and Directors shall immediately cease. The Corporation shall pay to the Estate of the decedent from the first proceeds of liquidation (after deducting or paying all liabilities of the Corporation), a sum equal to the purchase price for decedent's shares (as hereinafter provided), less a sum equal to all insurance proceeds received by such Estate from life insurance policies owned by the Corporation.

I. <u>Lifetime Sale Of Shares.</u> No Shareholder of the Corporation shall sell, transfer, pledge, hypothecate or assign or in any way dispose of all or any part of his stock except by sale to the Corporation or the other Shareholder as hereinafter provided. All of the stock certificates of the Corporation shall contain an endorsement that they are subject to the terms and provisions of this Agreement which shall state the following:

"The transferability of the stock represented by this Certificate is restricted by an Agreement filed with the Corporation among the parties hereto, bearing date the ___ day of _____, 199 , a copy of which Agreement may be examined at the office of the Corporation."

1. <u>Offer.</u> In the event a Shareholder desires to dispose of his stock in the Corporation, he shall offer by certified mail, return receipt requested, all of his shares to the Corporation and the other Shareholder at the purchase price set forth herein. The Corporation shall have the first option to purchase as many of the shares as it can legally purchase. If the Corporation cannot legally purchase all of the stock or fails to indicate acceptance of the offer by certified mail, return receipt requested, within twenty (20) days from the receipt of the offer, then the remaining Shareholder shall have the option to purchase all or the remaining balance of said shares. The remaining Shareholder if he desires to purchase the stock as offered, shall indicate his acceptance by certified mail, return receipt requested, to the seller and to the other Shareholder, within thirty (30) days after the receipt of the original offer.

The purchase price shall be the smaller of: (a) the agreed upon value of the Corporation as agreed upon by the parties in their most recent six (6) month determination or (b) one (1) times the gross commission income of the Corporation for the fiscal year preceding the year in which the Shareholder offers to sell his stock pursuant to this paragraph.

Closing shall be held no later than ten (10) days after the purchase price is determined. At closing the selling Shareholder shall deliver to the purchaser, his shares of stock duly endorsed for transfer, with the appropriate transfer tax stamps affixed thereon, together with his resignation as an Officer and Director of the Corporation and an instrument stating that he is terminating any employment agreement with the Corporation.

At closing the selling Shareholder shall have the option to purchase any and all life insurance policies owned by the Corporation or the other Shareholder, on his life, at a price equal to the then cash surrender value of such policies or the sum of Ten Dollars ($10.00), whichever is greater.

2. <u>Failure To Purchase.</u> In the event the Corporation is not legally able to purchase or does not purchase all or part of said shares and the remaining Shareholder fails or refuses to purchase all or the balance of such shares as hereinabove provided, and such failure or refusal continues for a period of ten (10) days after the original written notice of offer to sell, then the parties do hereby agree that the Corporation shall and will be liquidated and dissolved forthwith, that all salaries of all Shareholders, Officers and Directors shall immediately cease, and the net proceeds of liquidation shall be distributed to each shareholder pro rata to his interest in the Corporation.

3. <u>Default.</u> If either the Corporation or the remaining Shareholder defaults in payment after acceptance, and said default in payment continues for a period of ten (10) days after notice in writing, sent certified mail, return receipt requested from the seller, then the Corporation shall be liquidated and dissolved forthwith, all salaries of the Shareholders, Officers and Directors shall immediately cease, the purchase price for the seller's shares shall be paid out of the first proceeds of liquidation after deducting or paying all liabilities of the Corporation, and the accepting party or parties shall remain liable for any resulting deficiency and shall be required to pay the difference between the purchase price and the amount realized by the seller after liquidation.

4. <u>Deferred Payment</u>. That portion of the purchase price of the shares of a deceased Shareholder or selling Shareholder shall be paid as follows: Twenty-five percent (25%) at closing; and the balance in Thirty-Six (36) equal monthly consecutive payments. Such deferred payments shall commence one month after closing. All deferred payments shall be evidenced by a series of negotiable promissory notes bearing interest at the rate of eight percent (8%) per annum, and providing for acceleration in the event of default continuing ten (10) days after written notice of default. Starting one month after closing, the maker shall have the right to prepay all or any of said notes in the inverse order of their maturity without premium or penalty provided interest is paid to the date of payment.

5. <u>Escrow.</u> Upon the receipt of the purchase price in full or in cash and notes as hereinabove provided, the legal representative of the deceased Shareholder or the selling Shareholder, as the case may be, shall deliver the certificates for such shares (and all related documents) together with an executed standard form General Release in favor of the Corporation and the remaining Shareholder, to the attorney for the Corporation, who shall hold all such certificates and General Releases in escrow to secure payment therefor, until all of the unpaid balance has been received and collected by the seller, at which time he shall deliver them to the purchaser.

The shares shall be duly endorsed to the purchaser and have appropriate tax transfer stamps affixed thereto. The purchaser shall have all rights of ownership during the time the shares are held in escrow and shall be entitled to vote said shares, and shall be entitled to receive any dividends or other emoluments so long as the purchaser is not in default under the terms of this Agreement.

6. <u>Default.</u> Upon default in payment of the notes, the seller shall have all rights of a secured party under the applicable provisions of the Uniform Commercial Code concerning Secured Transactions, as then in effect under the laws of the State of [specify state] which rights are incorporated herein by reference. The sole obligation of the Escrowee is to produce the escrowed shares and general releases at the public or private sale held pursuant to said Code provision. The Escrowee shall not have any liability except for fraud or gross negligence. In addition to the foregoing, if the Corporation is the purchaser and there is a default in payment of any notes and said default in payment continues for a period of ten (10) days after notice in writing thereof from the seller, then the Corporation shall be liquidated and dissolved forthwith, all salaries of all Shareholders, Officers and Directors shall immediately cease, and the purchase price for the seller's shares shall be paid out of the first proceeds of liquidation after deducting or paying all liabilities of the Corporation.

7. <u>Additional Items At Closing</u>. The legal representative of a deceased Shareholder shall be required to deliver an appropriate tax waiver and a Certificate of Letters Testamentary or Letters of Administration to the attorney for the purchaser upon receipt of the purchase price in full or in cash and notes as hereinabove provided.

All credit cards and corporate property of the selling or deceased Shareholder shall be delivered to the Corporation. The seller shall agree to indemnify the Corporation against any unknown and/or unauthorized charges on such cards or property.

8. Loans. Any loans owed to the Corporation by the deceased or selling Shareholder shall be paid to the Corporation out of the first monies received on the sale of the shares hereunder, and any loans owed to the deceased or selling Shareholder by the Corporation shall be paid at the tine of closing,

9. Guaranty. The parties hereto further agree that in the event of a purchase or sale, the remaining Shareholder individually and/or his estate, shall remain personally liable to the seller.

J. Corporate Surplus. In the event the Corporation shall not have sufficient surplus to permit it to lawfully purchase the deceased or selling Shareholder's shares, the surviving Shareholder and the seller may promptly take such lawful measures, if any such measures are available, as may be appropriate or necessary in order to enable the Corporation to lawfully purchase and pay for seller's shares, including by way of limitation, a current appraisal of the assets of the Corporation to determine whether a reappraisal surplus is available.

K. Tax Liability. Acceptance by the seller of all or part of the purchase price of his stock pursuant to this Agreement shall constitute an agreement by the seller to indemnify the Corporation and its remaining Shareholder from and against any and all claims or liabilities of the Corporation which may arise subsequent to the date of closing with respect to taxes of any kind or nature found to be due to the United States or any State or Municipality for any periods prior to the date of closing. It is understood and agreed that liability of the selling Shareholder shall be limited to such proportion as is equivalent to his proportionate share or interest in the Corporation prior to closing. The seller shall be entitled to prompt notification by the Corporation of any and all notices of claims and shall have the right, at his sole cost and expense, to participate in any proceeding, legal or otherwise, with respect to such claim or liability. The indemnification provided for herein shall be a continuing one and shall survive closing.

L. Action In Violation Of This Agreement. In the event the shares of any Shareholder are transferred or disposed of in any manner without complying with the provisions of this Agreement, or if such shares are taken in execution or sold in any voluntary or involuntary legal proceeding, execution sale, bankruptcy, insolvency or in any other manner, the Corporation and the Shareholder shall, upon actual notice thereof, in addition to their rights and remedies under this Agreement, be entitled to purchase such shares from the transferee thereof, under the same terms and conditions set forth in this Agreement as if the transferee had offered to sell such shares, but in no event shall the purchase price exceed the amount paid for the said shares by the transferee if such shares were acquired by the transferee for consideration. The Corporation may, at its option, refuse to transfer on its books and records any shares transferred in violation of this Agreement.

Any Shareholder who shall petition any Court for the dissolution of the Corporation, other than pursuant to the specific right to cause the Corporation to be liquidated and dissolved as provided in this Agreement, shall be deemed to have offered his shares for sale under the same terms and conditions as set forth in this Agreement.

M. Illegality. If any provision of this Agreement shall be determined by the arbitrators or any Court having jurisdiction, to be invalid, illegal or unenforceable, the remainder of this Agreement shall not be affected thereby, but shall continue in full force and effect as though such invalid, illegal or unenforceable provision or provisions were not originally a part hereof.

N. Termination. This Agreement shall remain in full force and effect for as long as the two Shareholders of the Corporation, or until the adjudication of the Corporation as a bankrupt or until the dissolution of the Corporation.

O. Waiver. No waiver or modification of any of the provisions of this Agreement or any of the rights or remedies of the parties hereto shall be valid unless such change is in writing, signed by the party to be charged therewith. No waiver of any of the provisions of this Agreement shall be deemed a waiver of any other provision.

P. Arbitration. Any claim or controversy arising among or between the parties hereto pertaining to the Corporation, or any claim or controversy arising out of or respecting any matter contained in this Agreement or any differences as to the interpretation or performance of any of the provisions of this Agreement shall be settled by arbitration in [specify location] before three arbitrators of the American Arbitration Association under its then prevailing rules. In any arbitration involving this Agreement, the arbitrators shall not make any award which will alter, change, cancel or rescind any provision of this Agreement, and their award shall be consistent with the provisions of this Agreement. Any such arbitration must be commenced no later than one (1) year from the date such claim or controversy arose, or such claim shall be deemed to have been waived. The award of the arbitrators shall be final and binding and judgment may be entered thereon in any court of competent jurisdiction.

The arbitrators shall be specifically instructed to reduce the amount of money due a selling Shareholder pursuant to the terms of this Agreement by Thirty Three Percent (33%) in the event they determine that an Officer was discharged for cause, or was not working full-time and exclusively for the Corporation with the written consent of the other Officer as described in Article E of this Agreement, as well as award reasonable attorney fees and costs to the prevailing party.

Anything to the contrary herein contained notwithstanding, since the shares of the Corporation cannot be readily purchased or sold on the open market and the parties will be irreparably damaged in the event this Agreement is not specifically enforced, should any dispute concerning the sale or disposition of any of the shares of the Shareholders occur, or should any dispute arise to enforce the provisions of a restrictive covenant referred to in Article Q of this Agreement, a temporary restraining order or injunction may be obtained from a court of appropriate jurisdiction, restraining any sale or disposition of said shares, or restraining the seller from working for or being directly or indirectly involved with a competitor (or representing Principals previously solicited by the Corporation), pending the determination of such controversy, pursuant to the arbitration provision of this Agreement. In addition to the foregoing, any of the parties may apply to any court of appropriate jurisdiction for any of the provisional remedies to which such party may be entitled to under the laws of the State of [specify state], including, but not limited to, injunction, attachment or replevin, pending the determination of any claim or controversy, pursuant to the arbitration provision of this Agreement. Service of process and notice of arbitration may be made by either Certified or Registered Mail, return receipt requested, addressed to any party at the address listed in this Agreement.

Q. Restrictive Covenant. Upon the termination of this Agreement, for any reason whatsoever, neither party shall, for a period of Three (3) years after the termination of this Agreement, work for, own an interest in, operate, join, control, participate in or be connected, either directly or indirectly, as an officer, employee, agent, independent contractor, shareholder or principal of any of the Principals of the Corporation represented by the Corporation during the preceding Two (2) years of this Agreement. Notwithstanding the foregoing, neither party shall, for a period of Three (3) years after termination of this Agreement, undertake, plan or organize with other employees or sales associates of the Corporation, or former employees or sales associates of the Corporation, any business which competes, either directly or indirectly, with the business of the Corporation, and neither party will induce or influence any person who is engaged by the Corporation as an employee or sales associate to terminate his or her employment or to engage or otherwise participate in any business or activity which directly or indirectly competes with the Corporation. In the event this Restrictive Covenant is found to be breached by the arbitrators, the parties further agree that the arbitrators may award the prevailing party reasonable attorney fees, costs, and the cessation of any future payments due the seller pursuant to Article I of this Agreement.

R. Survival. This Agreement shall bind the parties hereto and their respective heirs, administrators, executors, successors and assigns.

S. Notices. Any notice required to be given under this Agreement shall be sent by certified mail, return receipt requested to the respective addresses of the parties as contained in this Agreement or in the records of the Corporation.

T. Construction Of Terms. As used in this Agreement, wherever necessary or appropriate, the singular shall be deemed to include the plural and vice versa, and the masculine gender shall be deemed to include the feminine and vice versa, as the context may require.

This Agreement has been prepared by [specify attorney]. In the event of any ambiguity concerning the intentions of the parties or the language used thereto, the arbitrators shall seek the counsel of [specify attorney], the preparer of this Agreement.

IN WITNESS WHEREOF, the parties hereto have hereunto set their hands and seals the day, month and year first above written.

DATE: By:

DATE: By:

STOCK PURCHASE AGREEMENT

AGREEMENT made this ____ day of _____ 199 , by and between [specify seller] (hereinafter referred to as "Seller"); and [specify buyer] (hereinafter referred to as the "Corporation").

WITNESSETH

WHEREAS Seller is hereby selling his ten (10) shares of stock representing his one-half (1/2) stock interest in the Corporation; and

WHEREAS the Corporation is hereby purchasing and redeeming said shares from the Seller; and

WHEREAS Seller is hereby resigning as an officer and Director of the Corporation effective as of [specify date];

NOW, THEREFORE, it is mutually agreed as follows:

FIRST: Seller is hereby selling and transferring back to the Corporation all of Seller's shares of stock in the Corporation, as evidenced by ten (10) shares of common stock, and the Corporation is hereby purchasing same under the terms and conditions set forth in this Agreement.

SECOND: The purchase price is the sum of [specify amount] Dollars, and shall be paid at the rate of [specify rate] Dollars per week over a period of [specify term] consecutive weeks commencing [specify date]. Payments are to be made on Wednesday of each week and includes interest at the rate of seven (7%) percent per annum, and are evidenced by a Non-Negotiable Promissory Note being signed and delivered simultaneously herewith.

THIRD: The entire purchase price shall become immediately due and payable upon any of the following occurrences:

A. In the event there is a default in any payment thereunder and such default continues over a period of five (5) days after notice is given to the Corporation of such default;

B. all of the remaining Shareholders of the Corporation sell all or substantially all of the shares of stock owned by them to any third party; or

C. all or substantially all of the assets of the Corporation are sold; or

D. the Corporation is liquidated or substantially liquidated. In the event of a liquidation, the obligation due to Seller shall have priority over any and all liquidating dividends given to Shareholders, as well as any and all accrued bonuses in excess of normal salaries that are made to the existing Shareholders.

FOURTH: Simultaneously herewith the Corporation is assigning to Seller all life insurance policies owned by the Corporation on the life of the Seller. The Corporation shall sign any and all further documents that may be required by the life insurance companies to effectuate the transfer of said policies including any Cash Surrender Value which may have accumulated.

FIFTH: Simultaneously herewith Seller is signing and delivering back to the Corporation a Stock Certificate for ten (10) shares, duly endorsed in blank for transfer.

SIXTH: Seller warrants and represents as follows:

A. Stock sold hereby is fully paid for, non-assessable and is owned by Seller free and clear of any liens and encumbrances of any nature whatsoever.

B. Seller hereby waives any and all dividends, interests, increments and claims which may be due him from the Corporation from the shares of stock being sold hereby.

C. Seller has incurred no liabilities, obligations or commitments of any nature, kind or description on behalf of the Corporation, except such liabilities or commitments which may be listed on the books and records of the Corporation.

SEVENTH: Seller is hereby resigning as an officer and Director of the Corporation effective [specify date]. However, Seller shall continue to remain as an employee of the Corporation under a separate Employment Agreement. General Releases are being signed simultaneously herewith between Seller, the Corporation, and Seller is hereby released from all personal liability he may have incurred on behalf of the Corporation.

EIGHTH: The parties hereto agree that all contracts heretofore existing between them, or all contracts which may be construed as continuing to exist in the future between them, either orally or in writing, of whatsoever kind, nature and description, hereinafter or by operation of law (except this Agreement and any other Agreement being signed simultaneously herewith), are hereby cancelled and declared null and void between the within parties and are of no effect.

NINTH: Each and all of the covenants and conditions of this Agreement shall be binding and inure to the benefit of the parties hereto, their respective heirs, legal representatives, successors and assigns, and shall not be changed or modified except in writing, signed by each of the parties hereto.

IN WITNESS WHEREOF the parties hereto have hereunto set their hands and seals the day, month and year first above written.

By: By: DATE:

NON-NEGOTIABLE PROMISSORY NOTE

FOR GOOD AND VALUABLE CONSIDERATION, the undersigned agrees to pay to the order of [specify] at such place or places as may be designated by [specify] the sum of [specify amount] Dollars, payable at the rate of [specify rate] Dollars per week, on the Friday of each and every week commencing [specify date] for a period of five hundred (500) consecutive weeks thereafter. Said sum includes interest at the rate of seven (7%) percent per annum.

This Note is being paid pursuant to a Stock Purchase Agreement being signed simultaneously herewith, and in the event there is a default in any of the payments hereunder as set forth in Article "THIRD" of said Stock Purchase Agreement, then and in such event interest shall accrue on the unpaid balance thereof as of date of default at the rate of one (1%) percent per month, and the maker hereof agrees to pay all costs of collection including, but not limited to, reasonable attorneys' fees.

DATE: BY:

CONSULTING AGREEMENT
(Used with Stock Purchase Agreement)

AGREEMENT made this _____ day of _____, 199 , by and between XYZ, Inc., a [specify state] corporation with principal offices at [specify address] (the "Company") and John Doe, residing at [specify address] ("Consultant").

WITNESSETH

WHEREAS, the Company desires to engage Consultant to render advisory and consulting services to it, and Consultant is willing to accept such engagement on the terms and conditions hereinafter set forth;

NOW, THEREFORE, in consideration of the premises and the mutual covenants hereinafter contained, the parties hereto agree as follows:

1. The Company hereby retains Consultant as a consultant to advise the Company in connection with its printing production and sales, and Consultant hereby accepts such retention and agrees to render, from time to time, upon request of the Company during the term hereof, such advisory and consulting services as the Company may reasonably request. In rendering such advisory and consulting services to the Company, Consultant shall not be required to report on any periodic basis to the Company's offices and may render all such advisory and consulting services by telephone or written communication.

2. The term of this consulting agreement shall be for a period of 10 years beginning on the date hereof, and shall expire on the earliest of (a) _____, __ ; or (b) the Consultant's death.

3. As the full and entire compensation for all of the services to be rendered by Consultant under this Agreement, the Company will pay to Consultant and Consultant hereby accepts, the sum of [specify amount]; payable in equal weekly installments of [specify amount] commencing [specify date] and continuing for [specify term] weeks thereafter.

4. Consultant shall not be deemed an employee of the Company by virtue of his retention hereunder, but shall, for all purposes be deemed an independent contractor. The Company shall not be obligated to deduct social security, withholding or other payroll or related taxes from any payments to be made to Consultant under this Agreement. Consultant shall not be deemed to have been granted any right or authority to assume or create any obligation or responsibility on behalf of or in the name of the Company except as may be specifically authorized or contemplated by this Agreement.

5. This agreement shall inure to the benefit of and shall be binding upon the respective heirs, personal representatives, successors and assigns of the parties hereto.

6. The failure of any party at any time to require performance of any other party of any provision hereof or to resort to his or its remedy at law or in equity or otherwise, shall in no way affect the right of such party to require full performance or to resort to such remedy at any time thereafter, nor shall a waiver by any party of any breach of any provision hereof be taken or held to be a waiver of any subsequent breach of any such provision, unless expressly so stated in writing. No waiver of any of the provisions hereof shall be effective unless in writing and signed by the party to be charged therewith.

7. All notices which any party may desire or be required to send to another party hereunder shall be delivered in person or mailed by certified or registered mail, return receipt requested, and if mailed, shall be deemed to have been given on the date of the posting of the mail to the party at his address as it appears on the first page of this Agreement or at such other address as may be designated by the parties, from time to time, by notice in accordance with this Paragraph.

8. No alteration, modification, variation or waiver of this Agreement or any of the provisions hereof shall be effective unless in writing and executed by the parties hereto, or in the case of a waiver, by the party or parties waiving compliance.

9. This Agreement shall be governed by, and interpreted and construed in accordance with, the laws of the State of [specify state].

10. During the term of this Consulting Agreement and for a period of three (3) years after its termination, the Consultant shall not, directly or indirectly, within the City of [specify location] and the counties of [specify], enter into or engage in a business which is competitive with that of the Company. This covenant shall apply to the Consultant as an individual for his own account, as a partner or joint venturer, as an employee, agent, or, salesman for any person, as an officer, director, or shareholder of a corporation, or otherwise. Solicitation or acceptance of orders outside the restricted territories for shipment to, or delivery in, any of the restricted territories shall constitute "engaging in business" in the restricted territories in violation of this Agreement. This covenant shall be construed as an agreement independent of any other provision in this Agreement.

The existence of any claim or cause of the Consultant against the Company, whether predicated on this Agreement or otherwise, shall not constitute a defense to the enforcement by the Company of this covenant.

The parties agree that there is no adequate remedy at law for the breach of this covenant; accordingly the Company shall have the right to enjoin such violation by injunction or other equitable remedy.

11. Notwithstanding anything to the contrary contained herein, this Agreement shall not become effective unless and until the following agreements are fully executed by the following persons: each of [specify] and [specify] shall have executed stock purchase agreements and consulting agreements with the Company and each of [specify] and [specify] shall have executed agreements waiving annual interest payments of [specify] in consideration of the Company agreeing to keep policies of insurance on their lives in force.

IN WITNESS WHEREOF, the undersigned have hereunto set their hands as of the date and year first above written.

DATE: By:

DATE: By:

DATE   By:

NON-SOLICITATION AGREEMENT
(Used with Stock Purchase Agreement)

THIS NON-SOLICITATION AGREEMENT is made this _____ day of _____ 19_, by and between John Doe, residing at [address] and ABC, Inc., a [specify state] corporation, doing business at [business address], hereinafter referred to as "Company".

RECITAL

Concurrently with the execution of this Agreement the Company and John Doe entered into an agreement ("Stock Purchase Agreement") providing for the sale by John Doe of his entire stock interest in the Company and his resignation as an officer, director, and employee of the Company, and a Consulting Agreement ("Consulting Agreement"). The parties now desire to provide for a restriction upon John Doe for the Company's benefit from the solicitation by John Doe of the Company's business accounts.

NOW, THEREFORE, it is agreed as follows:

1. For a period of five (5) years from the date hereof, John Doe shall not directly or indirectly, within 100 miles from the City of [city of operation], solicit orders from any of the Company's accounts, a schedule of which is annexed hereto and made a part hereof.

This covenant shall apply to John Doe as an individual for his own account, as a partner or joint venturer, as an employee, agent, or salesman for any person, as an officer, director, or shareholder of a corporation, or otherwise. Solicitation or acceptance of orders outside the restricted territory for shipment to, or delivery in, such territory shall constitute a violation of this Agreement. This covenant shall be construed as an agreement independent of any other provision in the Stock Purchase Agreement or the Consulting Agreement.

The existence of any claim or cause of action by John Doe against the Company, whether predicated on this Agreement or otherwise, shall not constitute a defense to the enforcement by the Company of this covenant.

The parties agree that there is no adequate remedy at law for the breach of this covenant; accordingly the Company shall have the right to enjoin such violation by injunction or other equitable remedy.

2. In consideration of this covenant not to solicit the Company's business accounts, the Company shall pay to John Doe, the following consideration: the sum of [amount] in [number of payments agreed upon] equal consecutive monthly installments of which shall become due on the first day of each calendar month following the execution of this Agreement, without interest. The first installment shall commence on [date of first payment], and shall continue on the first day of each successive month thereafter.

3. If the Company defaults in the timely payment of any installment under the Agreements, John Doe shall be released from the obligation of the covenant set forth herein, and at his option may declare the full unpaid balance of the consideration immediately due and payable; provided however, that any such default shall not become effective to permit the release of the covenant or the acceleration of the unpaid installments unless and until John Doe has notified the Company of such default in writing and has given the Company at least ten business days in which to cure the default.

4. The installment payments shall be made to John Doe at his address set forth above, or to such other address as he may designate by written notice to the Company by registered or certified mail, return receipt requested, and, if mailed, shall be deemed to have been given three days following the date of the posting of the mail.

5. This Agreement shall be governed by the laws of the State of [state of operation].

6. This Agreement contains the entire understanding and agreement of the parties with respect to the subject matter hereof, and may not be charged without the written consent of both parties.

IN WITNESS WHEREOF, the parties have executed this Agreement the day and year set forth above.

Date: By:

Date: By:

SAMPLE PURCHASE AGREEMENT

AGREEMENT made this _____ day of _____, 199 , between [specify seller] (hereinafter referred to as "Seller"), a [specify state] corporation having its offices at [specify address], [specify buyer] (hereinafter referred to as "Buyer"), a [specify state] corporation having its offices at [specify address], and [specify guarantor], (hereinafter referred to as "Guarantor"), a [specify state] corporation having its offices at [specify address].

FIRST: Seller is hereby selling and Buyer is hereby purchasing the following assets ("Assets") of Seller at the price, terms and conditions hereinafter set forth:

A. All accounts receivable owned by Seller as of [specify date] as listed on "Schedule A," annexed hereto and made a part hereof.

B. All right, title and interest in and to the name [specify name], which name Seller warrants and represents to be the only trade name and trademark used by Seller in the course of its business.

C. All inventory listed on "Schedule B" annexed hereto and made a part hereof. Seller represents that said inventory provides certain of the parts, supplies and other items necessary to fill the orders listed on "Schedule C" hereof.

D. All of Seller's orders from customers as listed on "Schedule C," annexed hereto and made a part hereof. Said orders are represented by Seller to have a net sales value of no less than Five Hundred Eighty Five Thousand Dollars ($585,000) as of this date. The term "net sales value" is hereby defined as the sales price, less any trade or cash discounts and allowances, returns or reworks which may have been granted to the customer prior to date hereof.

E. Certain machinery, equipment, molds, tools and dyes listed on "Schedule D". Certain items of the equipment are owned by Seller and certain items are owned by a joint venture consisting of [specify partners] (the joint venture hereinafter referred to as "F&W"). The equipment owned by F&W is included in this sale, and [names of partners], by consenting to this Agreement, agree to transfer the F&W equipment concurrently with the transfer of the remaining Assets.

F. All of seller's right, title and interest in and to its list of customers (although some may not be currently active), together with all other historical records, documents, blueprints, part specifications and quantities sold. The list of customers is represented by Seller to be essentially all significant customers sold by Seller within the past five (5) years and is set forth on "Schedule E", annexed hereto and made a part hereof.

SECOND: A. Annexed hereto, made a part hereof and marked "Schedule F" is a full and complete list of liabilities and creditors of Seller. As of this date said liabilities and creditors are separated into the following: secured creditors, lessors of machinery and equipment, etc., tax liabilities and unsecured creditors. Except for the orders which are being assigned to Buyer, Buyer shall not assume or pay any of Seller's liabilities. The proceeds of closing shall be applied towards payment of all secured creditors and unsecured creditors, with the exception of those set forth on Schedule G, annexed hereto and made a part hereof, and said proceeds shall be delivered to [specify address], the attorneys for Seller, to be used specifically for payment of all of such liabilities. Annexed hereto and made a part hereof as Schedule H is an Escrow Agreement to be signed by such attorneys, to that effect. All liens on machinery and equipment sold hereby will be satisfied from the proceeds of closing. The remainder of all liabilities and obligations of Seller shall be paid from the first proceeds Seller receives from the commissions due to Seller pursuant to Article "THIRD B" hereof.

B. Seller and [specify partner] by consenting hereto, shall indemnify, defend and hold Buyer harmless from any and all liability for any of Seller's obligations or liabilities, existing, accrued or contingent and any and all expenses including reasonable attorneys' fees therewith, which indemnity shall survive closing of this Agreement. In the event a claim is made against Buyer for any of Seller's obligations or liabilities, Buyer shall notify Seller, in writing, of such claim. In the event Seller fails to obtain a release to Buyer from the claimant within thirty (30) days after notice is given to Seller thereof, then in addition to any and all rights and remedies, Buyer shall be entitled to offset the amount of such claim against the following monies due:

i) any monies due to Seller representing commissions due hereunder pursuant to Article "THIRD" hereof; or ii) any monies due to [specify partner] under a Sales Agent Agreement being signed simultaneously herewith.

The amount of offset shall be an amount equal to any claims made against Buyer for any liabilities or obligations of Seller and the amount offset shall be held until such time as such claims are either paid or resolved to the reasonable satisfaction of Buyer, at which time the withheld amount shall be paid to the Seller according to entitlement.

THIRD: A. The purchase price for all assets purchased hereunder is the sum of Six Hundred Fifty Thousand Dollars ($650,000), which sum shall be delivered to Seller's attorney upon approval of this transaction by the Trustee in Bankruptcy of [partner], as provided in separate Letter Agreement being signed simultaneously herewith.

B. In addition thereto, Buyer shall pay to Seller commissions equal to five (5%) percent of the net monies received and retained from sales made of [specify] products by Buyer to Seller's customers listed on "Schedule C" hereof. Payment of said commissions shall be made for all sales made over a period of seven (7) years from date hereof or until the total commissions paid to Seller total the sum of One Million Fifty Thousand Dollars ($1,050,000), whichever event occurs first. However, if during the foregoing seven (7) year period the net monies received and retained from sales made to the aforesaid customers exceed the sum of Twenty One Million ($21,000,000) Dollars, then Buyer shall pay to Seller an additional commission of five (5%) percent of said amount which exceeds Twenty One Million Dollars ($21,000,000). Payment of the aforesaid commissions shall be paid within thirty (30) days after each quarter-annual period, based upon net monies received from sales to such customers during said quarter-annual period. The term "net monies received and retained", shall be defined as the net proceeds realized from the sales to the customers listed on Schedule C after deduction of any returns and allowances. Seller shall provide Buyer with quarterly reports stating how the amount of commissions was arrived at and listing all such sales, and Seller shall have the right, at its expense, to audit such reports, at times and places convenient to Buyer.

FOURTH: The purchase price of Six Hundred Fifty Thousand Dollars ($650,000) is allocated as follows:

Assets	Allocation
A. Accounts Receivable	280,000
B. Inventory	100,000
C. Seller's Machinery and Equipment, etc.	140,000
D. Machinery and Equipment	130,000

FIFTH: Annexed hereto and made a part hereof is a list of all leases, union agreements, employment agreements and any other contracts, commitments or obligations of Seller of a continuing nature. Said list is designated as "Schedule I". Buyer shall in no way assume or be responsible for any of said commitments and obligations and the indemnity provision of Article "SECOND" hereof shall apply thereto.

SIXTH: A. That upon transfer of title to all Assets sold hereunder, such Assets shall be delivered free and clear of any and all liens, encumbrances and obligations.

B. That this transaction was duly authorized by the Board of Directors of Seller, and Seller is hereby submitting a certified copy of the Resolution of the Board of Directors of Seller authorizing this transaction.

C. That it has entered into no other contract or commitment to sell, assign, mortgage or otherwise encumber the Assets being sold hereunder or any portion thereof.

D. That the accounts receivable to be sold hereunder are represented to be bona fide in all respects. In the event the net monies received from said accounts receivable is less than the total face value thereof, Seller shall indemnify Buyer for the amount of such deficiency. Buyer shall be entitled to a credit for the amount of such deficiency which may, at Seller's option, be offset against the commissions due to Seller after closing. Buyer shall use its best efforts to collect all accounts receivable and will apply receipts to the oldest accounts unless otherwise directed by the customer.

E. That the annual net sales volume for the last fiscal or calendar year of Seller is in excess of [specify amount] Dollars.

F. That, the orders being transferred and assigned to Buyer are bona fide in all respects. If said orders are canceled for any reason whatsoever, except if said cancellation is due to the fault of the Buyer, then Buyer shall be entitled to be reimbursed by Seller for the cost of all inventory which was specifically produced by Seller prior to date hereof to fill said canceled order.

G. That there are no judgments, liens, actions or proceedings pending against it in any court, nor is there any litigation, proceeding, governmental or United Postal Service investigation presently pending to be paid from the purchase price.

H. Except as provided in a separate agreement pertaining to the requirement of the consent of the Trustee of [specify partner name], neither the execution and delivery of this Agreement nor the consummation of the contemplated transactions herein will conflict with or result in a breach of any of the terms, conditions or provisions of any law or any regulations, order, writ, injunction or decree of any court or governmental instrumentality, or of any agreement or other instrument to which it is a party or by which it is bound.

I. This Agreement is a legal, valid and binding obligation of the Seller.

J. That all of the machinery, equipment, tools and dyes being sold to Buyer are owned by either Seller or F&W and shall be delivered free and clear of any and all liens and encumbrances and in working condition.

K. That Seller shall cause the owner of the premises in which Seller is located to permit all of the machinery and equipment, tools and dyes to remain in the premises presently occupied by Seller, without charge, for a period of ninety (90) days after same is transferred to Buyer, to permit Buyer and/or its Assignee to conduct an auction sale on said premises of said equipment. During said period of time, said equipment may be used by Buyer who shall provide appropriate liability and other insurance to protect Seller during the course of access to said premises and the sale thereof. Said sale shall not use the name of Seller.

SEVENTH: Buyer and Guarantor hereby represent as follows:

A. Neither the execution and delivery of this Agreement nor the consummation of the contemplated transactions herein will conflict with or result in a breach of any of the terms, conditions or provisions of any law or any regulation, order, writ, injunction or decree of any court or governmental instrumentality or of any agreement or instrument to which it is a party or by which it is bound.

B. This Agreement is a legal, valid and binding obligation of the Buyer and Guarantor and Buyer and Guarantor are hereby delivering their Corporate Resolutions authorizing this transaction.

C. Buyer and Guarantor are [specify state] corporations having been duly incorporated under the laws of the State of [specify state] and have the authority to execute this Agreement and all documents pursuant thereto.

D. Buyer shall not assign its obligations hereunder nor will it take any action such as liquidation, dissolution or merger to avoid its obligations hereunder.

E. Buyer is a wholly owned subsidiary of Guarantor, which, by executing this Agreement, guarantees all the obligations of Buyer hereunder and agrees not to allow Buyer to take any action such as liquidation, dissolution or merger to avoid its obligations hereunder.

EIGHTH: All of the warranties and representations of both Seller, Buyer and Guarantor shall survive closing of this contract.

NINTH: The parties acknowledge that the sole broker that brought about this sale is [specify broker] and Seller shall pay said broker all commissions due hereunder as per separate Agreement, and shall indemnify and hold Buyer harmless therefrom.

TENTH: Simultaneously herewith, the following documents are being signed and delivered:

A. Seller is delivering to Buyer a Bill of Sale transferring to Buyer all of the Assets sold hereunder, free and clear of any and all liens, encumbrances, security interests, debts or taxes of any nature whatsoever. Said Bill of Sale shall contain an Affidavit of Title together with an Affidavit providing for the payment to Seller's creditors as set forth in this Agreement.

B. Seller is signing a document notifying all of Seller's accounts receivable to pay said accounts receivable to Buyer. Said document does provide that in the event any payments thereof are made to Seller, then Seller shall immediately turn over said payments to Buyer.

C. Seller shall sign a document in such form as may be designated by Buyer notifying its customers that their orders have been assigned and assumed by Buyer.

D. Seller shall sign a document assigning all of its right, title and interest in and to the name [specify name] to the Buyer. Within twenty (20) days from date hereof, Seller shall execute and file in the appropriate [specify state] office, a change of name certificate changing the name of its corporation to a name completely dissimilar to [specify name].

E. Seller is delivering to Buyer all of the records, documents, blueprints, specifications, etc. of its customers.

F. Seller's attorney is delivering to Buyer an Opinion Letter in the form annexed hereto, made a part hereof and marked "Schedule J".

G. A Sales Agent Agreement is being signed with [specify name] a copy of which is annexed hereto and marked "Schedule K".

H. In addition to the foregoing, Seller is hereby signing and delivering all other documents necessary to effectuate the transfer of the ownership of the Assets being sold hereby and if any additional documents are necessary to complete said transfer, Seller agrees to sign same.

ELEVENTH: Seller and [specify partner] individually, hereby jointly and severally agree that except as provided in the Sales Agent Agreement with [specify name] they shall not engage in or in any manner become interested in, either directly or indirectly, as an owner, partner, shareholder or employee (jointly or otherwise), in any business, trade or occupation which sells to the customers (as hereinafter defined) of Seller, any products which were sold by Seller during the calendar years _____ and _____ to date. Said covenant shall continue in full force and effect for a period of six (6) years from date hereof and may be enforced by injunctive relief in any court of competent jurisdiction. In the event of a breach hereof, Buyer shall have the right (in addition to all other rights and remedies), to terminate and reduce any commissions or payments due to Seller and/or [specify partner], pursuant to Article "THIRD" hereunder, or pursuant to the Sales Agent Agreement being signed by [specify partner]. Such termination and/or reduction of commissions or payments shall not be considered a default by Seller. In the event there be a default (as hereinafter defined) by Seller in payment of said commissions under Article "THIRD B" hereunder, or in the payment of any monies due to [specify partner] under the Sales Agent Agreement, then the foregoing restrictive covenant shall terminate. The term "default" shall mean an adjudication by a court of competent jurisdiction or an arbitration tribunal that Seller is in default. The term "customers" as used herein shall mean all customers sold by Seller during the five (5) year period immediately preceding date hereof.

TWELFTH: Any claim or controversy arising among or between the parties hereto pertaining to this Agreement and any claim or controversy arising out of or respecting any matter contained in this Agreement or any difference as to the interpretation of any of the provisions of this Agreement shall be settled by arbitration in [specify location] by three (3) arbitrators under the then prevailing rules of the American Arbitration Association.

THIRTEENTH: This writing is intended by the parties as a final expression of their agreement and is intended also as a complete and exclusive statement of the terms of their agreement. No course of prior dealings between the parties and no usage of the trade shall be relevant to supplement or explain any term used in this Agreement. Whenever a term defined by the Uniform Commercial Code is used in this Agreement, the definition contained in the code is to control.

FOURTEENTH: This Agreement can be modified or rescinded only by a writing by both parties or their duly sworn authorized agents.

FIFTEENTH: No claim or right arising out of the breach of this Agreement can be discharged in whole or in part by a waiver or renunciation of such claim or right unless the waiver or renunciation is in writing signed by the aggrieved party.

SIXTEENTH: The invalidity or unenforceability of any particular provision of this Agreement shall not affect other provisions hereof and this Agreement shall be construed in all respects as if such invalid or unenforceable provisions were omitted.

SEVENTEENTH: This Agreement shall inure to the benefit of and be binding upon the parties named herein as the Seller and the Buyer and, except as heretofore provided, to their respective successors, assigns, heirs, executors, legal representatives and administrators.

EIGHTEENTH: This Agreement shall be executed simultaneously in two or more counterparts, each of which shall be deemed an original but all of which together shall constitute one and the same instrument, and this Agreement shall be construed under the laws of the State of [specify state].

NINETEENTH: All notices hereunder shall be sent by certified mail, return receipt requested, with copies to the parties' attorneys by regular mail as follows:

[specify seller's address]
[specify seller's attorneys' address]
[specify buyer's address]
[specify buyer's attorneys' address]

IN WITNESS WHEREOF the parties hereto have set their hands and seals the day and year first above written.

CONSENTED AND AGREED TO:

BY: **BY:**

BILL OF SALE
(Used with Sample Purchase Agreement)

KNOW ALL MEN BY THESE PRESENTS, that [specify seller], an Ohio corporation (the "Seller"), in consideration of the promises, covenants, conditions and agreements of [specify buyer], a [specify state] corporation ("Purchaser"), pursuant to a certain Purchase Agreement (the "Agreement") among seller and Purchaser, does hereby grant, bargain, sell, transfer, convey, assign and deliver to Purchaser, certain assets of Seller's business consisting of the following:

(a) All accounts receivable owned by Seller as of [specify date] as listed on Schedule A annexed hereto and made a part hereof.

(b) All right, title and interest in and to the name [specify name] which name Seller warrants and represents to be the only tradename and trademark used by Seller in the course of its business.

(c) All inventory listed on Schedule B annexed hereto and made a part of. Seller represents that said inventory provides certain of the parts, supplies and other items necessary to fill the orders on Schedule C hereof.

(d) All of Seller's orders from customers as listed on Schedule C annexed hereto and made a part hereof. Said orders are represented by Seller to have a net sales value of not less than [specify amount] as of [specify date]. The term "Net Sales Value" is hereby defined as the sales price, less any trade or cash discounts or allowances, returns or reworks which may have been granted to the customer prior to the date hereof.

(e) Certain machinery, equipment, molds, tools and dies listed on Schedule D.

(f) All of Seller's right, title and interest in and to its list of customers (although some may not be currently active), together with all other historical records, documents, blueprints, parts specifications and quantities sold. The list of customers is represented by Seller to be essentially all significant customers sold by Seller within the last five (5) years and is set forth on Schedule E annexed hereto and made a part hereof.

TO HAVE AND TO HOLD THE SAME UNTO THE PURCHASER AND ITS SUCCESSORS AND ASSIGNS FOREVER.

And said Seller hereby covenants to and with the said Purchaser that Seller has good and marketable title to all items to be sold, transferred, assigned and conveyed hereunder, subject to no liens, claims, encumbrances or restrictions of any kind, has the right, power and authority to, and hereby does, sell, transfer, assign and convey all of said assets free and clear of such liens, claims, encumbrances and restrictions. Said Seller hereby covenants that it will warrant and defend same against all lawful claims whatsoever.

IN WITNESS WHEREOF, the Seller has set its hand this ___ day of _____, 199 .

WITNESSES:

STATE OF [SPECIFY STATE]   )
                                  : SS:
COUNTY OF [SPECIFY COUNTY]   )

BEFORE ME, the Subscriber, a Notary Public in and for said County and State, personally appeared [specify name] of [specify company], the corporation which executed the foregoing instrument, who acknowledged he did sign said instrument as such officer on behalf of said corporation, and by authority of its Board of Directors, and that the execution of said instrument is his free and voluntary act and deed individually and as such officer, and the free and voluntary act and deed of said corporation.

IN TESTIMONY WHEREOF, I have hereunto subscribed my name and affixed my Notarial Seal this ___ day of _____, 199 .

Notary Public, State of [specify]

TECHNICAL EMPLOYMENT AGREEMENT AND RELATED DOCUMENTS WITH A FOREIGN EMPLOYER

ACTION OF THE INCORPORATOR
OF
XYZ, INC.

The undersigned, being the sole incorporator of (USA) Inc., a Delaware corporation (the "Corporation"), acting without a meeting pursuant to Section 108 (c) of the Delaware General Corporation Law in lieu of an organization meeting, hereby takes the following action and adopts the following resolutions:

RESOLVED, that a copy of the Certificate of Incorporation of the Corporation, as filed with the Secretary of State of the State of Delaware on [specify date], shall be kept in the minute book of the Corporation.

RESOLVED, that the form of By-Laws for the Corporation, as attached to this certificate, be and it hereby is adopted as the By-Laws of the Corporation, and a copy thereof shall be kept in the minute book of the Corporation.

RESOLVED, that the form of seal for the Corporation, as imprinted in the margin of this certificate, be and it hereby is approved.

RESOLVED, that the form of certificate for shares of the capital stock of the Corporation, as attached to this certificate, be and it hereby is approved.

RESOLVED, that the Board of Directors of the Corporation shall consist of three Directors.

RESOLVED, that the following persons be and they hereby are elected Directors of the Corporation, to hold office in accordance with the By-Laws until the first annual meeting of the stockholders and until their successors, if any, are elected and qualified:

[specify names of Directors]

RESOLVED, that the Directors of the Corporation be and they hereby are authorized and empowered in their discretion to issue shares of the capital stock of the Corporation to the full amount authorized by the Certificate of Incorporation, in such amounts and for such consideration as from time to time shall be determined by the Board of Directors and as permitted by law.

Dated:

_____
Sole Incorporator

WRITTEN CONSENT
OF THE
BOARD OF DIRECTORS
OF
XYZ, INC.

The undersigned, being all the Directors of XYZ, INC., a Delaware corporation (the "Corporation"), acting without a meeting pursuant to Section 141(f) of the Delaware General Corporation Law, hereby take the following action and adopt the following resolutions:

RESOLVED, that the action of and resolutions adopted by the Incorporator of the Corporation on [specify date], as set forth in his certificate thereof, be and they hereby are in all respects approved, ratified and confirmed.

RESOLVED, that the following persons be and they hereby are elected to the offices of the Corporation set opposite their respective names, to hold office in accordance with the By-Laws until the next annual meeting of the Board of Directors and until their successors, if any, are elected and qualified:

President:
Vice President:
Secretary:
Assistant Secretary:

RESOLVED, that the officers of the Corporation be and they hereby are authorized and directed to offer for sale and to sell (i) to [specify party] 60 shares of the Corporation's Common Stock, without par value, at a purchase price of $_____ per share to be paid in aggregate $_____ in cash and by the execution and delivery of a promissory note in the amount of $_____ in form as annexed hereto as Exhibit A; and (ii) to [specify party] 40 shares of the Corporation's Common Stock, without par value, at a purchase price of $_____ per share to be paid in aggregate by the execution and delivery of a bill of sale respecting the inventory described therein in form as annexed hereto as Exhibit B; and to issue such shares as fully paid and nonassessable shares of the Corporation's Common Stock, upon receipt of the full purchase price therefor; some or all of such shares may be uncertificated shares pursuant to Section 158 of the Delaware General Corporation Law.

RESOLVED, that the form of Corporate Resolutions of the Bank as annexed hereto, for the purpose of opening and maintaining one or more bank accounts and transacting other banking business of the Corporation at said Bank, authorizing the persons specified therein to exercise the powers set forth therein, be and it hereby is adopted and the appropriate officers of the Corporation be and they hereby are authorized and directed to certify the same to such Bank.

RESOLVED, that each of the officers of the Corporation be and hereby is authorized and empowered to execute, deliver and file on behalf of the Corporation any and all documents and to take such other action, from time to time, as may be necessary or desirable to qualify the

Corporation to transact business in any state in which the President or Vice President, upon the advice of counsel to the corporation, determines to be necessary or desirable.

RESOLVED, that the fiscal year of the Corporation shall end on October 31 of each year, and the first fiscal year shall commence on the date of incorporation of the Corporation.

RESOLVED, that [specify accounting firm] be engaged as auditors of the Corporation on such terms and conditions as are set forth on Exhibit C hereto.

RESOLVED, that the Corporation proceed to carry on the business for which it was incorporated.

RESOLVED, that each of the (i) President and the (ii) Vice President of the Corporation, acting singly, and such other officers as either of them may designate, be and they hereby are authorized and directed on behalf of the Corporation to negotiate and agree to the terms and provisions of, and to execute and deliver, all agreements, instruments and consents in connection with [description of transaction and related agreements], in form as circulated for signature, with such changes, insertions and deletions therein as any of them, with the advice of counsel to the Corporation, shall approve, such approval to be conclusively expressed by their execution thereof.

RESOLVED, that each of the (i) President and the (ii) Vice President of the Corporation, acting singly, and such other officers as either of them may designate, be and they hereby are authorized and directed on behalf of the Corporation to do and perform such other acts and execute such other documents, instruments and certificates as they shall deem necessary or desirable to further the intent and purposes and otherwise to effectuate the foregoing resolutions.

Dated:

_____

_____

CERTIFICATE OF INCORPORATION
OF
XYZ INC.

THE UNDERSIGNED, in order to form a corporation under and pursuant to the General Corporation Law of the State of Delaware, does hereby certify as follows:

FIRST: The name of the Corporation is XYZ Inc.

SECOND: The registered office of the Corporation is at [specify address], and its registered agent at such address is [specify registered agent].

THIRD: The purpose of the Corporation is to engage in any lawful act or activity for which corporations may be organized under the General Corporation Law of Delaware.

FOURTH: The total number of shares of stock which the Corporation is authorized to issue is one thousand (1000) shares of Common Stock, with no par value, all of which shall be of the same class. Each holder thereof shall be entitled to one vote at all meetings of stockholders for each share of such stock standing in his name on the books of the Corporation on the record date fixed for such meeting.

FIFTH: The name and mailing address of the Incorporator is [specify address].

SIXTH: A director of the Corporation shall not be personally liable to the Corporation or its stockholders for monetary damages for breach of fiduciary duty as a director, except as otherwise provided by the Delaware General Corporation Law as the same exists or may hereafter be amended.

SEVENTH: The stockholders, or the Board of Directors of the Corporation without the assent or vote of the stockholders, shall have the power to adopt, alter, amend or repeal the By-Laws of the Corporation.

EIGHTH: The Corporation reserves the right to amend, alter, change or repeal any provision set forth in this Certificate of Incorporation in the manner now or hereafter prescribed by law.

IN WITNESS WHEREOF, I have hereunto set my hand this ___ day of ___ 199_.

_____
Sole Incorporator

BY-LAWS
OF
XYZ INC.

(A Delaware Corporation)

ARTICLE I
OFFICES

Section 1.01 <u>Offices.</u> The Corporation shall have its registered office in the State of Delaware, and may have such other offices and places of business within or without the State of Delaware as the Board of Directors may from time to time determine or the business of the Corporation may require.

ARTICLE II
STOCKHOLDERS

Section 2.01 <u>Place of Meetings</u>. Meetings of stockholders for any purpose may be held at such place or places, either within or without the State of Delaware, as shall be designated by the Board of Directors, or by the President with respect to meetings called by him.

Section 2.02 <u>Annual Meeting</u>. The annual meeting of stockholders shall be held on such date as may be determined by the Board of Directors. At such meeting, the stockholders shall elect a Board of Directors and transact such other business as may properly come before the meeting.

Section 2.03 <u>Special Meetings</u>. Special meetings of stockholders may be called at any time by the Board of Directors or by the President, and shall be called by the President or Secretary at the written request of stockholders owning a majority of the shares of the Corporation then outstanding and entitled to vote.

Section 2.04 <u>Notice of Meetings</u>. Written notice of the annual meeting or any special meeting of stock shall be given to each stockholder entitled to vote thereat, not less than ten nor more than sixty days prior to the meeting, except as otherwise required by statute, and shall state the time and place and, in the case of a special meeting, the purpose or purposes of the meeting. Notice need not be given, however, to any stockholder who submits a signed waiver of notice, before or after the meeting, or who attends the meeting in person or by proxy without objecting to the transaction of business.

Section 2.05 <u>Quorum</u>. At all meetings of stockholders, the holders of a majority of the stock issued and outstanding and entitled to vote thereat, present in person or represented by proxy, shall constitute a quorum for the transaction of business, except as otherwise provided by statute, the Certificate of Incorporation or these By-Laws. When a quorum is once present to organize a meeting, it is not broken by the subsequent withdrawal of any stockholder.

Section 2.06 <u>Voting</u>. (a) At all meetings of stockholders, each stockholder having the right to vote thereat may vote in person or by proxy, and, unless otherwise provided in the Certificate of

Incorporation or in any resolution providing for the issuance of any class or series of stock adopted by the Board of Directors pursuant to authority vested in the Board by the Certificate of Incorporation, shall have one vote for each share of stock registered in his name. Election of directors shall be by written ballot.

(b) When a quorum is once present at any meeting of stockholders, a majority of the votes cast, whether in person or represented by proxy, shall decide any question or proposed action brought before such meeting, except for the election of directors, who shall be elected by a plurality of the votes cast, or unless the question or action is one upon which a different vote is required by express provision of statute, the Certificate of Incorporation or these By-Laws or an agreement among stockholders, in which case such provision shall govern the vote on the decision of such question or action.

Section 2.07 <u>Adjourned Meetings</u>. Any meeting of stockholders may be adjourned to a designated time and place by a vote of a majority in interest of the stockholders present in person or by proxy and entitled to vote, even though less than a quorum is present, or by the President if a quorum of stockholders is not present. No notice of such adjourned meeting need be given, other than by announcement at the meeting at which adjournment is taken, and any business may be transacted at the adjourned meeting which might have been transacted at the meeting as originally called. However, if such adjournment is for more than thirty days, or if after such adjournment a new record date is fixed for the adjourned meeting, a notice of the adjourned meeting shall be given to each stockholder of record entitled to vote at such meeting.

Section 2.08 <u>Action by Written Consent of Stockholders</u>. Any action of the stockholders required or permitted to be taken at any regular or special meeting thereof may be taken without any such meeting, notice of meeting or vote if a consent in writing setting forth the action thereby taken is signed by the holders of outstanding stock having not less than the number of votes that would have been necessary to authorize such action at a meeting at which all shares entitled to vote were present and voted. Prompt notice of the taking of any such action shall be given to any stockholders entitled to vote who have not so consented in writing.

Section 2.09 <u>Stockholders of Record</u>. (a) The stockholders from time to time entitled to notice of or to vote at any meeting of stockholders or any adjournment thereof, or to express consent to any corporate action without a meeting, or entitled to receive payment of any dividend or other distribution or the allotment of any rights, or entitled to exercise any rights in respect of any change, conversion or exchange of stock or for the purpose of any other lawful action, shall be the stockholders of record as of the close of business on a date fixed by the Board of Directors as the record date for any such purpose. Such a record date shall not precede the date upon which the resolution fixing the record date is adopted by the Board of Directors, and shall not, with respect to stockholder meetings, be more than sixty days nor less than ten days before the date of such meeting, or, with respect to stockholder consents, more than ten days after the date upon which the resolution fixing the record date is adopted by the Board of Directors.

(b) If the Board of Directors does not fix a record date, (i) the record date for the determination of stockholders entitled to notice of or to vote at a meeting of stockholders shall be as of the close of business on the day next preceding the day on which notice of such meeting is given, or, if notice is waived as provided herein, on the day next preceding the day on which the meeting is held; (ii) the record date for determining stockholders entitled to express consent to corporate action in writing without a meeting, where no prior action by the Board of Directors is necessary, shall be the close of business on the day on which the first signed written consent setting forth the action taken or proposed to be taken is delivered to the Corporation; and (iii) the record date for determining stockholders for any other purpose shall be at the close of business on the day on which the resolution of the Board of Directors relating thereto is adopted.

ARTICLE III
DIRECTORS

Section 3.01 <u>Board of Directors</u>. The management of the affairs, property and business of the Corporation shall be vested in a Board of Directors, the members of which need not be stockholders. In addition to the power and authority expressly conferred upon it by these By-Laws and the Certificate of Incorporation, the Board of Directors may take any action and do all such lawful acts and things on behalf of the Corporation and as are not by statute or by the Certificate of Incorporation or these By-Laws required to be taken or done by the stockholders.

Section 3.02 <u>Number.</u> The number of directors shall be as fixed from time to time by the Board of Directors.

Section 3.03 <u>Election and Term of Directors</u>. At each annual meeting of the stockholders, the stockholders shall elect directors to hold office until the next annual meeting. Each director shall hold office until the expiration of such term and until his successor, if any, has been elected and qualified, or until his earlier resignation or removal.

Section 3.04 <u>Annual and Regular Meetings</u>. The annual meeting of the Board of Directors shall be held promptly after the annual meeting of stockholders, and regular meetings of the Board of Directors may be held at such times as the Board of Directors may from time to time determine. No notice shall be required for the annual or any regular meeting of the Board of Directors.

Section 3.05 <u>Special Meetings</u>. Special meetings of the Board of Directors may be called by the President, by an officer of the corporation who is also a director or by any two directors, upon one day's notice to each director either personally or by mail, telephone, telecopier or telegraph, and if by telephone, telecopier or telegraph confirmed in writing before or after the meeting, setting forth the time and place of such meeting. Notice of any special meeting need not be given, however, to any director who submits a signed waiver of notice, before or after the meeting, or who attends the meeting without objecting to the transaction of business.

Section 3.06 <u>Place of Meetings</u>. (a) The Board of Directors may hold its meetings, regular or special, at such places, either within or without the State of Delaware, as it may from time to time determine or as shall be set forth in any notice of such meeting.

(b) Any meeting of the Board of Directors may be held by means of conference telephone or similar communications equipment whereby all persons participating in the meeting can hear each other, and such participation shall constitute presence at the meeting.

Section 3.07 Adjourned Meetings. A majority of the directors present, whether or not a quorum, may adjourn any meeting of the Board of Directors to another time and place. Notice of such adjourned meeting need not be given if the time and place thereof are announced at the meeting at which the adjournment is taken.

Section 3.08 Quorum of Directors. A majority of the total number of directors shall constitute a quorum for the transaction of business. The total number of directors means the number of directors the Corporation would have if there were no vacancies.

Section 3.09 Action of the Board of Directors. The vote of a majority of the directors present at a meeting at which a quorum is present shall be the act of the Board of Directors, unless the question or action is one upon which a different vote is required by express provision of statute, the Certificate of Incorporation or these By-Laws, in which case such provision shall govern the vote on the decision of such question or action. Each director present shall have one vote.

Section 3.10 Action by Written Consent of Directors. Any action required or permitted to be taken at any meeting of the Board of Directors or of any committee thereof may be taken without a meeting, if a written consent thereto is signed by all members of the Board of Directors or of such committee, and such written consent is filed with the minutes of proceedings of the Board of Directors or committee.

Section 3.11 Resignation. A director may resign at any time by giving written notice to the Board of Directors, the President or the Secretary of the Corporation. Unless otherwise specified in the notice, the resignation shall take effect upon receipt by the Board of Directors or such officer, and acceptance of the resignation shall not be necessary.

Section 3.12 Removal of Directors. Any or all of the directors may be removed with or without cause by the stockholders.

Section 3.13 Newly Created Directorships and Vacancies. Newly created directorships resulting from an increase in the number of directors or vacancies occurring in the Board of Directors for any reason except the removal of directors without cause may be filled by a vote of the majority of the directors then in office, although less than a quorum. Vacancies occurring by reason of the removal of directors without cause shall be filled by a vote of the stockholders. A director elected to fill a newly created directorship or to fill any vacancy shall hold office until the next annual meeting of stockholders, and until his successor, if any, has been elected and qualified.

Section 3.14 Chairman. At all meetings of the Board of Directors the Chairman of the Board or, if one has not been elected or appointed or in his absence, a chairman chosen by the directors present at such meeting, shall preside.

Section 3.15 Committees Appointed by the Board of Directors. The Board of Directors may, by resolution passed by a majority of the entire Board of Directors or by written consent of all of the directors, designate one or more committees, each committee to consist of one or more of the directors. The Board may also designate one or more directors as alternate members of any committee who may replace any absent or disqualified committee member at any committee meeting. Any such committee, to the extent provided in the resolution, except as restricted by law, shall have and may exercise the powers of the Board of Directors in the management of the affairs, business and property of the Corporation, and may authorize the seal of the Corporation to be affixed to all papers which may require it.

Section 3.16 Compensation. No compensation shall be paid to directors, as such, for their services, but the Board of Directors may authorize payment of an annual retainer and/or fixed sum and expenses for attendance at each annual, regular or special meeting of the Board of Directors. Nothing herein contained shall be construed to preclude any director from serving the corporation in any other capacity and receiving compensation therefor.

ARTICLE IV
OFFICERS

Section 4.01 Offices, Election and Term. (a) At its annual meeting the Board of Directors shall elect or appoint a President and a Secretary and may, in addition, elect or appoint at any time such other officers as it may determine. Any number of offices may be held by the same person.

(b) Unless otherwise specified by the Board of Directors, each officer shall be elected or appointed to hold office until the annual meeting of the Board of Directors next following his election or appointment and until his successor, if any, has been elected or appointed and qualified, or until his earlier resignation or removal.

(c) Any officer may resign at any time by giving written notice to the Board of Directors, the President or the Secretary of the Corporation. Unless otherwise specified in the notice, the resignation shall take effect upon receipt thereof, and the acceptance of the resignation shall not be necessary to make it effective.

(d) Any officer elected or appointed by the Board of Directors may be removed by the Board of Directors with or without cause. Any vacancy occurring in any office by reason of death, resignation, removal or otherwise may be filled by the Board of Directors.

Section 4.02 Powers and Duties. The officers, agents and employees of the corporation shall each have such powers and perform such duties in the management of the affairs, property and business of the Corporation, subject to the control of and limitation by the Board of Directors, as generally pertain to their respective offices, as well as such powers and duties as may be authorized from time to time by the Board of Directors.

Section 4.03 Sureties and Bonds. If the Board of Directors shall so require, any officer, agent or employee of the Corporation shall furnish to the Corporation a bond in such sum and with such surety or sureties as the Board of Directors may direct, conditioned upon the faithful performance of his duties to the Corporation and including responsibility for negligence and for the accounting for all property, funds or securities of the corporation which may come into his hands.

ARTICLE V
CERTIFICATES AND TRANSFER OF SHARES

Section 5.01 <u>Certificates</u>. Unless otherwise provided pursuant to the General Corporation Law of the State of Delaware, the shares of stock of the Corporation shall be represented by certificates, as provided by the General Corporation Law of the State of Delaware. They shall be numbered and entered in the books of the Corporation as they are issued.

Section 5.02 <u>Lost or Destroyed Certificates</u>. The Board of Directors may in its discretion authorize the issuance of a new certificate or certificates in place of any certificate or certificates theretofore issued by the Corporation, alleged to have been lost, stolen or destroyed. As a condition of such issuance, the Board of Directors may require, either generally or in each case, the record holder of such certificates, or his legal representative, to furnish an affidavit setting forth the facts of such alleged loss, theft or destruction, together with proof of advertisement of the alleged loss, theft or destruction, and a bond with such surety and in such form and amount as the Board may specify indemnifying the Corporation, any transfer agent and registrar against any claim against any of them relating to such lost, stolen or destroyed certificates.

Section 5.03 <u>Transfer of Shares</u>. (a) Upon surrender to the Corporation or the transfer agent of the Corporation of a certificate for shares or other securities of the Corporation duly endorsed or accompanied by proper evidence of succession, assignment or authority to transfer, the corporation shall issue a new certificate to the person entitled thereto, and cancel the old certificate, except to the extent the Corporation or such transfer agent may be prevented from so doing by law, by the order or process of any court of competent jurisdiction, or under any valid restriction on transfer imposed by the Certificate of Incorporation, these By-Laws, or agreement of security holders. Every such transfer shall be entered on the transfer books of the Corporation.

(b) The Corporation shall be entitled to treat the holder of record of any share or other security of the Corporation as the holder in fact thereof and shall not be bound to recognize any equitable or other claim to or interest in such share or security on the part of any other person whether or not it shall have express or other notice thereof, except as expressly provided by law.

ARTICLE VI
INDEMNIFICATION

Section 6.01 <u>Indemnification</u>. The Corporation shall indemnify the directors, officers, agents and employees of the Corporation in the manner and to the full extent provided in the General Corporation Law of the State of Delaware. Such indemnification may be in addition to any other rights to which any person seeking indemnification may be entitled under any agreement, vote of stockholders or directors, any provision of these By-Laws or otherwise. The directors, officers, employees and agents of the Corporation shall be fully protected individually in making or refusing to make any payment or in taking or refusing to take any other action under this Article VI in reliance upon the advice of counsel.

ARTICLE VII
MISCELLANEOUS

Section 7.01 <u>Corporate Seal</u>. The seal of the Corporation shall be circular in form and bear the name of the Corporation, the year of its organization and the words, "Corporate Seal, Delaware". The seal of the certificates for shares or any corporate obligation for the payment of money, or on any other instrument, may be a facsimile, engraved, printed or otherwise reproduced.

Section 7.02 <u>Execution of Instruments</u>. All corporate instruments and documents shall be signed or countersigned, executed, and, if desired, verified or acknowledged by a proper officer or officers or such other person or persons as the Board of Directors may from time to time designate.

Section 7.03 <u>Fiscal Year</u>. The fiscal year of the Corporation shall be as determined by the Board of Directors.

ARTICLE VIII
AMENDMENTS

Section 8.01 <u>Amendments</u>. These By-Laws may be altered, amended or repealed from time to time by the stockholders or by the Board of Directors without the assent or vote of the stockholders.

ARTICLE IX
STOCKHOLDERS AGREEMENT

Section 9.01 <u>Stockholders Agreement.</u> Should the Corporation at any time, or from time to time, be party to a stockholders agreement (a "Stockholders Agreement"), then notwithstanding anything to the contrary contained in these By-Laws, in the event of any conflict between any provision of such Stockholders Agreement and any provision of these By-Laws, such conflicting provision of the Stockholders Agreement shall be incorporated herein as a By-Law and shall control.

APPLICATION FOR AUTHORITY
of
XYZ, INC.
UNDER SECTION 1304 OF THE BUSINESS CORPORATION LAW

Pursuant to the provisions of the New York Business Corporation Law, the undersigned corporation hereby applies for authority to transact business in New York, and for that purpose submits the following:

1. The name of the corporation is: XYZ, INC.

2. It is incorporated under the laws of the State of Delaware.

3. The date of its incorporation is [specify date].

4. The business which the corporation proposes to conduct in New York State is as follows:

   To engage in any lawful act or activity for which corporations may be organized under the Business Corporation Law provided that the corporation shall not engage in any act or activity which requires the consent or approval of any state official, department, board, agency or other body, without such consent or approval first being obtained.

5. The office of the corporation within the State of New York is to be located in the county of [specify county].

6. The corporation hereby designates the Secretary of State as its agent upon whom all process in any action or proceeding against it may be served within the State of New York.

7. The address to which the Secretary of State shall mall a copy of process, in any action or proceeding against the corporation which may be served upon him is: [specify address].

8. Since the date of its incorporation, the corporation has not engaged in any activity in New York.

9. The corporation hereby appoint [specify registered agent and address] as its registered agent in New York upon whom process against it may be served.

   IN WITNESS WHEREOF, XYZ, INC., the corporation hereinbefore mentioned and described has caused this certificate to be signed in its name by its (President or Vice President] this ____ day of _____, 199 and the statements contained therein are affirmed as true under penalties of perjury.

By:

**SHAREHOLDER'S AGREEMENT
AMONG
[SPECIFY PARTIES TO AGREEMENT]
AND
XYZ, INC.**

Dated:

SHAREHOLDERS AGREEMENT

AGREEMENT made this ____ day of _____ 199 , by and among ABC, SA, a <u>societe anonyme</u> organized and existing under the laws of the Republic of France, having a place of business at [specify address], John Doe, residing at [specify address], and XYZ, INC. ("The Corporation"), a corporation organized and existing under the laws of the State of Delaware, having a place of business at [specify address].

WITNESSETH:

WHEREAS, prior to the execution of this Agreement ABC, SA and John Doe (each a "Shareholder" and together the "Shareholders" caused the incorporation of the Corporation, with a total authorized capital stock of 1,000 shares of common stock, no par value per share (the "Shares"), all of which are of the same class (the "Authorized Stock");

WHEREAS, ABC, SA is in the business of manufacturing, marketing and selling [specify product], and John Doe is experienced in marketing and selling [specify product] in the United States;

WHEREAS, the parties intend the Corporation to be engaged in the marketing, distribution and sale of [specify product] in the United States and in such other activities as may be decided from time to time; and

WHEREAS, the parties believe that their best interests will be served by reaching certain agreements respecting the disposition of the Corporation's capital stock , the management of the Corporation, and other matters respecting the Corporation and its affairs as set forth below;

NOW, THEREFORE, in consideration of the premises and the mutual promises and covenants contained in this Agreement, it is agreed by and among the parties as follows:

1. <u>Organization of the Corporation</u>.

    1.1 <u>Certificate of Incorporation, By-Laws, Principal Offices</u>. The Certificate of Incorporation and By-Laws of the Corporation, copies of which are annexed hereto as Exhibits A and B, respectively, shall remain in full force and effect unless duly amended in a manner not inconsistent with the provisions hereof. The principal offices of the Corporation shall be located in the State of [specify state] or such other place or places as shall be decided in a manner not inconsistent with the provisions hereof.

2. <u>Capitalization and Share Issuance</u>.

    2.1 <u>The Shares</u>. Promptly subsequent to the execution of this Agreement, in consideration of the capital contributions set forth in Section 2.2, 60 Shares of Authorized Stock shall be issued and delivered to ABC, SA and 40 shares of Authorized Stock shall be issued and delivered to John

Doe. Upon such issuance and delivery, the total number of issued and outstanding Shares of Authorized Stock shall be 100.

2.2 **Capital Contribution.** Each of ABC, SA and John Doe shall contribute to the Corporation as a capital contribution in consideration of the foregoing issuance of Shares that consideration set forth opposite its respective name:

ABC, SA............................... $_____ cash and the execution and delivery of a promissory note in form as annexed hereto as Exhibit C.

Doe....................................... the execution and delivery of a bill of sale in form as annexed hereto as Exhibit D respecting the inventory of shoes described therein having a value as at June 30, 199 of _____

3. **Management.**

3.1 **Board of Directors.** The Board of Directors of the Corporation (the "Board") shall consist of three directors.

3.2 **Meetings of Board of Directors.** The presence in person of a majority of the directors shall constitute a quorum for the transaction of business. The Board of Directors may take action only by the affirmative vote of a majority of votes cast.

3.3 **Telephone Meetings and Written Consents.**

(a) Meetings of the Board may be conducted by means of telephone or other communications facilities as permit all persons participating in the meeting to hear each other, and a member of the Board participating in such a meeting by such means is deemed present at the meeting.

(b) Any matter to be decided by the Board may be passed by resolution signed by all of the members of the Board. Any resolution so signed is as valid and effective as if passed at a meeting duly called, constituted and held for that purpose with all directors present in person.

3.4 **Officers.** The Corporation shall have a President, Vice President and a Secretary to be nominated by the Board. The Corporation shall also have such other officers as may be elected in accordance with the provisions of the By-Laws. The specific powers and duties of the officers shall be provided for in the By-Laws or otherwise, as determined by the Board.

3.5 **Compensation.** The members of the Board and the officers of the Corporation shall serve in such capacities without compensation but with reimbursement of reasonable and necessary out-of-pocket expenses incurred in such capacities, provided that any such director or officer who is also an employee of, or consultant or other independent contractor to, the Corporation shall be entitled to receive compensation in such capacity pursuant to an employment, consulting, or other contract with the Corporation.

3.6 **Employment of Doe.** Doe shall be employed by the Corporation pursuant to an employment contract in form as annexed hereto as Exhibit E (the "Doe Employment Agreement"), subject to revision only in a manner not inconsistent with the provisions thereof and hereof.

3.7 **No Personal Liability.** No officer or director of the Corporation shall incur any personal liability arising from the corporate activities conducted by such officer or director in his capacity as such, except in the case of gross negligence or wilful misconduct. The Corporation shall indemnify its officers and directors and their heirs and legal representatives against all damages, judgments and other liabilities, including all reasonable costs, charges and expenses, including attorneys' fees and costs, and any amount paid to settle any action provided such settlement has been approved by the Corporation, incurred by them in respect of any civil, criminal or administrative action or proceeding to which such person is made a party by reason of being or having served in such capacity if (a) such person acted honestly and in good faith with a view to the best interests of the Corporation, (b) in the case of a criminal or administrative action or proceeding such person had reasonable grounds for believing that his or her conduct was lawful, and (c) whether or not such person is still serving in such capacity at the time of such action or judgment.

4. Restrictions on Stock Transfer.

4.1 **Stock Transfer Restrictions.** No Shareholder shall give, sell, assign, transfer, encumber, create a security interest in or lien on, place in trust, bequeath or otherwise dispose of in any manner whatsoever (individually and collectively, "Transfer") all or any part of his Shares, and such Shares shall not be transferred on the books of the Corporation, unless and until he has obtained the prior written consent of all of the other Shareholders (the "Other Shareholders"), or has otherwise complied with the requirements of this Article 4.

4.2 **Right of First Refusal.** If a Shareholder (a "Transferor") desires to Transfer all or any part of his Shares, he shall give to the Other Shareholders and the Corporation written notice (the "Notice") of this desire including written evidence of a bona fide arm's length offer from a third party (the "Third Party") to purchase such Shares (the "Offered Shares") plus all of the other issued and outstanding Shares of Authorized Stock (the "Other Shares") for a price and on such other terms and conditions as are specified in such writing (the "Terms and Conditions") . Such Notice shall be deemed an "Offer" on the part of the Transferor for a period of 45 days to sell to the Corporation and to the Other Shareholders all of the Offered Shares. The Corporation shall have the first option to purchase all or any part of the Offered Shares on the Terms and Conditions on a per Share basis. A decision by the Corporation with respect to such Offer shall be made by the Board acting unanimously, except, however, not including the director who is, or who is nominated by, the Transferor, if any. Each of the Other Shareholders shall have the option to accept the offer to purchase all or any part of any of the offered Shares with respect to which the Corporation has not accepted the Offer (the "Rejected Shares") in an amount equal to its proportionate ownership of the Shares (excluding Offered Shares) on the Terms and Conditions on a per Share basis. If any Other Shareholder does not desire to purchase its proportionate share of the Rejected Shares, then the other Shareholders shall have the right to purchase such Rejected Shares in a manner similarly proportionate on the Terms and Conditions on a per Share basis. During such 45-day period the Corporation and the Other Shareholders shall keep each other informed as to each of their intentions with respect to the offer so that each may, within such 45-day period, exercise the rights granted in this Section 4.2. For a period of 15 days commencing on the expiration of the foregoing 45-day period, the Transferor may Transfer to the Third Party the Offered Shares with respect to which neither the Corporation nor the Other Shareholders has accepted an offer (the "Third Party Transfer Shares") provided that a simultaneous Transfer is made to the Third Party of such number of Other Shares as the holders thereof desire to Transfer on the Terms and Conditions on a per Share basis. Subsequent to such 15-day period the Transferor shall be required to provide the Corporation and the Other Shareholders with a new opportunity, in accordance with the procedures set forth in this Section 4.2, before Transferring the Third Party Transfer Shares. The failure of the Corporation or the Other Shareholders to accept an Offer pursuant to this Section 4.2 shall not constitute a waiver of any of the provisions of this Agreement with respect to any proposed subsequent Transfer of Shares.

4.3 Agreement Required. It shall be a condition of any Shareholder's Transfer of any Shares to a Third Party, except to the extent that such Transfer is of all issued and outstanding Shares of Authorized Stock, that (i) such Third Party shall have delivered to the Corporation and the Other Shareholders an agreement, in form and substance reasonably satisfactory to the Corporation and the other Shareholders, assuming all obligations of the Transferor under this Agreement and agreeing to abide by all of the provisions of this Agreement; and (ii) such Third Party shall possess, to the reasonable satisfaction of the Corporation and the other Shareholders, sufficient creditworthiness and other ability to enable the fulfillment of obligations pursuant to this Agreement.

4.4 Permitted Dispositions. Subject to Section 4.3, but notwithstanding any other provisions of this Agreement, ABC, SA shall be entitled to Transfer any and all of its Shares, at any time and from time to time, to any corporation or other entity which would constitute an "Affiliate" of ABC, SA as such term is defined in Regulation C of the Securities Act of 1933.

4.5 Transfer on the Termination of Employment, Death or Disability of Doe. In the event of the termination of employment under the Doe Employment Agreement or any successor thereto, or the death or disability (as defined below) of Doe, he or his estate or his representative, as the case may be, shall sell to the Corporation, and the Corporation shall purchase, all of the Shares owned by Doe, and if Doe or any nominee of his is serving as a director or officer of the Corporation such service shall immediately terminate. The purchase price for such Shares shall be the fair market value of such Shares as determined by the Corporation's auditors, such determination to be conclusive and binding for such purpose. For the purposes of this Section 4.5 disability shall have the same meaning provided in the policy of buy-sell insurance referred to in Section 5.4; provided, however, that if no such insurance policy is in effect at the time the determination of disability must be made, disability shall mean a condition preventing Doe from performing his duties under the Doe Employment Agreement, or any successor thereto, in a manner satisfactory to the Corporation, as determined by the Board.

5. Covenants.

5.1 Preservation of Corporate Existence and Compliance with Laws and Regulations. The parties shall cause to be done all things necessary to preserve, renew and keep in full force and effect and good standing the corporate existence, rights, licenses, permits and franchises of the

Corporation, and shall cause the Corporation to comply in all material respects with all applicable laws and regulations.

5.2 <u>Budgets</u>. The Corporation shall prepare, subject to approval by the Board, budgets for ____ month periods. Each such budget shall be prepared and approved during the ____ month preceding the period to which such budget relates.

5.3 <u>Financial Statements</u>. The Corporation shall cause to be prepared and delivered to each Shareholder monthly, quarterly and annual income statements and balance sheets ("Financial Statements") . The monthly and quarterly Financial Statements shall be delivered to each Shareholder within ____ days of the end of the period to which they relate, and the annual Financial Statements shall be delivered to each shareholder within ____ days of the end of the year to which they relate.

5.4 <u>Buy-Sell Insurance</u>. The Corporation, unless otherwise determined by the Board, shall at all times keep in full force and effect buy-sell insurance respecting Doe as insured naming the Corporation as owner beneficiary in such amounts, and on such other terms and conditions, as the Board shall decide. Such amounts and other terms and conditions shall be reviewed as frequently as may be necessary to provide for insurance proceeds in adequate amounts to satisfy the requirements of Section 4.5.

5.5 <u>Confidentiality</u>. Each party hereby covenants and agrees (a) not to disclose, except in accordance with any future agreement made by the parties respecting such disclosure, to any person other than the other parties, any information acquired in its dealings with the others, and (b) to exercise due care when exchanging or in any way transferring information proprietary to any party. In recognition of the importance of the confidentiality agreement contained in this Section 5.5, and without limiting the generality of the provisions of Section 6.2, the parties shall have the right to enforce their rights under this Section 5.5 by means of an action for injunctive relief and for specific performance as well as to pursue any other remedy or remedies available in any action at law or at equity.

5.6 <u>Further Assurances</u>. Each Shareholder shall from time to time execute and deliver all such further documents and instruments and do all acts and things as the other Shareholders or the Board may reasonably require to carry out effectively or better evidence or perfect the full intent and meaning of this Agreement and to further the operations and activities of the Corporation.

6. <u>Miscellaneous</u>.

6.1 <u>Uncertificated Shares; Stock Certificate Legend</u>. The Corporation shall be authorized to issue some or all of the Authorized Stock as uncertificated shares pursuant to Section 158 of the General Corporation Law of the State of Delaware. To the extent certificates representing Shares of Authorized Stock shall nevertheless be issued, all such certificates shall have endorsed upon them a legend substantially as follows:

"The shares represented by this certificate have not been registered under the Securities Act of 1933, as amended, or under any state securities law, and may not be sold or otherwise transferred in the absence of such registration or an exemption therefrom under such Act or applicable state law. Any proposed reliance on any such exemption is subject to the opinion of legal counsel to the Corporation that such exemption is available. Such shares may be sold or otherwise transferred only in compliance with the conditions specified in an Agreement dated as of [specify date], by and among ABC, SA, John Doe, and the Corporation, a complete and correct copy of which is available for inspection at the principal office of the Corporation. The Corporation is empowered to issue stop transfer instructions in connection with the foregoing restrictions."

6.2 <u>Specific Performance; Other Rights</u>. The parties recognize that various of the rights granted under this Agreement are unique and, accordingly, the parties shall, in addition to such other remedies as may be available to them at law or in equity, have the right to enforce their rights under this Agreement by actions for injunctive relief and specific performance.

6.3 <u>Notices.</u> All Notices and other communications under this Agreement shall be in writing and shall be deemed to have been given upon acknowledgement of receipt of transmission by telefax, telex, telegram or other means of electronic communication, or ten days following first class certified airmail posting, addressed to all parties at their respective addresses set forth at the beginning of this Agreement, or at such other address or addresses as may be designated for such purpose from time to time.

6.4 <u>Prior Agreements; Construction; Entire Agreement</u>. This Agreement constitutes the entire agreement of the parties with respect to the subject matter hereof and supersedes all prior agreements and understandings between them as to such subject matter. The headings contained in this Agreement are for convenience only and shall not in any way affect the meaning or interpretation of any term or provision of this Agreement. References to Sections and Exhibits in this Agreement are to the Sections and Exhibits to this Agreement. References to "parties" in this Agreement are to the parties to this Agreement. The Exhibits are part of this Agreement. In this Agreement, to the extent the context requires, the singular includes the plural, the plural the singular, the masculine gender includes both male and female referents, and the word "or" is used in the disjunctive and conjunctive sense. The word "person" as used in this Agreement includes, without limitation, an individual, corporation, partnership, trust, association, business, firm or other entity.

6.5 <u>Waivers and Further Agreements</u>. The waiver of any term or condition of this Agreement shall not operate as a waiver of any other breach of such term or condition or of any other term or condition, nor shall any failure to enforce any provision hereof operate as a waiver of such provision or of any other provision hereof.

6.6 <u>Amendments</u>. This Agreement may not be amended nor shall any waiver, change, modification, consent or discharge be effected except by an instrument in writing executed by and on behalf of all the parties.

6.7 <u>Assignment; Successors and Assigns</u>. Each party enters into this Agreement in reliance upon the other party's specific personal qualities including ability, skill, trust, experience, character and judgment, and no party shall assign, mortgage or pledge this Agreement or any of the rights or obligations contained in this Agreement. This Agreement shall be binding upon and inure to the benefit of the parties and their respective successors and permitted assigns.

6.8 <u>Severability</u>. If any provision of this Agreement shall be held or deemed by a final order of a competent authority to be invalid, inoperative or unenforceable, such circumstance shall not have the effect of rendering any other provision or provisions herein contained invalid, inoperative or unenforceable, but this Agreement shall be construed as if such invalid, inoperative or unenforceable provision had never been certified herein so as to give full force and effect to the remaining such terms and provisions.

6.9 <u>Counterparts</u>. This Agreement may be executed in two or more counterparts, each of which shall be deemed an original, but all of which together shall constitute one and the same instrument.

6.10 <u>Governing Law</u>. This Agreement shall be governed by and construed, interpreted and enforced in accordance with the law of the State of [specify state] without regard to the law of the conflicts of law of such State.

6.11 <u>No Rights of Third Parties</u>. This Agreement sets forth the relationship among the parties, and shall not confer any rights or privileges on any third parties.

6.12 <u>Books and Records</u>. The Shareholders, upon reasonable notice to the Corporation, shall have access to the books and records of the Corporation, with reasonable frequency, for the purpose of examination and inspection during normal business hours at the offices where such books and records are maintained.

IN WITNESS WHEREOF, the parties have executed this Agreement as of the date first above written.

By:

Name:
Title:

NON-NEGOTIABLE DEMAND
PROMISSORY NOTE

[specify dollar amount of note]

[specify location]
[specify date]

FOR VALUE RECEIVED, ABC, SA, a societe anonyme organized and existing under of the Republic of France, hereby promises to pay XYZ, INC. a corporation organized and existing under the laws of the State of Delaware the principal sum of [specify amount] with interest accrued thereon at a rate per annum equal to [the prime commercial lending rate of ___], as in effect from time to time, in accordance with the provisions hereof.

1. <u>Payment</u>. The principal amount of this Note or any part thereof, along with all interest accrued and unpaid thereon, shall be payable to XYZ, INC. by ABC, SA within thirty days of XYZ, INC's written demand upon ABC, SA therefor.

2. <u>Prepayment</u>. ABC, SA may prepay this Note in whole or in part, at any time, and from time to time, without premium or penalty.

3. <u>Governing Law</u>. This Note shall be construed, interpreted and enforced in accordance with the law of the State of [specify state] without regard to the law of the conflicts of laws of such State.

4. <u>Return of Note</u>. This Note shall be returned to ABC, SA upon the payment in full of the amount of this Note.

5. <u>Non-Negotiability</u>. This Note is non-negotiable and may not otherwise be transferred.

IN WITNESS WHEREOF, ABC, SA has caused this Note to be duly executed and delivered as of the day and year first above written.

By:

Name:

Title:

ASSIGNMENT AND BILL OF SALE

Pursuant to a shareholders agreement of even date herewith, by and among ABC, SA, a <u>societe anonyme</u> organized and existing under the laws of The Republic of France, having a place of business at [specify address], John Doe, residing at [specify address], and XYZ, INC., a corporation organized and existing under the laws of the State of Delaware, having a place of business at [specify address] (The Corporation"), and in consideration of the issuance to Doe of 40 shares of the Corporation's Common Stock, with no par value, Doe does hereby assign, sell, transfer and convey to the Corporation all of Doe's right, title and interest as of the date hereof in and to the property and assets of which are listed on Schedule I hereto (the "Assets").

TO HAVE AND TO HOLD, the Assets hereby conveyed, all and singular, unto the Corporation, to and for its use and benefit.

Doe represents and warrants to the Corporation that he has good and valid title to and is the lawful owner of the assets, and that Doe has the right to sell the Assets free and clear of all liens, claims and encumbrances.

Doe will, at any time and from time to time after the date hereof, upon the reasonable request of the Corporation, do, execute, acknowledge and deliver, or will cause to be done, executed, acknowledged or delivered, all such further acts, deeds, assignments, transfers, conveyances, powers of attorney or assurances as may be required for the better transferring, assigning, conveying and confirming to the Corporation, or for aiding and assisting in reducing to possession by the Corporation, any of the Assets or rights being purchased hereunder, or to vest in the Corporation good, valid and marketable title to such Assets and rights.

This Assignment and Bill of Sale shall inure to the benefit of the Corporation and shall be binding upon Doe and his successors and assigns.

IN WITNESS WHEREOF, Doe has caused this Assignment and Bill of Sale to be duly executed this ____ day of _____, 199 .

By:

DISTRIBUTION AND LICENSE AGREEMENT

THIS AGREEMENT, made as of [specify date] by and between ABC, SA, a societe anonyme organized and existing under the laws of the Republic of France, with an office at [specify address] and XYZ, INC., a corporation organized and existing under the laws of the State of Delaware, with an office at [specify address].

WITNESSETH:

WHEREAS, ABC, SA is in the business of manufacturing, marketing and selling [specify product] (the "Product") in France for distribution there and for export internationally, and possesses all rights to the trademarks, trade names, copyrights, and designs identified in Exhibit A hereto;

WHEREAS, XYZ, INC. is in the business of importing the Product into the United States for marketing, sale and distribution there; and

WHEREAS, ABC, SA and XYZ, INC. (collectively the "Parties") desire to enter into a distribution and license agreement on the terms set forth herein (the "Agreement"),

NOW, THEREFORE, in consideration of the mutual promises contained herein, and for other good and valuable consideration, the receipt and sufficiency of which is hereby acknowledged, the Parties agree as follows:

1. <u>Grant of Rights; Territory; Non-Exclusivity</u>.

1.01 ABC, SA hereby appoints XYZ, INC. as its non-exclusive distributor for the term of this Agreement for the importation, marketing, sale and distribution of the Product in the fifty states of the United States, the District of Columbia, Puerto Rico, the United States Virgin Islands and all other United States territories and possessions, and duty free markets located therein (the "Territory") and XYZ, INC. hereby accepts such appointment.

1.02 ABC, SA hereby grants to a non-exclusive license to XYZ, INC. within the Territory in connection with its activities hereunder the trademarks, trade names, copyrights and designs concerning the Product as identified in Exhibit A hereto. In consideration of this license XYZ, INC. shall pay to ABC, SA eighteen percent of the invoice price of all Product purchased by XYZ, INC. pursuant hereto. Such license fee shall be paid by to ABC, SA quarterly, in French francs, within 30 days following the end of each fiscal quarter to which such fee relates.

1.03 XYZ, INC. shall pay to DEF, Inc., a French <u>societe anonyme</u> and majority shareholder of ABC, SA, $1.00 for each pair of the Product sold by XYZ, INC., up to a total of $150,000, provided, however, that each such payment shall be made in the French franc equivalent of such amount as in effect at the time of payment, up to the French franc equivalent of $150,000 as in effect at the time each amount is attained.

1.04 To the extent that ABC, SA sells Product into the Territory other than to XYZ, INC., ABC, SA shall pay to XYZ, SA five percent of the Net Sales (as defined below) respecting such Product. Such payment shall be paid by ABC, SA to XYZ, INC. quarterly within 30 days following the end of each fiscal quarter to which such fee relates. Net Sales shall mean actual receipts received by ABC, SA from the sale of Product to its purchasers in the Territory after any applicable discounts are applied and exclusive of amounts received for taxes, handling, shipping, insurance and similar costs. ABC, SA may not sell Product directly to any person in the Territory who at the time of such sale is a customer of XYZ, INC. except with the consent of Doe.

2. Term of Agreement; Renewal.

2.01 The initial term of this Agreement shall commence upon the execution hereof, and shall, provided this Agreement has not previously been terminated, continue until the first anniversary of the date hereof (the "Initial Term").

2.02 Upon the expiration of the Initial Term, and provided this Agreement has not previously been terminated, the term of this Agreement may continue for an indefinite term subject to termination by either Party upon not less than six (6) months' prior written notice to the other Party of its decision so to terminate.

2.03 Whenever use is made hereinof the word "term" to refer to the term of this Agreement, such word shall be deemed to refer to the Initial Term or any subsequent renewal or extension thereof.

3. Purchase and Sales; Price; Delivery.

3.01 During the term of this Agreement, XYZ, INC. shall, from time to time, submit to ABC, SA purchase orders for quantities of the Product. Upon ABC, SA's receipt of any such order, ABC, SA shall promptly advise XYZ, INC. of ABC, SA's acceptance or rejection of the order. In the event of any conflict between the terms of such order and this Agreement, the terms of this Agreement shall prevail.

3.02 Quantities of the Product sold to XYZ, INC. pursuant ABC, SA's acceptance of orders pursuant to Section 3.01 shall be delivered to XYZ, INC. Upon such delivery by ABC, SA, all risk of loss and damage shall be borne by XYZ, INC.

3.03 The initial prices of the various Product shall be as set forth in a writing to be delivered to XYZ, INC. by ABC, SA upon, or prior to, the execution of this Agreement. At any time, and from time to time, shall provide XYZ, INC. with written notice of the prices of the various Product to be effective as of the delivery of such notice, and to remain effective until the next notice is given as provided herein.

3.04 Payment for the Product delivered to XYZ, INC. as provided in Section 3.03 shall be made by XYZ, INC. to ABC, SA by direct bank-to-bank wire transfer in French francs to an account designated by ABC, SA, or by such other means as ABC, SA may advise XYZ, INC. from time to time, payable [_____ days] subsequent to the date of invoice for the Product so delivered. Any payment outstanding subsequent to the due date shall bear interest from the due date until the date of payment at the compounded rate charged to ABC, SA by [_____ Bank] in France on short term unsecured loans as may be in effect from time to time.

4. <u>Duties of XYZ, INC.</u> Without limiting the generality of the other provisions of this Agreement imposing obligations upon XYZ, INC., XYZ, INC. shall fully and faithfully carry out the following duties:

4.01 XYZ, INC. shall utilize its best efforts to promote, extend and maximize sales of the Product, and the reputation of the Product, throughout the Territory, and shall conduct its business, and otherwise act, in all matters concerning ABC, SA and the Product, in a manner which will benefit and enhance ABC, SA's and the Product's interests and reputation.

4.02 XYZ, INC. shall maintain at least ____ months' inventory of the Product, and shall encourage its purchasers to maintain at least ____ months' inventory of the Product.

4.03 XYZ, INC. shall provide ABC, SA with written reports respecting the Product, broken down by states in the United States and appropriate geographic entities outside the states of the United States within the Territory, setting forth (a) on a monthly basis (i) XYZ, INC.'s billings to its customers and (ii) depletions by its customers (sales by XYZ, INC.'s customers to their purchasers as provided to XYZ, INC. by its customers); and (b) on a quarterly basis (i) inventories of XYZ, INC. and its customers within the Territory and (ii) such current information as may be available to XYZ, INC. concerning competition within the Territory.

4.04 XYZ shall sell the Product in the Territory only under the trademark and trade name normally used for the Product by ABC, SA and, except to the extent otherwise agreed in writing by ABC, SA, only in the packaging and in the same condition as that in which the Product is dispatched by ABC, SA and with all packaging intact.

4.05 Except to the extent otherwise provided in Section 1.02, XYZ, INC. acknowledges the right of ABC, SA to all patents, trademarks, trade names, copyrights and designs concerning the Product. XYZ, INC. shall not apply for registration or other rights to any of the foregoing, or the rights to anything similar to any of the foregoing, and all literature supplied by ABC, SA concerning ABC, SA or the Product shall be and remain the property of ABC, SA and no rights to use such property shall accrue to XYZ, INC. as a result of this Agreement other than as authorized by ABC, SA.

4.06 XYZ, INC. shall inform ABC, SA of any infringement or threatened infringement of any trademark, trade name, copyright or design concerning the Product in the Territory, and in any legal proceeding or other effort taken by, or on behalf of, ABC, SA concerning any such infringement or threatened infringement, XYZ, INC. shall provide ABC, SA or anyone acting on ABC, SA's behalf whatever assistance ABC, SA shall reasonably request, provided, however, that XYZ, INC. shall have no responsibility for incurring legal fees or other costs with respect to rendering such assistance.

4.07 XYZ, INC. shall, on or before [specify date] of each year, notify ABC, SA in writing of its anticipated purchase requirements, broken down by month, for each of the Product during the coming year (such notice of anticipated requirements shall not operate as, or be deemed to be, a guarantee by XYZ, INC. to attainment of such volume, or a guarantee by ABC, SA as to the availability of such volume).

4.08 XYZ, INC. shall comply with all applicable Federal, State and local laws and regulations.

4.09 XYZ, INC. shall bring to the attention of ABC, SA any information received by XYZ, INC. which is likely to be of interest, use or benefit to ABC, SA in relation to the marketing of the Product in the Territory.

4.10 XYZ, INC. shall not, in the event of damage to any of the Product which affects the contents thereof, or renders the packaging unsightly or of less than first class condition, sell or otherwise dispose of such Product or permit the same to become the property of any insurer, carrier or salvage company, except in accordance with prior written instruction from ABC, SA. XYZ, INC. shall be credited by ABC, SA for ABC, SA's invoiced price to XYZ, INC. of such Product.

5. <u>Duties of ABC, SA</u> Without limiting the generality of the other provisions of this Agreement imposing obligations upon ABC, SA, ABC, SA shall fully and faithfully carry out the following duties:

5.01 ABC, SA shall fill XYZ, INC.'s orders for the Product which are accepted by ABC, SA pursuant to Section 3.01 in accordance with the specifications in each such order except to the extent that ABC, SA is unable to do so as a result of circumstances reasonably beyond the control of ABC, SA.

5.02 ABC, SA shall take reasonably necessary steps to ensure that deliveries of the Product under this Agreement will be of good quality, properly packaged in France, in conformity with applicable laws, regulations and requirements in effect within the Territory, as ABC, SA shall be notified by XYZ, INC. ABC, SA's obligation with respect to this Section 5.02 and any breach thereof shall be limited solely to replacement of the Product except that, at XYZ, INC.'s option exercised by written notice to ABC, SA, ABC, SA will credit XYZ, INC. for the Product at ABC, SA's invoiced price to XYZ, INC. rather than replace it, provided that XYZ, INC. complies with ABC, SA's instructions as to the disposition of the Product with respect to which XYZ, INC. is to receive such credit. The foregoing shall be XYZ, INC.'s sole remedy and ABC, SA's sole obligation with respect to the provisions of this Section 5.02; provided, however, that the remedy granted to XYZ, INC pursuant to this Section 5.02 shall not be available does not provide ABC, SA with written notice of XYZ, INC.'s alleged claim to entitlement to such remedy as soon as XYZ, INC. learns of, or should have learned of, facts which would give rise to such alleged claim. THERE ARE NO OTHER WARRANTIES, EXPRESS OR IMPLIED, INCLUDING ANY WARRANTY OF MERCHANTABILITY OR OF FITNESS FOR ANY PARTICULAR PURPOSE.

5.03 ABC, SA shall not be liable for any damages for business interruption, injury to property, increased expenses of operation, lost sales, lost profits, or any other incidental or consequential damages of any kind, whether based on warranty, contract, negligence, strict liability or otherwise.

5.04 ABC, SA shall take reasonably necessary steps to safeguard XYZ, INC.'s rights granted herein including, but at ABC, SA's sole discretion the taking of such steps as my be available to ABC, SA to prevent the infringement of those rights by any company or other person and to prevent the infringement of any of ABC, SA's patents, trademarks, trade names, emblems, designs or other similar industrial or commercial property rights within the Territory.

5.05 ABC, SA shall provide promptly to XYZ, INC. such material and other information as may reasonably be required to enable XYZ, INC to carry out its obligation under Section 4.08.

5.06 ABC, SA shall bear the reasonable cost of any disposition of the Product which XYZ, INC. may be obligated to effect under Section 4.10.

6. <u>Advertising and Promotion</u>.

6.01 ABC, SA and XYZ, INC. shall consult with each other to prepare and execute annual marketing and promotional plans and programs, and otherwise to determine when and how the Product shall be advertised in the Territory, what expenditures should be made for advertising and sales promotion purposes, how and through which media such expenditures should be made, and who among advertising agencies and public relations firms should be retained, provided that with respect to all of the foregoing, ABC, SA shall have sole decision authority.

7. <u>Confidentiality</u>.

Neither Party shall at any time divulge or make known to any company or other person, directly or indirectly, any Confidential Information concerning the other Party. For the purposes of this Section 7, "Confidential Information" shall mean information disclosed or obtained during the term of this Agreement by ABC, SA as a result of or related to its relationship to XYZ, INC. not generally know by, or otherwise available to, ABC, SA or XYZ, INC., as applicable, or to the public or any company or other person, concerning ABC, SA's or XYZ, INC.'s, as applicable, products, processes, services, customer or vendor lists or cost and pricing policies, including, but not limited. to, information relating to research, development, inventions, manufacture, purchasing, accounting, marketing, merchandising, selling, specifications, formulas, methods and techniques.

8. <u>Force Majeure</u>.

An "Event of Force Majeure" shall mean any Act of God, war, riot, mobilization, embargo, governmental rules, regulations or decrees, drought, typhoon, flood, fire, earthquake, strike, lockout, labor disturbance,. difference with workers, accident to machinery, failure of sources of supply of materials ordinarily used for the production of the Product, shortage of ships, or any other event beyond the control of the Party affected, whether similar or dissimilar to any of the foregoing. ABC, SA shall not be required to deliver any Product if prevented from so doing by an Event of Force

Majeure. XYZ, INC. shall not be required to accept delivery of any if prevented by an Event of Force Majeure, except with respect to any delivery already in transit on the date written notice is received by ABC, SA pursuant to the subsequent sentence of this Section 8. Each Party shall promptly notify the other in writing of the existence of an Event of Force Majeure and, to the extent possible, of the duration of any disability caused thereby. ABC, SA is not, however, thereby relieved from making delivery, or XYZ, INC. from accepting delivery, pursuant to this Agreement when the Event of Force Majeure no longer exists. XYZ, INC.'s failure to accept delivery or to make payment for any quantity of the Product pursuant to this Section 8 shall, at ABC, SA's option, release ABC, SA from making any further deliveries until the Event of Force Majeure no longer exists.

9. <u>Termination</u>.

9.01 Either Party may immediately terminate this Agreement, without prejudice to whatever other remedies it may have, by giving notice in writing to the other Party of its decision so to terminate, upon the occurrence of any of the following:

(a) If the other Party shall be in breach of any of the provisions of this Agreement, and shall not remedy such breach to the satisfaction of the terminating Party within thirty (30) days after the service of written notice of and requirement to remedy such breach served by the terminating Party and referring to this Section 9.01(a), unless such breach is not capable of being remedied, in which event this Agreement may be terminated forthwith by serving written notice thereof referring to this Section 9.01(a);

(b) If (i) the other Party shall become insolvent or admit in writing its inability to pay its debts as they mature; (ii) the other Party shall make any assignment to or for the benefit of creditors or seek to obtain an extension of time within which to pay obligations; (iii) the other Party suffers any distress or execution to be levied on a substantial part of its property; (iv) the other Party applies for, consents to, or acquiesces in the appointment of a trustee, receiver or custodian for it or any of its property; (v) in the absence of an application, consent or acquiescence, a trustee, receiver or custodian is appointed for the other Party or any of its property; or (vi) any bankruptcy, reorganization, debt arrangement, or other proceeding under any bankruptcy or insolvency law, or any dissolution or liquidation proceeding, is instituted by or against the other Party;

(c) If the other Party, directly or indirectly, becomes controlled by any company or other person other than any company or other person which may have such control as of the date of the execution it of this Agreement.

9.02 Upon any termination of this Agreement (a) XYZ, INC. shall (i) immediately cease use of the property licensed to it hereunder and identified in Exhibit A hereto and in this regard shall take all corporate action necessary to change its corporate name in compliance with this provision, and (ii) promptly return or otherwise dispose of as directed by ABC, SA, pamphlets, catalogues, advertising materials, specifications and other materials which XYZ, INC. may have in its possession or under its control relating to ABC, SA or the Product, and (b) ABC, SA shall repurchase, or XYZ, INC. shall sell to any person as directed by ABC, SA, all inventory of the Product held by XYZ, INC. at the time of such termination for a purchase price equal to ABC, SA's original cost of such inventory of the Product pursuant to ABC, SA invoice. XYZ, INC. shall then deliver the inventory so purchased to any person or place as directed by ABC, SA, provided, however, that XYZ, INC. shall not be responsible for paying the cost of such delivery.

10. **Miscellaneous**.

10.01 **No Assignment**. Each Party enters into this Agreement in reliance upon the other Party's specific personal qualities including ability, skill, trust, experience, credit, character and judgment, and neither Party shall assign, mortgage or charge this Agreement or any of the rights or obligations contained in this Agreement.

10.02 **Construction; Entire Agreement; Applicable Law**.
This Agreement constitutes the entire agreement and understanding of the Parties with respect to its subject matter, supersedes all prior negotiations, understandings and agreements concerning the subject matter thereof, and shall be construed and interpreted in accordance with the laws of the State of [specify state], without regard to the law of the conflicts of law of said State. Any headings in this Agreement are for convenience only and not intended to influence its construction. In this Agreement, unless the context requires otherwise, the singular includes the plural, and the plural includes the singular, and all references to Sections shall be to sections of this Agreement.

10.03 **Counterparts**. This Agreement may be executed in counterparts, each of which shall be deemed an original, and which together shall constitute one and the same instrument.

10.04 **Amendment and Modification**. This Agreement may not be amended or otherwise modified except by a writing referring to this Agreement duly executed by both of the Parties.

10.05 **Notices**. Any written notice or other communication required or permitted hereunder shall be deemed given when delivered personally or deposited in the mails of the country of origin of such written notice by air mail, registered or certified, or its equivalent in the country of origin, postage prepaid, addressed as follows, or when sent by telefax providing proof of receipt is received by the sender:

    (a)   If sent to ABC, SA to:
              [specify address, contact]

    (b)   If sent to XYZ, INC. to:
              [specify address, contact]

or to such other address or telefax number as may be furnished in writing in such manner by either Party. Any written notice or other communication given in any manner other than as provided in this Section 10.05 shall be deemed to have been given only when actually received.

10.06 **Further Assurances**. The Parties shall execute and deliver such documents and take such other actions as may reasonably be required, from time to time, in order to effectuate the purpose and to carry out the terms of this Agreement.

10.07 <u>No Waiver.</u> The failure or omission by either Party to insist upon or to enforce any of the terms hereof shall not be deemed a waiver by such Party of the right to protest or terminate this Agreement for breach of any such terms, unless such waiver shall be in a writing referring to this Agreement and duly executed by such Party. A waiver of any right on one occasion shall not constitute a bar to, or a waiver of, any such right on any future occasion.

10.08 <u>Relationship Between the Parties</u>. The relationship between the Parties is as between principals and not as between principal and agent. Neither Party shall have the authority to bind the other in any manner whatsoever, and neither Party shall hold itself out, or otherwise describe itself as, agent for the other by way of correspondence, document, nameplate, sign or any other oral or written notice or other communication.

10.09 <u>Survival.</u> The provisions of Section 7 shall survive any termination of this Agreement as a separate agreement of the Parties.

IN WITNESS WHEREOF, the undersigned, have caused this Agreement to be executed as of the date first written above.

By:

Name:

Title:

By:

Name:

Title:

MANAGEMENT, ADMINISTRATIVE AND TECHNICAL SERVICES AGREEMENT

This Agreement made this _____ day of _____ 199_ between DEF, Inc., a <u>societe anonyme</u> organized and existing under the laws of the Republic of France, with a place of business at [specify address] and XYZ, INC., a Corporation organized and existing under the laws of the State of Delaware (the "Corporation") with a place of business at [specify address].

WITNESSETH

WHEREAS, DEF, Inc., through certain of its affiliates, is in the business of manufacturing, marketing and selling [specify product] in France for distribution there and for export internationally; and

WHEREAS XYZ, INC. is in the business of importing [specify product] into the United States for marketing, sale and distribution there; and

WHEREAS, DEF, Inc., and certain of its affiliates, has certain resources and experience which enable it to provide benefit to XYZ, Inc. in its business activities; and

WHEREAS, DEF, Inc. and XYZ, INC. (collectively the "Parties") desire to enter into this agreement on the terms set forth herein,

NOW, THEREFORE, in consideration of the mutual promises contained herein, and for good and valuable consideration, the receipt and sufficiency of which is hereby acknowledged, the Parties agree as follows:

1. <u>Services to be Provided</u>. DEF, Inc., directly or indirectly as provided in Section 1.2, agrees to provide to XYZ, INC. from time to time, the following services (the "Services") as reasonably required and requested by XYZ, INC., and subject to the availability of resources:

    (a) general management services, including (i) the services of executive, operating, legal and financial officers and other personnel; (ii) advice concerning the preparation of budgets, forecasts, capital expenditures, financing, and long range strategic planning; and (iii) such other general management services as may from time to time reasonably be requested by XYZ, Inc.; and

    (b) general administrative and technical services, advice and direction, including (i) accounting, including cost accounting, inventory control, tax compliance and reporting systems services; (ii) legal, trademark and patent advice, including advice with respect to compliance with applicable legal regulations, patent applications and prosecutions; (iii) market servicing, product pricing and costs controls and evaluations; (iv) preparation of advertising and publicity literature and other materials; (v) providing, training and supervising sales representatives and support staff and providing guidelines and policies for sales representatives and other direction, as may be necessary, for promoting sales; (vi) compensation planning, pension, if any, and human resources services; (vii) purchasing services; (viii) import export advice; (ix) preparation of reporting forms; and (x) such other general administrative and technical services as may from time to time reasonably be requested by XYZ, INC.

1.1. It is understood that DEF, Inc. may provide any of the Services directly or through any of its affiliates, professional advisors or other representatives. (The entity providing such Services is hereinafter referred to as the "Services Provider".)

1.2. The Services Provider shall, in its provision of Services hereunder, utilize a standard of duty and care equal to that of a reasonably prudent person acting on its own behalf in similar circumstances.

2. <u>Payment; Reimbursement of Expenses</u>. In consideration for the provision of Services under this agreement, DEF, Inc. shall be entitled to payment from XYZ, INC. as follows:

(a) two percent of the invoice price of the Product (as defined in the Distribution and License Agreement of even date herewith between ABC, SA and XYZ, INC.) purchased and paid for pursuant to the Distribution and License Agreement, it being agreed that the variety and frequency of the Services to be provided make difficult a calculation of a charge therefor otherwise than on the basis of a percentage of sales as provided herein; and

(b) reimbursement of reasonable out-of-pocket expenses actually and necessarily incurred for travel of the Services Provider's personnel in connection with providing Services hereunder. Such travel costs shall include hotel accommodation and meals and local transportation during the period services are provided.

2.1. DEF, Inc. shall, on a quarterly basis, invoice for Services provided. All invoices and payments shall be rendered in French francs. Payment shall be due 30 days after invoicing.

3. <u>Term and Termination</u>. The term of this agreement shall begin on the date hereof and shall continue thereafter unless DEF, Inc. or XYZ, INC. shall serve notice to the other in writing of its decision to terminate the provisions of this agreement, in which event such agreement shall terminate at the conclusion of the fiscal quarter in which such notice is given.

3.1. In addition to the provisions of Section 3 hereof, the provisions of this agreement may be terminated immediately upon written notice as follows:

(a) by either Party in the event the other Party shall fail to perform any of its obligations hereunder and shall fail to remedy such non-performance within 30 days after written demand therefor;

(b) by either Party, upon notice to the other Party, in the event that the other Party shall be declared insolvent or bankrupt or make any assignment or other arrangement for the benefit of its creditors or to be dissolved or liquidated.

3.2. Upon termination of the provisions of this agreement all rights and obligations hereunder shall forthwith terminate, except for rights and obligations in respect of payment for Services and reimbursement pursuant to Section 2.

IN WITNESS WHEREOF, the Parties have caused this Agreement to be duly executed this ____ day of _____, 199 .

By:

Name:

Title:

By:

Name:

Title:

EMPLOYMENT AGREEMENT

THIS AGREEMENT made this _____ day, of _____, 199 between XYZ, INC., a Delaware corporation with a place of business at [specify address] ("Employer"), and John Doe, residing at [specify address] ("Employee").

WITNESSETH:

WHEREAS, the Employer desires to employ the Employee, and the Employee desires to be employed by the Employer, on the terms and conditions contained herein,

NOW, THEREFORE, in consideration of the mutual covenants, conditions and agreements as hereinafter set forth, the parties agree as follows:

1. Employment. The Employer hereby employs the Employee, and the Employee hereby accepts employment as [position], upon the terms and conditions hereinafter set forth.

2. Duties. The Employee shall perform his duties as [position] at the Employer's place of business in New York. The Employee shall be responsible for all duties commensurate with his position of [position], as directed, established and assigned by the Employer from time to time including, without limitation, the marketing, promotion and sales of the Employer's products throughout the United States market.

The Employer, in its discretion, shall have the right, at any time during the term of this Agreement, to assign the Employee to perform duties different in any manner whatsoever from the duties originally assigned and specified.

3. Compensation. During the term of this Agreement, the Employee shall receive as full compensation for services rendered, payable in accordance with the prevailing payroll practices of the Employer, ten percent of the Net Sales (as defined below) of the Employer as determined by the Employer's auditors, such determination to be conclusive and binding on the Employer and the Employee for such purpose, less $5,000 per annum. Net sales shall mean actual receipts received by the Employer from the sale of its products to its purchasers after any applicable discounts are applied and exclusive of amounts received for taxes, handling, shipping, insurance and similar costs. Such Net Sales shall be determined by the Employer's auditors no later than the conclusion of each calendar month following the month to which such determination relates. The Employer shall pay to the Employee his compensation based upon such determination at the conclusion of the month in which such determination is made.

To the extent that with respect to any month the application of the foregoing provisions of this Article 3 result in the Employee's receiving less than $_____ in compensation for such month (the "Minimum Amount"), then the Employee shall be entitled to receive as a draw (the "Draw") against future compensation hereunder, and in addition to the compensation otherwise payable to him hereunder with respect to such month (the "Monthly Compensation"), the lesser of (i) the difference between the Monthly Compensation and the Minimum Amount, or (ii) ten percent of the Employer's accounts receivable generated during such month by reference to invoices of the Employer dated and dispatched during such month for product of the Employer sold and dispatched during such month. The full amount of the Draw shall be repaid to the Employer as a deduction against compensation payable to the Employee hereunder in the month next succeeding the month in which such Draw is received, and such immediately succeeding months as may be necessary to reimburse the Employer in full for the amount of the Draw. Notwithstanding anything to the contrary contained herein, the Employee shall only be entitled to a Draw hereunder to the extent that all previous Draws have been fully reimbursed to the Employer. Any unreimbursed Draw outstanding upon the termination of this Agreement or other termination of the employment of the Employee shall immediately be reimbursed by the Employee to the Employer, and shall be applied as a setoff against any amounts which might otherwise be owing by the Employer to the Employee at the time of such termination.

The Employer shall reimburse the Employee for all reasonable and necessary expenses incurred by the Employee in connection with the Employer's business, provided that (i) such expenses are within the annual budget established by the Employer, (ii) such expenses are deductible to the Employer and (iii) such expenses are properly documented and accounted for in accordance with the policies of the Employer as in effect from time to time, and in accordance with the requirements of the Internal Revenue Service, as in effect from time to time.

From time to time the Employee may propose to the Employer that additional persons be engaged to assist the Employee in his efforts hereunder. The Employee shall be free in his discretion to effect such engagements, it being understood, however, that any engagements shall be at the sole expense of the Employee, and that the Employer shall have the right to reject any such proposed engagements, or terminate any person so engaged, for cause.

4. <u>Holidays; Vacation</u>. The Employee shall be entitled to holidays and vacation in accordance with the prevailing policies of the Employer as in effect from time to time.

5. <u>Death or Disability</u>. If the Employee dies or becomes disabled so that he cannot perform his duties under this Agreement in a manner satisfactory to the Employer, in its discretion, the Employer may terminate this Agreement, and thereupon the Employer shall pay to the representative of the Employee's estate or to the Employee any compensation which would otherwise be payable to the Employee up to the end of the month in which such termination occurs.

6. <u>Covenant Not to Disclose Information; Exclusive Employment, Remedies</u>. The parties hereto recognize that Proprietary Information (as hereinafter defined) is important, material and confidential. Accordingly, the Employee shall not, directly or indirectly, during the term of this Agreement or at any time thereafter, without the prior written consent of the Employer, disclose, use or permit any other business, firm, corporation, person or other entity to disclose, use or have access to Proprietary Information, except as may be necessary in connection with the Employee's provision of services under this Agreement. As used in this Agreement, "Proprietary Information" means information disclosed to or obtained by the Employee as a result of or related to his relationship with the Employer, whether or not acquired during business

hours, including, but not limited to, information concerning the Employer's business, customers, operations, and services. During the course of the Employee's employment under this Agreement and at all times thereafter, the Employee shall not, without the prior written consent of the Employer, directly or indirectly, record, photograph, photocopy or by any other means copy or cause to be copied any document, list or other writing or material that embodies or relates to Proprietary Information except as may be necessary in connection with the Employee's provision of services under this Agreement.

Immediately upon the termination of this Agreement and the Employee's employment under this Agreement, the Employee shall return to the Employer everything in the Employee's possession or custody or under the Employee's control which contains or relates to any Proprietary Information.

All business conducted, generated, or produced by the Employee must be through the Employer, unless the Employer previously has otherwise specifically consented in writing.

The covenants contained in this paragraph 6 shall be construed as an agreement independent of any other provision of this Agreement, and the existence of any claim or cause of action of the Employee against the Employer, whether predicated on this Agreement or otherwise, shall not constitute a defense to the enforcement by the Employer of this independent agreement in this paragraph 6.

In the event of an actual or threatened breach by the Employee of any of the covenants contained in this paragraph 6, the Employer shall be entitled to an injunction restraining the Employee from such action or threatened action. In addition, the Employer may pursue any other remedies available for such actual or threatened breach, including recovery of damages from the Employee.

7. <u>Termination</u>. The Employee or the Employer may terminate this Agreement and the Employee's employment hereunder at any time, upon one,month's prior notice, for any reason, or no reason, without cause. The Employer may terminate this Agreement and the Employee's employment hereunder at any time, without prior notice, for cause. This Agreement and the Employee's employment hereunder shall automatically terminate upon the Employee' s ceasing to be a stockholder of the Employer. Subsequent to any termination hereunder, the Employee shall have no right to receive any further compensation from the Employer whatsoever beyond that which has become due and payable to the Employee, pursuant to the terms of this Agreement, as of the date of such termination,, provided, however, that the agreements contained in paragraph 6 shall survive any termination of this Agreement.

8. <u>Assignment</u>. The rights of this Agreement, including paragraph 6 of this Agreement, may be assigned, conveyed or sold by the Employer and shall be binding upon the Employee, his heirs and permitted assigns. The Employer has entered into this Agreement in reliance upon the Employee's specific personal qualities including ability, skill, trust, experience, character and judgment, and this Agreement is not assignable by the Employee to any entity or person without the express consent in writing of the Employer.

9. <u>Notices</u>. Any and all notices or other communications required or permitted to be given under any of the provisions of this Agreement shall be in writing and shall be deemed to have been duly given when personally delivered or mailed by first class, certified mail, return receipt requested, addressed to the party to whom the notice is directed at its address appearing above, or at such other addresses as the parties may designate from time to time.

10. <u>Severability</u>. If any provision of this Agreement shall be held or deemed to be invalid, such circumstance shall not have the effect of rendering any other provision of this Agreement invalid, inoperative or unenforceable, but such invalid provision shall, to the extent possible, be modified to render it valid, and if such provision is not capable of being so modified, this Agreement shall be construed as if such invalid, inoperative or unenforceable provision had never been contained herein so as to give full force and effect to the remaining such terms and provisions.

11. <u>Entire Agreement; Amendment</u>. This writing constitutes the entire agreement of the parties with respect to the subject matter hereof and may not be modified, amended or terminated except by written agreement specifically referring to this Agreement signed by all of the parties hereto.

12. <u>Waiver</u>. No waiver of any breach or default hereunder shall be considered valid unless in writing and signed by the party giving such waiver, and no such written waiver shall be deemed a waiver of any subsequent breach or default of the same or similar nature.

13. <u>Binding Agreement</u>. This Agreement shall be binding upon and inure to the benefit of each party hereto, its successors and permitted assigns.

14. <u>Counterparts</u>. This Agreement may be executed in counterparts, each of which shall constitute an original and all of which taken together shall constitute one agreement.

15. <u>Governing Law</u>. This Agreement shall be governed by and construed in accordance with the laws of the State of New York without regard to the law of the conflicts of law of such state.

16. <u>Paragraph Headings; Construction</u>. The headings in this Agreement are for convenience only and are not intended to influence its construction. Any references to "Articles", "Paragraphs" or "Exhibits" in this agreement are to the articles, paragraphs, and exhibits to this Agreement. Any Exhibits are part of this Agreement. In this Agreement, the singular includes the plural, the plural the singular, and the words "and" and "or" are used in the disjunctive and conjunctive sense, as the sense and circumstances may require.

IN WITNESS WHEREOF, the parties have caused this Agreement to be executed, delivered and effective as of the day and year first above written.

XYZ, INC.

By:

Name:

Title:

OPTION AND PURCHASE AGREEMENT

THIS OPTION AND PURCHASE AGREEMENT ("Agreement") is made and entered into this _____ day of _____, 199 , by and among [specify purchaser], a [specify state] corporation, or its nominee(s) ("Purchaser"), and [specify seller], a [specify state] corporation ("Seller"), and [specify shareholder], a [specify state] corporation ("Shareholder").

WITNESSETH:

WHEREAS, Seller is a wholly owned subsidiary of Shareholder, whose home office is in [specify home office]; and

WHEREAS, Seller is engaged in the business of [specify business activity]; and

WHEREAS, Purchaser desires to acquire from Seller, and Seller desires to sell to Purchaser, certain of the assets and property of Seller upon the terms hereinafter set forth.

NOW, THEREFORE, in consideration of the promises and mutual covenants herein contained, and for other good and valuable consideration, the mutual receipt and sufficiency of which are hereby acknowledged, the parties hereby agree as follows:

1. Sale and Purchase of Assets; Assumption of Liabilities.

1.1 Option: Seller hereby grants to Purchaser an option (the "Option") to purchase the "Acquired Assets", as defined below, on the terms and conditions set forth in this Agreement. The Option may be exercised at any time on or before [specify effective date], on five days prior written notice to Seller. In consideration of the grant of the Option, Purchaser shall pay to Seller, on or before [specify payment date], an Option payment of [specify amount], all of which shall be credited against the purchase price to be paid by Purchaser at the Closing.

1.2 Assets: At the Closing (as defined herein) the Seller shall sell, deliver, transfer, assign, and convey to Purchaser, free and clear of all liens, claims, charges, restrictions, and encumbrances of every kind, nature, and description, and Purchaser shall purchase for the considerations herein provided, the following assets ("Acquired Assets"):

    a. All patents, copyrights, trademarks, trade names, and product licenses set forth on Schedule 1(a) hereto;

    b. Such of Seller's inventory of [specify industry] related finished goods as Purchaser and Seller reasonably agree are current and merchantable in the ordinary course of Seller's business;

c. All operating assets employed in Seller's ordinary course of business, including those set forth on Schedule 1(c);

d. The office and warehouse furniture and equipment employed in the operation of Seller's business as Purchaser shall select and as set forth in Schedule 1(d);

e. All right, title and interest of Seller in, to, and under all executory contracts, including purchase, sale, and supply contracts, sale representative contracts, supplier and manufacturer warranties, and all leases of personal property as Purchaser shall select and as set forth on Schedule 1(e) hereto;

f. Seller's customer lists and records, supplier lists, sales representative lists, advertising and promotional materials and records and other business records related to Seller's operations;

g. Seller's research and development, engineering drawings and designs and other records related to the design, manufacture, assembly and packaging of Seller's products;

h. A covenant not-to-compete as hereinafter provided in Section 7.4.

1.3 Liabilities: At the Closing, Purchaser shall assume in writing those liabilities and obligations of Seller set forth on Schedule 1.3 (the "Assumed Liabilities"). All other liabilities or obligations of any nature shall not be assumed by Purchaser hereunder, but instead shall remain liabilities and obligations of Seller.

2. Considerations for Acquired Assets

2.1 Operating Assets: The aggregate purchase price for the assets described in Sections 1.2(a), 1.2(c), 1.2(e), 1.2(f), 1.2(g) and 1.2(h) to be paid at the Closing shall be [specify sale amount], which is allocated as follows:
- Section 1.2(a) - $[specify amount]
- Section 1.2(c) - $[specify amount]
- Section 1.2(e) - $[specify amount]
- Section 1.2(f) - $[specify amount]
- Section 1.2(g) - $[specify amount]

2.2 Inventory: In partial consideration for the assets described in Section 1.2(b), Purchaser shall pay at the Closing an amount equal to $[specify amount]. Purchaser and Seller shall arrange for a physical inventory of the assets described in Section 1.2(b) on the Closing Date, which shall be conducted by Seller and observed by [specify inventory observer], Seller's independent accountants, subject to an engagement letter among the parties. Purchaser may if it so chooses observe such inventory. The inventory to be purchased shall consist only of new merchantable [specify industry] related products currently sold by Seller in the ordinary course of its business and shall specifically exclude defective and obsolete products. The pricing of the inventory shall be at the lower of (i) Seller's landed cost, which shall consist of those invoiced costs in effect from suppliers at [specify date], plus all of Seller's costs incurred through payment to third parties for freight, duties, brokerage fees, handling charges, and insurance with respect to the products, or (ii) market, or (iii) 50% of the actual aggregate invoiced selling prices Seller charged its customers for the same goods in the months of [specify time frame], and shall be further valued for purchase hereunder by application to a percentage of said costs as follows:

(a) All new finished goods in final packaging at 100%.

(b) All new finished goods in other than final packaging at 90%.

(c) All new finished goods returned for repackaging at 90%.

(d) Usable packaging, raw materials, supplies and the like in original, unbroken, purchase quantities at 100%.

(e) Inventory that is defective, obsolete, or otherwise deemed not merchantable at 0%.

Purchaser will pay Seller in cash the difference between the amount paid at Closing for the inventory and the aggregate value thereof determined at the above values within ten (10) days after completion of the physical inventory and receipt of the valuation thereof. The cost of [inventory observer] observing the physical inventory shall be borne equally by Purchaser and Seller.

All new finished goods in final packaging in transit to Seller on the Closing Date, which goods are listed by purchase order in <u>Schedule 2.2</u>, will be purchased from Seller upon arrival at 100% of landed costs as described above.

2.3 <u>Office and Warehouse Equipment:</u> The purchase price for the assets described in Section 1.2(d) to be paid at the Closing shall be the net book value thereof established on the Seller's normal method of accounting consistently applied on the Closing Date.

2.4 <u>Accounts Receivable:</u> Purchaser will collect Seller's accounts receivable not paid directly to Seller, account to Seller for such collections and pay to Seller the amounts collected [specify day of week] of each week. Seller will promptly advise Purchaser of collections received by Seller. The first amounts customers of Seller remit to Purchaser shall be paid to Seller to the extent of the customers balance due to Seller that is not in dispute. Purchaser shall have no obligation to pursue collection of accounts of Seller that are not paid and shall return the unpaid accounts to Seller for collection by Seller 120 days following the Closing Date.

3. The Closing:

3.1 Date, Time and Place of Closing: Consummation of the sale and purchase set forth herein (the "Closing") shall take place on the date specified by Purchaser in the notice exercising the option but no later than [specify date], (the "Closing Date"), at [specify time of day] local time at the offices of [specify offices and address].

3.2 Deliveries by Seller: The Seller shall deliver the following documents to the Purchaser at or before the Closing, all of which shall be in form and substance acceptable to the Purchaser and its counsel:

(i) Such bills of sale, endorsements, assignments, and other instruments of sale, transfer, conveyance, and assignment as shall be necessary or desirable to vest in Purchaser good and marketable title to the Acquired Assets free and clear of all liens, security interests, charges, mortgage executions, and encumbrances of any type;

(ii) Consents and approvals of all third parties necessary for the Seller to execute, deliver, or perform this Agreement;

(iii) Certified copies of the corporate actions taken by the Board of Directors of Seller and Shareholder authorizing the execution, delivery, and performance of this Agreement;

(iv) Certificates of Good Standing for Seller from the Secretary of State of [specify state] no earlier than ten (10) days prior to the Closing Date;

(v) The JKL option agreement described in Section 4 below; and

(vi) Such other and further documentation as Purchaser may reasonably require.

3.3 Deliveries by Purchaser: Purchaser shall deliver certified or bank cashier's checks for the amount to be paid on the Closing Date under Sections 2.1, 2.2, and 2.3, less deductions provided for in Sections 1.1 and 7.2. Purchaser will also deliver to Seller an assumption of liabilities in form satisfactory to the parties pursuant to Section 1.3, and to Seller's suppliers a Letter or Letters of Credit in replacement of Seller's Letters of Credit currently with such suppliers, which are set forth in Schedule 5.11, or shall assume Seller's Letters of Credit pursuant to a form of assumption reasonably satisfactory to the issuer thereof.

4. <u>JKL Company Contract</u>: Seller and Shareholder agree to cause JKL Company (hereinafter referred to as "JKL"), another subsidiary of Shareholder, for a period ending on [specify date], to accept orders from and to sell to Purchaser for delivery before [specify date], and Purchaser hereby agrees to place orders with and purchase from JKL during the same period, products now being manufactured and sold by JKL to Seller. The price to be paid by Purchaser for such products shall be no higher than the prices paid by Seller at [specify date], subject to adjustment for changes in the NT/U.S. Dollar exchange rate from the rate in effect at the Closing Date. It is agreed that the current exchange rate is [list current NT exchange rate] to one U.S. Dollar. The operating assets sold to Purchaser hereunder being used by JKL will remain in JKL's possession for use in producing products for JKL's present customers listed in Schedule 4 until [specify date]; provided, however, following the Closing Date, JKL will not otherwise produce, sell, or distribute products that would violate the provisions of Section 7.4 hereof.

Shareholder hereby grants to Purchaser, effective as of the Closing, the option to purchase, at Purchaser's election, the outstanding stock or tangible assets of JKL, at a purchase price equal to the value of JKL's tangible assets at the date of purchase. The price for the option shall be $[specify amount], payable at the Closing hereunder. The option payment shall be credited towards the purchase price for the JKL stock or assets. The option shall expire on [specify date] and must be exercised in writing prior to that date, with the purchase and sale to be consummated pursuant to an agreement substantially similar to the provisions hereof with such changes as are necessary to reflect the purchase and sale of stock and providing for completion of such purchase and sale, and the payment of the purchase price, by [specify date].

5. <u>Representations and Warranties of the Seller and the Shareholder:</u> Seller and the Shareholder, jointly and severally, hereby represent and warrant to Purchaser the following:

5.1 <u>Organization:</u> The Seller is a corporation duly organized, validly existing, and in good standing under the laws of the State of [specify state]. The Shareholder is a corporation duly organized, validly existing, and in good standing under the laws of the State of [specify state]. The Seller is qualified to do business and is in good standing in each jurisdiction listed on <u>Schedule 5.1</u> which are all jurisdictions in which the failure to be so qualified would have a material adverse effect on the business of Seller.

The Seller has all corporate power and authority and all licenses to own its property and to carry on its operations as now conducted by it and as contemplated by this Agreement.

5.2 <u>Corporate Action; Valid and Binding Agreements:</u> All corporate and shareholder action of Seller and Shareholder necessary to authorize the execution, delivery, and performance of this Agreement and each of the other agreements, instruments, and other documents to be delivered by the Seller and Shareholder in connection herewith has been properly taken. This Agreement and all such other agreements, instruments, and other documents have been duly and validly executed and delivered by, and constitute a valid and binding agreement of the Seller and Shareholder enforceable in accordance with its terms, subject as to enforcement to applicable equitable principles or bankruptcy, insolvency, reorganization, moratorium or other similar laws now or hereafter in effect generally affecting creditors' rights.

5.3 No Violation: Except as set forth on Schedule 5.3, neither the execution, the delivery of this Agreement, nor the consummation of the transaction contemplated hereby constitutes a violation of, or results in a breach of, or gives rise to a right of acceleration or termination under, (a) any term or provision of the respective Articles or Certificate of Incorporation or Bylaws of Seller or Shareholder, (b) any agreement or commitment material to the business of Seller to which the Seller or Shareholder is bound, (c) any agreement, understanding, or commitment relating to any bank or other institutional loans or indebtedness of the Seller or Shareholder, or (d) any judgment, decree, order, regulation or rule of any court or governmental authority, or any statute or law. The execution, delivery, and consummation of this Agreement will neither result in the imposition of any lien, mortgage, pledge, encumbrance, easement, claim, or other restriction or charge on the Acquired Assets nor disrupt nor impair any material business relationship which the Seller currently has with any dealer, distributor, sales representative, supplier, or customer. No consent, registration, or filing with any federal, state or local authority or other public or private body or person is required in connection with the execution and delivery of this Agreement and the performance of the transactions contemplated hereby or is required with respect to the transfer, except as set forth in Schedule 5.3.

5.4 Tax Returns: The Shareholder and the Seller have duly filed all tax reports and returns which are required to be filed with respect to Seller and have fully paid or provided for all taxes and other charges due or claimed to be due by all federal, state, county, city, local, and foreign taxing authorities with respect to Seller. Seller has set up on its books adequate reserves for the payment of all taxes attributable for the period up to and including the Closing Date. There are no federal, state, county, city, local, or foreign tax liens upon any property or assets of Seller, and there are no unpaid taxes, interest, or penalties which are or could become a lien on the Acquired Assets or require payment by Purchaser. Except as set forth on Schedule 5.4, there are no present audits or other discussions by any state, city, county, local, or foreign government concerning any income, property (tangible and intangible), franchise, sales, or any other tax returns filed by Seller. The Seller does not have any liability or deficiency (including, without limitation, interest and penalties) for taxes to any federal, state, county, city, local, or foreign taxing authority attributable to any fiscal period ending prior to the Closing Date for which the statutory period of limitations is still open. There are no outstanding agreements or waivers extending the statutory period of limitations applicable to any federal, state, county, city, local, or foreign tax return of Seller for any period.

5.5 Financial Statements: Seller will deliver to Purchaser its balance sheets and related statements of income for the years ended [specify dates], and for the interim period ended [specify dates], and like statements for JKL for [specify dates](the "Financial Statements"). The Financial Statements fairly present the financial condition and results of operations of Seller and JKL as of the respective dates prepared in accordance with generally accepted accounting principles consistently applied throughout. The Financial Statements provide for all fixed and noncontingent liabilities of a type required to be disclosed or provided for in financial statements.

5.6 Title to and Condition of Assets: Seller has good, valid, and marketable title to all of the Acquired Assets except as set forth on Schedule 5.6, none of the Acquired Assets is subject to any imperfection in title, pledge, lien, encumbrance, security interest, charge or other similar restriction of any nature whatsoever. Each of the Acquired Assets is in good operating condition and repair commensurate with its age and use, and capable of being used for its intended purpose in the ordinary course of business. All of the assets listed in Schedule 1(c) and 1(d) are located in the premises described thereon. Except as set forth on Schedule 5.6, no other person or entity has any rights to the use thereof and said assets are all the assets necessary to the conduct of the business of Seller. Except as set forth on Schedule 5.6, the patents, copyrights, trademarks, and trade names set forth on Schedule 1(a) hereto are owned by Seller free and clear of all liens, charges, or encumbrances of any nature whatsoever without any material known conflict with the rights of others and the same are valid and enforceable and have been maintained and prosecuted by Seller.

5.7 Litigation: Except as set forth in Schedule 5.7, there is no action, suit, proceeding, or investigation pending or, to the knowledge of the Seller or the Shareholder, threatened against or involving Seller before any court, administrative agency or other governmental body; and neither the Seller nor the Shareholder know of any reasonable basis for any action, suit, proceeding, or investigation by any court, administrative agency, or other governmental body against or involving the Seller. No unsatisfied judgment, order, writ, injunction, decree or assessment or other command of any court or any federal, state, municipal, foreign, or other governmental department, commission, board, bureau, agency, or instrumentality has been entered against and served upon Seller. There is no action, proceeding or investigation pending, or to the knowledge of the Seller or Shareholder, threatened, which questions or challenges the validity of this Agreement or any of the transactions contemplated by this Agreement or otherwise seeks to prevent or have the effect of preventing the consummation of the transactions contemplated hereby.

5.8 Insurance: A description of all of the Seller's insurance, together with the limits of coverage, are set forth in Schedule 5.8 attached hereto and made a part hereof.

5.9 Employee Contracts: The Seller has no obligations, contingent or otherwise, under any employment, consulting or similar agreement, collective bargaining agreement or other contract with a labor or employee group or under any executive or employee's compensation, life insurance, disability, medical, or other employee benefit plan or agreement, including, without limitation, any pension, profit sharing, stock purchase, stock option, bonus or savings plan or agreement, except as disclosed in Schedule 5.9 attached hereto and made a part hereof (the "Employee Contracts"). All contracts listed in Schedule 5.9 are valid and binding on all of the parties thereto, are in full force and effect and no party to any such contract is in default thereunder and, to the knowledge of the Seller and the Shareholder, no default is threatened. Schedule 5.9 also sets forth the names, currently hourly and annual salary rates and other compensation arrangements of all employees of the Seller.

5.10 Absence of Labor Difficulties: There is no unfair labor practice charge or complaint against Seller pending before the National Labor Relations Board or any labor related agency. There is no strike, picketing, slowdown or work stoppage or organizational attempt actually pending or, to the knowledge of the Seller or Shareholder, threatened against or involving Seller. No representation question is pending or, to the knowledge of Seller or Shareholder, is threatened respecting the employees of Seller. There is no collective bargaining or similar employee agreement which is binding on the Seller or, to the knowledge of the Seller or Shareholder, is being asserted as binding by any person or entity on Seller. Seller has paid in full or accrued for all employees all wages, salaries, commissions, bonuses, and other direct compensation for services performed by them. Upon termination of the employment of any said employees, neither the Seller nor the Purchaser will, by reason of anything done prior to or at the Closing, be liable to any of said employees for so-called "severance pay" or any other similar payments, except as is set out in Schedule 5.10.

5.11 Contracts: Schedule 5.11 to this Agreement, attached hereto and made a part hereof, lists all outstanding contracts, agreements, commitments, guarantees of payment or performance by third parties, rental agreements and leases (for both real and personal property) including but not limited to all arrangements with distributors, conditional sales agreements, and lease purchase agreements for tangible personal property to which the Seller is a party or by which the Seller is bound and incorporates by reference the Employee Contracts (Schedule 5.9) (the "Contracts"); provided, however, that the term "Contract" does not include (a) agreements relating to office equipment, production support equipment, maintenance, security or utilities which do not individually result in the incurrence of greater than $[specify amount] in annual expense by the Seller, (b) any other individual agreement creating a liability to the Seller of less than $[specify amount], so long as the total of such agreements do not aggregate in excess of $[specify amount] (such agreements and understandings so excluded in subsections "(a)" and 11(b)" above are herein referred to as the "Additional Contracts"), or (c) any purchase or sale orders entered into in the ordinary course of business. As to the Seller and, to the knowledge of Seller and Shareholder, as to the other parties thereto, the Contracts and Additional Contracts are valid, binding, in full force and effect, enforceable in accordance with their terms subject as to enforcement to applicable equitable principles or bankruptcy, insolvency, reorganization moratorium, or other similar laws now or hereafter in effect generally affecting creditors' rights, and are not subject to termination except in accordance with the respective terms thereof. True and complete copies of all Contracts listed in Schedule 5.11 which Purchaser shall request, including, without limitation, all changes, additions, or modifications thereof, will be delivered to the purchaser within ten (10) days of the date of execution hereof. Neither the seller nor, to the knowledge of the Seller and the Shareholder, any other party thereto, is in material default under any of the Contracts or Additional Contracts and no event has occurred which but for notice or lapse of time or both, would constitute such a default and no default is threatened. The contracts and the Additional Contracts have been entered into in the ordinary course of business. Seller will, at Purchaser's request, assist Purchaser in obtaining assignments of such of the Contracts and Additional Contracts as Purchaser shall direct.

5.12 Operation of JKL: JKL is now, and will continue to be throughout the term of this Agreement as required for the supply of product to Purchaser as set forth in Section 4 above, financially and operationally capable of providing the products currently required for the business being acquired hereunder; and, JKL will perform its agreement as provided in Section 4 and will continue in its normal course of business during the entire term of the Agreement and any extensions thereof.

5.13 Government Regulation; Compliance with Laws: The Seller complies with, and neither the Seller nor the Shareholder have received any notice of a failure to comply with, any statutes, laws, ordinances, rules, regulations, orders or directives applicable to the operations of the Seller. Seller has complied with all workers' compensation and unemployment compensation laws of the State of [specify state] and any other applicable jurisdiction, and has paid all premiums and amounts due thereunder. The Seller has all material permits, licenses, orders, approvals, authorizations, concessions and franchises of any governmental or regulatory authority that are necessary in the conduct of its business, all of which are set forth on Schedule 5.13.

5.14 Operation in Ordinary Course of Business: Since [specify date], the business of Seller has been operated only in the ordinary course, and except as set forth on Schedule 5.14, there has not been to a material degree with respect to the Seller:

>(a) Any adverse change in the aggregate in its condition (financial or otherwise), assets, liabilities, business, earnings or prospects;

>(b) Any damage, destruction or loss in the aggregate adversely affecting its properties, business, or prospects, or any taking of or the creation of any immediate threat to take any real property

owned or leased by the Seller by condemnation or eminent domain;

(c) Any forward purchase commitments in excess of the normal business requirements or other than for normal operating inventories or at prices higher than current market prices;

(d) Any increase in any rate or rates of salaries or compensation of salaried employees or agents, or any specific increases in the salary or compensation paid to or accrued for the benefit of any employee or agent or any increase in the benefit payable under any bonus, insurance, pension or other benefit plan of the Seller;

(e) Any mortgage, pledge or subjection to lien, charge, security interest or to any other encumbrance of any of its assets or properties;

(f) Any waiver or release of any rights of material value;

(g) Any transfer or grant of any rights under any concessions, leases, licenses, agreements, patents, inventions, trademarks, trade names, service marks, copyrights or with respect to any know-how.

Seller will continue to operate its business in the ordinary course from the date of execution hereof to the Closing Date.

5.15 Completeness: The Seller owns or has under lease or by contract all of the properties and assets, tangible and intangible, necessary in order to operate the business of the seller as currently conducted.

5.16 General Representation and Warranty: None of the representations and warranties of the Seller and Shareholder made in this Agreement or in the Schedules of Exhibits contains any untrue statement of material fact or omits to state any material fact necessary in order to make said representations and warranties not misleading.

6. Representations and Warranties of the Purchaser: The Purchaser represents and warrants to the Seller as follows:

6.1 Organization, Standing, and Power of Purchaser: Purchaser is a corporation duly organized, validly existing and in good standing under the laws of the State of [specify state]. Purchaser is qualified and in good standing as a foreign corporation in all jurisdictions in which the failure so to be qualified would have a material adverse effect upon its business. Purchaser has the corporate power and corporate authority to hold, own, operate, and lease its properties and otherwise carry on its business as presently conducted.

6.2 <u>Authority</u>: The execution, delivery, and performance by purchaser of this Agreement and all other agreements contemplated hereby have been duly and validly authorized by the Board of Directors of Purchaser and by all other necessary corporate action on the part of Purchaser, and, assuming due authorization, execution, and delivery by the other parties hereto and thereto, this Agreement and such other agreements constitute legal, valid, and binding agreements of Purchaser, enforceable against Purchaser in accordance with their terms, subject as to enforcement to applicable equitable principles and bankruptcy, insolvency, reorganization, moratorium, or other similar laws now or hereafter in effect generally affecting creditors rights.

6.3 <u>No Conflicts</u>: The execution, delivery, and performance of this Agreement and the consummation of the transactions contemplated thereby by Purchaser have not and will not (i) violate, conflict with, or breach any provision of the Articles of Incorporation or Bylaws of Purchaser or any presently existing order, writ, injunction, judgment, decree, law, ordinance, rule, or regulation applicable to Purchaser or any of its properties, or (ii) violate, conflict with, require consent under, breach, cause a default, or provide grounds for termination, cancellation, or acceleration of performance in respect of, or result in the creation or imposition of a lien or other encumbrance Pursuant to, any agreement material to the business of Purchaser to which Purchaser is a party or to which it may be bound.

6.4 <u>Litigation</u>: There is no action, proceeding or investigation pending or, to the knowledge of Purchaser, threatened which questions or challenges the validity of this Agreement or any of the transactions contemplated by this Agreement or otherwise seeks to prevent or have the effect of preventing the consummation of the transactions contemplated hereby.

7. <u>Additional Agreements:</u>

7.1 <u>Further Assurances</u>:   After the Closing, the parties hereto agree to take whatever further action is necessary and to execute whatever further documents, instruments of assignment, transfer, conveyance or authorization and agreements as may be reasonably requested by the Purchaser in order to fulfill the purposes and the intent of this Agreement.

7.2 <u>Defective Goods</u>: Seller represents its net costs attributable to returns, allowances, repairs and replacements for defective goods has historically been [list percentage] of gross sales or less as set forth in <u>Schedule 7.2</u>. Seller has no reason to believe its historical experience will change significantly for products sold since [specify date]. Purchaser shall assume all obligation and liability for the repair or replacement of defective goods by Seller prior to the Closing and returned after the Closing. Seller agrees to reimburse Purchaser $[specify amount] in [specify number of payments] monthly installments of $[specify amount] each from and after the Closing Date to pay all costs it incurs in repairing or replacing such products; and in the event those costs exceed $[specify amount] in the aggregate, Purchaser, on 30 days notice to Seller, may deduct the excess from amounts Purchaser is obligated to pay Seller at any time after Closing. Seller shall have the right to examine Purchaser's return records and returned goods (excluding those items returned in the ordinary course of business).

7.3 <u>Use of Seller's Facilities:</u> Purchaser shall occupy up to [specify number of square feet] square feet of segregated office and warehouse space in Seller's facility for not less than ninety (90) days following the Closing Date and shall pay Seller $[specify amount] per month for the use thereof and a pro rata share of utility and other charges (for the warehouse space only and not for Seller's equipment operation) until such time as Purchaser or Seller relocates its operations to another facility. Until such time as Purchaser converts to its own computer system, but not to exceed 6 months, Purchaser will have the right to utilize Seller's computer system at a rental and use rate of $[specify amount] per month.

7.4 <u>Nondisclosure, Noncompetition and Noninterference:</u> The Seller and the Shareholder, and all other subsidiaries of shareholder shall: (i) at all times hold in strictest confidence any and all confidential nonpublic data and information within their knowledge concerning the products, services, businesses, representatives, suppliers, distributors, and customers of the business of the Seller; (ii) not, for a period of six (6) years after Closing Date, without the prior written consent of Purchaser, either directly or indirectly operate or perform any advisory or consulting services for, invest in or otherwise operate or become associated with in any capacity, any company, partnership, organization, proprietorship or other entity which competes with Purchaser in any geographic or product market in which Seller and/or Purchaser currently conduct business including each county in [specify state] and the remainder of Northern America; and (iii) not, at any time, without the prior written consent of Purchaser, directly or indirectly induce or attempt to induce any employee, agent or other representative or associate of the Purchaser to terminate its relationship with the Purchaser or in any way interfere with such a relationship or a relationship between the Purchaser and any of its suppliers, customers or distributors. Seller and the Shareholders acknowledge that compliance with the covenants in this Section 7.4 is necessary to protect the Purchaser, and that a breach of these covenants will result in irreparable and continuing damage for which there will be no adequate remedy at law and agree that in the event of any breach of said covenants, Purchaser and its respective successors and assigns, shall be entitled to injunctive relief and to such other and further relief as is proper.

8. <u>Survival of Representations, Warranties and Indemnities:</u>

8.1 <u>Survival:</u> The representations, warranties and indemnities contained in this Agreement shall be deemed to be renewed at the Closing Date and shall survive the Closing.

8.2 <u>Representation and Warranty Indemnification by the Seller and Shareholder:</u>
The Seller and Shareholder, jointly and severally, shall indemnify Purchaser against and hold it harmless from (i) any and all loss, damage, liability or

deficiency resulting from or arising out of any inaccuracy in or breach of any representation, warranty, covenant, or obligation made or incurred by the indemnifying person herein; and (ii) any and all costs and expenses (including reasonable legal and accounting fees) related to any of the foregoing; <u>provided, however</u>, that Seller and Shareholder shall only be required to indemnify Purchaser for losses, costs and expenses under this Section 8.2 and Section 8.3 to the extent the same exceed [specify amount].

8.3 <u>Product Liability Indemnification by Seller:</u> The Seller and Shareholder shall indemnify Purchaser against and hold it harmless from any accident or occurrence with respect to products manufactured or sold by Seller prior to the Closing Date which result in personal injury, sickness, death, property damage, destruction or loss of use, or economic loss arising out of or resulting from the use of such products and all costs and expenses (including reasonable legal and accounting fees). The Seller and Shareholder agree to cooperate with Purchaser in the defense of any product liability claims asserted against Purchaser relating to products sold by Seller prior to Closing.

8.4 <u>Indemnification by Purchaser:</u> Purchaser shall indemnify Seller and the Shareholder against and hold them harmless from (i) any and all loss, damage, liability or deficiency resulting from or arising out of any inaccuracy in or breach of any representation, warranty, covenant, or obligation made or incurred by Purchaser herein and (ii) any and all costs and expenses (including reasonable legal and accounting fees).

8.5 <u>Defense of Third Party Claims and Extension of Statute of Limitations:</u> The party to this Agreement against which a claim for an indemnification is asserted (the "Indemnifying Party") shall have a right in its discretion and at its expense to participate in and control (a) the defense or settlement of any claim, suit, action or proceeding (including appeals) in respect of such item (or items) by any other person other than a party hereto insofar as the Indemnified Party shall claim indemnification hereunder in respect thereof, (b) any and all negotiations with respect thereto and (c) the assertion of any claim against any insurer with respect thereto, and the Indemnified Party shall not settle any such claim, suit, action or proceeding or agree to extend any applicable statute of limitation without the prior written approval of the Indemnifying Party. The rights of participation, control and approval granted to the Indemnifying Party shall be subject to the following conditions precedent: (a) such party's acknowledging to the Indemnified Party, in writing, the obligation of the Indemnifying Party to indemnify the other party hereto in respect of such third party's claim, suit, action or proceeding giving rise to such item; and (b) the Indemnifying Party posting a bond or making other arrangements satisfactory to the Indemnified Party to assume full funding of the Indemnifying Party's obligation to indemnify the Indemnified Party as hereinabove provided. Upon satisfaction of such conditions precedent, the Indemnified Party will provide the Indemnifying Party with all reasonably available information, assistance and authority to enable the Indemnifying Party to effect such defense or settlement and upon the Indemnifying Party's payment of any amounts due in respect of such claim, suit, action or proceeding. The indemnified Party will, to the extent of such payment, assign or cause to be assigned to the Indemnifying Party the claims of the indemnified Party, if any, against such third parties in respect of which such payment is made.

If the Indemnifying Party is not so willing to acknowledge such obligation the parties shall jointly consult and proceed as to any such third party claim, suit, action or proceeding, but the Indemnified Party shall control the defense, negotiation or settlement thereof.

9. <u>Bulk Sales Compliance:</u> Seller shall cooperate fully with and provide all necessary documents and assistance to Purchaser in complying with the transferee notice to creditor requirements of the Bulk Sales Laws of the State of [specify state] and any other applicable jurisdiction prior to the Closing Date.

10. <u>Transition of Operations; Change of Name:</u> Seller agrees to assist Purchaser with the resolution of such transitional matters as may arise in connection with the consummation of the transactions contemplated hereby. Promptly following the Closing, the Purchaser agrees to change its corporate name and to execute such documents as shall be necessary for Purchaser to utilize its corporate name.

11. <u>General Provisions:</u>

11.1 <u>Notices:</u> All notices and other communications given pursuant to this Agreement shall be deemed to have been properly given or delivered if hand delivered or if mailed, by certified mail, postage prepaid, addressed to the appropriate party, at the following addresses:

    A.   To the Seller:

and

    B.   To the Shareholder:

With a copy to:

    C.   To the Purchaser:

With a copy to:

Any party may from time to time designate by written notice pursuant to this Section 11.1 any other address or party to which such notice or communication or copies thereof shall be sent.

11.2 <u>Brokerage Commissions and Fees:</u> Seller represents and warrants to Purchaser that other than as described on <u>Schedule 11.2</u>, no broker, finder or other person or entity acting in a similar capacity has participated on its behalf in bringing about the sale herein contemplated, rendered any services with respect thereto, or been involved in any way therewith. Seller shall be responsible for the fees payable to the broker identified on <u>Schedule 11.2</u>. Purchaser hereby represents and warrants to Seller that no broker, finder or other person or entity acting in a similar capacity has participated on its behalf in bringing about the sale herein contemplated, rendered any service with respect thereto, or been involved in any way therewith.

11.3 <u>Payment of Professional Fees and Other Expenses:</u> The professional fees of each party in connection with the transactions contemplated in this Agreement (including, but not limited to, legal and accounting fees) shall be borne by the respective parties incurring such fees, provided that the expense of [inventory conductor] with respect to the physical inventory under Section 2.4 shall be borne equally by Purchaser and Seller.

11.4 <u>No Publicity:</u> Seller and the Shareholder agree that except for disclosures required by law, they shall not make any Public announcement or otherwise disclose the transaction contemplated hereby without the prior written consent of Purchaser.

11.5 <u>Miscellaneous:</u> This Agreement shall be construed in accordance with, and governed by, the internal domestic laws of the State of [specify state] applicable to contracts made and to be wholly performed within such State. This Agreement shall be binding upon and inure to the benefit of and be enforceable by the parties hereto and their respective successors and assigns. Headings and subheadings herein are for convenience only and are not of substantive effect. There are no oral agreements in connection with this Agreement. This Agreement constitutes the entire agreement of the parties hereto, and supersedes any prior agreements or understandings, whether oral or written, between the parties hereto with respect to the subject matter thereof. This Agreement may not be terminated, modified or amended orally or by any course of conduct or usage of trade but only by an agreement in writing duly executed by the parties hereto. This Agreement may be executed simultaneously or in one or more counterparts, each of which shall be deemed an original and all of which together shall constitute one and the same instrument. Any waiver of a breach of any of the provisions of this Agreement shall not be deemed a waiver of any other provision of this Agreement. If any provision of this Agreement shall be determined to be unenforceable or invalid such provision shall remain in force and effect to the maximum extent allowable and the remainder of this Agreement shall be and remain binding and effective as against all parties hereto.

IN WITNESS WHEREOF, the parties have duly executed this Agreement as of the date first above written.

PURCHASER:

By:_____
     President

Attest:

By:_____
     Secretary

SELLER: Affix Corporate Seal if Applicable

By:_____
     President

Attest:

By:_____
     Secretary

SHAREHOLDER: Affix Corporate Seal if Applicable

By:_____
     President

Attest:

By:_____
     Secretary

SECTION FIVE:
Glossary of Terms

GLOSSARY OF TERMS

Abuse of process A cause of action which arises when one party intentionally misuses the legal process to injure another.

Accord and satisfaction An agreement by the employee and his or her company to compromise disputes concerning outstanding debts, compensation or terms of employment. Satisfaction occurs when the terms of the compromise are fully performed.

Action in accounting A cause of action in which one party seeks a determination of the amount of money owed by another.

Admissible Capable of being introduced in court as evidence.

Advance Sometimes referred to as "draw," it is a sum of money which is applied against money to be earned.

Affidavit A written statement signed under oath.

Allegations Written statements of a party to a lawsuit which charge the other party with wrongdoing. In order to be successful, these must be proven.

Answer The defendant's reply to the plaintiff's allegations in a complaint.

Anticipatory breach A breach of contract that occurs when one party, i.e., the employee, states in advance of performance that he or she will definitely not perform under the terms of his or her contract.

Appeal A proceeding whereby the losing party to a lawsuit applies to a higher court to determine the correctness of the decision.

Arbitration A proceeding whereby both sides to a lawsuit agree to submit their dispute to arbitrators, rather than judges. The arbitration proceeding is expeditious and is legally binding on all parties.

Assignment The transfer of a right or interest by one party to another.

Attorney in fact A person appointed by another to transact business on his or her behalf; the person does not have to be a lawyer.

At-will-employment See *Employment-at-will*.

Award A decision made by a judicial body to compensate the winning party in a lawsuit.

Bill of particulars A document used in a lawsuit which specifically details the loss alleged by the plaintiff.

Breach of contract A legal cause of action for the unjustified failure to perform a duty or obligation specified in an agreement.

Brief A concise statement of the main contentions of a lawsuit.

Burden of proof The responsibility of a party to a lawsuit to provide sufficient evidence to prove or disprove a claim

Business deduction A legitimate expense that can be used to decrease the amount of income subject to tax.

Business slander A legal wrong committed when a party orally makes false statements which impugn the business reputation of another (e.g., imply that the person is dishonest, incompetent or financially unreliable).

Calendar A list of cases to be heard each day in court.

Cause of action The legal theory upon which the plaintiff seeks to recover damages.

Caveat emptor A Latin expression frequently applied to consumer transactions; translated as "Let the buyer beware."

Cease-and-desist letter A letter, usually sent by a lawyer, notifying an individual to stop engaging in a particular type of activity, behavior or conduct which infringes upon the rights of another.

Certificate of incorporation A document which creates a corporation.

Check A negotiable instrument; the depositor's written order requesting his or her bank to pay a definite sum of money to a named individual, entity or to the bearer.

Civil court Generally, any court which presides over noncriminal matters.

Claims court A particular court which hears tax disputes.

Clerk of the court A person who determines whether court papers are properly filed and court procedures followed.

Closely held business A business typically owned by fewer than ten owners.

Collateral estoppel See *Estoppel*. Collateral estoppel is where a prior but different legal action is conclusive in a way to bring about estoppel in a current legal action.

Common law Law which evolves from reported case decisions which are relied upon for their precedential value.

Compensatory damages A sum of money awarded to a party which represents the actual harm suffered or loss incurred.

Complaint A legal document which commences the lawsuit; it alleges facts and causes of action which the plaintiff relies upon to collect damages.

Conflict of interest The ethical inability of a lawyer to represent a client because of competing loyalties, e.g. representing both employer and employee in a labor dispute.

Consideration An essential element of an enforceable contract; something of value given or promised by one party in exchange for an act or promise of another.

Constitutional Recognized as legal or valid.

Contempt A legal sanction imposed when a rule or order of a judicial body is disobeyed.

Contingency fee A type of fee arrangement whereby a lawyer is paid a percentage of the money recovered. If unsuccessful, the client is only responsible for costs already paid by the lawyer.

Continuance The postponement of a legal proceeding to another date.

Contract An enforceable agreement, either written, oral, or implied by the actions or intentions of the parties.

Contract modification The alteration of contract terms.

Counterclaim A claim asserted by the defendant in a lawsuit.

Covenant A promise.

Credibility The believability of a witness as perceived by a judge or jury.

Creditor The party to whom money is owed.

Cross-examination The questioning of a witness by the opposing lawyer.

Damages An award, usually money, given to the winning party in a lawsuit as compensation for the wrongful acts of another.

Debtor The party who owes money.

Decision The determination of a case or matter by a judicial body.

Deductible The unrecoverable portion of insurance proceeds.

Defamation An oral or written statement communicated to a third party which impugns a person's reputation in the community.

Default judgment An award rendered after one party fails to appear in a lawsuit.

Defendant The person or entity who is sued in a lawsuit.

Defense The defendant's justification for relieving himself or herself of fault.

Definite term of employment Employment for a fixed period of time.

Deposition A pretrial proceeding in which one party is questioned, usually under oath, by the opposing party's lawyer.

Disclaimer A clause in a sales, service, or other contract which attempts to limit or exonerate one party from liability in the event of a lawsuit.

Discovery A general term used to describe several pretrial devices (e.g., depositions and interrogatories) that enable lawyers to elicit information from the opposing side.

District court A particular court that hears tax disputes.

Dual Capacity A legal theory, used to circumvent Worker's Compensation laws, that allows an injured employee to sue his or her employer directly in court.

Due process Constitutional protections which guarantee that a person's life, liberty or property cannot be taken away without the opportunity to be heard in a judicial proceeding.

Duress Unlawful threats, pressure, or force that induces a person to act contrary to his or her intentions; if proved, it allows a party to disavow a contract.

Employee A person who works and is subject to an employer's scope, direction and control.

Employment-at-will Employment which does not provide an employee with job security, since the person can be fired on a moment's notice with or without cause.

Employment discrimination Conduct directed at employees and job applicants that is prohibited by law.

Equity Fairness; usually applied when a judicial body awards a suitable remedy other than money to a party (e.g., an injunction).

Escrow account A separate fund where lawyers are obligated to deposit money received from or on behalf of a client.

Estoppel Estoppel is a legal bar to prevent a party from asserting a fact or claim inconsistent with that party's prior position which has been relied on or acted on by another party.

Evidence Information in the form of oral testimony, exhibits, affidavits, etc., used to prove a party's claim.

Examination before trial A pretrial legal device; also called a "deposition."

Exhibit Tangible evidence used to prove a party's claim.

Exit agreements Agreements sometimes signed between employers and employees upon resignation or termination of an employee's services.

Express contract An agreement whose terms are manifested by clear and definite language, as distinguished from those agreements inferred from conduct.

False imprisonment The unlawful detention of a person who is held against his or her will without authority or justification.

Filing fee Money paid to start a lawsuit

Final decree A court order or directive of a permanent nature.

Financial statement A document, usually prepared by an accountant, which reflects a business's (or individual's) assets, liabilities and financial condition.

Flat fee A sum of money paid to a lawyer as compensation for services.

Flat fee plus time A form of payment in which a lawyer receives one sum for services and then receives additional money calculated on an hourly basis.

Fraud A false statement that is relied upon and causes damages to the defrauded party.

General denial A reply contained in the defendant's answer.

Ground The basis for an action or an argument.

Guaranty A contract where one party agrees to answer for or satisfy the debt of another.

Hearsay evidence Unsubstantiated evidence that is often excluded by a court.

Hourly fee Money paid to a lawyer for services, computed on an hourly basis.

Implied contract An agreement that is tacit rather than expressed in clear and definite language; an agreement inferred from the conduct of the parties.

Indemnification Protection or reimbursement against damage or loss. The indemnified party is protected against liabilities or penalties from that party's actions; the indemnifying party provides the protection or reimbursement.

Infliction of emotional distress A legal cause of action in which one party seeks to recover damages for mental pain and suffering caused by another.

Injunction A court order restraining one party from doing or refusing to do an act.

Integration The act of making a contract whole by integrating its elements into a coherent single entity. An agreement is considered integrated when the parties involved accept the final version as a complete expression of their agreement.

Interrogatories A pretrial device used to elicit information; written questions are sent to an opponent to be answered under oath.

Invasion of privacy The violation of a person's constitutionally protected right to privacy.

Judgment A verdict rendered by a judicial body; if money is awarded, the winning party is the "judgment creditor" and the losing party is the "judgment debtor."

Jurisdiction The authority of a court to hear a particular matter.

Legal duty The responsibility of a party to perform a certain act.

Letter of agreement An enforceable contract in the form of a letter.

Letter of protest A letter sent to document a party's dissatisfaction.

Liable Legally in the wrong or legally responsible for.

Lien A claim made against the property of another in order to satisfy a judgment.

Lifetime contract An employment agreement of infinite duration which is often unenforceable.

Liquidated damages An amount of money agreed upon in advance by parties to a contract to be paid in the event of a breach or dispute.

Malicious interference with contractual rights A legal cause of action in which one party seeks to recover damages against an individual who has induced or caused another party to terminate a valid contract.

Malicious prosecution A legal cause of action in which one party seeks to recover damages after another party instigates or institutes a frivolous judicial proceeding (usually criminal) which is dismissed.

Mediation A voluntary dispute-resolution process in which both sides attempt to settle their differences without resorting to formal litigation.

Misappropriation The unlawful taking of another party's personal property.

Misrepresentation A legal cause of action which arises when one party makes untrue statements of fact that induce another party to act and be damaged as a result.

Mitigation of damages A legal principle which requires a party seeking damages to make reasonable efforts to reduce damages as much as possible; for example, to seek new employment after being unfairly discharged.

Motion A written request made to a court by one party during a lawsuit.

Negligence A party's failure to exercise a sufficient degree of care owed to another by law.

Nominal damages A small sum of money awarded by a court.

Noncompetition clause A restrictive provision in a contract which limits an employee's right to work in that particular industry after he or she ceases to be associated with his or her present employer.

Notary Public A person authorized under state law to administer an oath or verify a signature.

Notice to show cause A written document in a lawsuit asking a court to expeditiously rule on a matter.

Objection A formal protest made by a lawyer in a lawsuit.

Offer The presentment of terms, which, if accepted, may lead to the formation of a contract.

Opinion letter A written analysis of a client's case, prepared by a lawyer.

Option An agreement giving one party the right to choose a certain course of action.

Oral contract An enforceable verbal agreement.

Parol evidence Oral evidence introduced at a trial to alter or explain the terms of a written agreement.

Partnership A voluntary association between two or more competent persons engaged in a business as co-owners for profit.

Party A plaintiff or defendant in a lawsuit.

Perjury Committing false testimony while under oath.

Petition A request filed in court by one party.

Plaintiff The party who commences a lawsuit.

Pleading A written document that states the facts or arguments put forth by a party in a lawsuit.

Power of attorney A document executed by one party allowing another to act on his or her behalf in specified situations.

Pretrial discovery A legal procedure used to gather information from an opponent before the trial.

Process server An individual who delivers the summons and/or complaint to the defendant.

Promissory note A written acknowledgment of a debt whereby one party agrees to pay a specified sum on a specified date.

Proof Evidence presented at a trial and used by a judge or jury to fashion an award.

Punitive damages Money awarded as punishment for a party's wrongful acts.

Quantum meruit An equitable principle whereby a court awards reasonable compensation to a party who performs work, labor or services at another party's request; also referred to as "unjust enrichment."

Rebuttal The opportunity for a lawyer at a trial to ask a client or witness additional questions to clarify points elicited by the opposing lawyer during cross-examination.

Release A written document which, when signed, relinquishes a party's rights to enforce a claim against another.

Remedy The means by which a right is enforced or protected.

Reply A written document in a lawsuit conveying the contentions of a party in response to a motion.

Restrictive covenant A provision in a contract which forbids one party from doing a certain act, e.g., working for another, soliciting customers, etc.

Retainer A sum of money paid to a lawyer for services to be rendered.

Service letter statutes Laws in some states that require an employer to furnish an employee with truthful written reasons for his discharge.

Sex harassment Prohibited conduct of a sexual nature which occur in the workplace.

Shop rights The rights of an employer to use within the employer's facility a device or method developed by an employee.

Slander Oral defamation of a party's reputation.

Small claims court A particular court that presides over small disputes (e.g., those involving sums of less than $2,500).

Sole proprietorship An unincorporated business.

Statement of fact Remarks or comments of a specific nature that have a legal effect.

Statute A law created by a legislative body.

Statute of frauds A legal principle requiring that certain contracts be in writing in order to be enforceable.

Statute of limitations A legal principle requiring a party to commence a lawsuit within a certain period of time.

Stipulation An agreement between parties.

Submission agreement A signed agreement whereby both parties agree to submit a present dispute to binding arbitration.

Subpoena A written order requiring a party or witness to appear at a legal proceeding; a subpoena duces tecum is a written order requiring a party to bring books and records to the legal proceeding.

Summation The last part of the trial wherein both lawyers recap the respective positions of their clients.

Summons A written document served upon the defendant giving notification of a lawsuit.

Temporary decree A court order or directive of a temporary nature, capable of being modified or changed.

Testimony Oral evidence presented by a witness under oath.

"Time is of the essence" A legal expression often included in agreements to specify the requirement of timeliness.

Tort A civil wrong.

Unfair and deceptive practice Illegal business and trade acts prohibited by various federal and state laws.

Unfair discharge An employee's termination without legal justification.

Verdict The decision of a judge or jury.

Verification A written statement signed under oath.

Void Legally without merit.

Waiver A written document that, when signed, relinquishes a party's rights.

Whistleblowing Protected conduct where one party complains about the illegal acts of another.

Witness A person who testifies at a judicial proceeding.

Worker's compensation A process in which an employee receives compensation for injuries sustained in the course of employment.

INDEX

INDEX

Accident/work Injury Report 181
Action of the Incorporator 288
Agreements
    Action of the Incorporator 288
    Application for Authority 299
    Assignment and Bill of Sale 309
    Bill of Sale 286
    By-laws 292
    Certificate of Incorporation 291
    Confidential Settlement Agreement, Mutual Release, and Covenant 226
    Confidentiality and Non-competition Agreement 42
    Consulting Agreement 84, 274
    Cover Letter and Release 215
    Distribution and License Agreement 310
    Employment Agreement 321
    Employment Agreement Alternative Long Version 56
    Employment Agreement—letter Version 77
    Employment Agreement—long Version 50
    Employment Agreement—short Version 74
    General Release—version One 211
    General Release—version Two 213
    Independent Sales Representative Agreement 91
    Independent Sales Representative Agreement (Short Version) 104
    Management, Administrative and Technical Services Agreement 318
    Non-solicitation Agreement 277
    Option and Purchase Agreement 326
    Outside Consultants and Independent Contractors 87
    Partnership Agreement 249
    Purchase Agreement 279
    Sales Employee Agreement Short Version 71
    Sales Employee Agreement—letter Version 79
    Sales Employee Agreement—long Version 62
    Separation Agreement and Release 202, 206
    Settlement Agreement and Mutual Release 230
    Shareholder Agreement 262
    Shareholders Agreement 300
    Standard Employment 45

Stock Purchase Agreement 271
Technical Employment Agreement with a Foreign Employer 288
Written Consent of the Board of Directors 289
Application for Authority 299
Attendance Log 154
Bill of Sale 286
Business Voucher Receipts Form 155
By-laws 292
Certificate of Incorporation 291
Checklists
Contract Execution 32
Drugs and Alcohol 137
Employee Termination Action 221
Employment Negotiating 29
Final Supervisor's Approval for Termination 223
Hiring Concerns 27
Independent Contractor V. Employee Status 33
Lawsuit Exposure 191
Legal and Illegal Hiring Questions 6
On-the-job Policies 134
Overtime Liability under the Fair Labor Standards Act 37
Pre-hiring Concerns 3
Pretermination Consideration 192
Sales Employment 30
Sexual Harassment Investigations 185
Trade Secret Concerns 121
Workplace Accidents 182
Code of Ethics Policy Statement 113
Confidential Settlement Agreement, Mutual Release, and Covenant 226
Confirmation of At-Will Employment Form 41
Confirmation of Job Offer 40
Consent Form to Investigate and Disclose Data 13
Consent to Medical Examination 144
Consulting Agreement 84, 274
Contract Execution 32
Cover Letter and Release 215
Direct Deposit Consent Form 151
Distribution and License Agreement 310
Drugs and Alcohol 137
EEO Compliance Statement and Plan 125
Employee Records 148
Employee Referral Policy and Award 180
Employee Status or Fact Change Form 159
Employee Termination Action 221
Employment Agreement Alternative Long Version 56
Employment Agreement—letter Version 77

358

Employment Agreement—long Version	50
Employment Agreement—short Version	74
Employment Application	11
Employment Negotiating	29
Exit Interview Form	219
Expense Report	156
Final Disciplinary Warning	196
Final Supervisor's Approval for Termination	223
Financial Disclosure Form	146
General Release—version One	211
General Release—version Two	213
Hiring Concerns	27
Hiring Results Summary Form	39
Immigration Control & Reform Act List of Acceptable Documents	24
Independent Contractor V. Employee Status	33
Independent Sales Representative Agreement	91
Independent Sales Representative Agreement (Short Version)	104
Interrogation Confirmation and Release Form	145
Job Applicant Summary Review Forms	
Clerical Appraisal	10
Comparison Form	9
Numerical Grade Form	8
Job Description	21
Job Elimination Notification	201
Job Hiring Progress Summary	23
Job Log	153
Job Requirements Summary	19
Judgment by Confession	238
Lawsuit Exposure	191
Leave of Absence Letter	197
Leave of Absence Request Form	149
Legal and Illegal Hiring Questions	6
Lie Detector Disclaimer and Release Form	147
Management, Administrative and Technical Services Agreement	318
Model Disciplinary Warning	195
Non-solicitation Agreement	277
Notice of Termination	200
On-the-job Policies	134
Option and Purchase Agreement	326
Outside Consultants and Independent Contractors	87
Overtime Liability under the Fair Labor Standards Act	37, 38
Partnership Agreement	249
Payment Calculation Sheet	205
Payroll or Other Deductions	157
Personal Guaranty	237

Personnel Action Form	187
Pre-hiring Concerns	3
Pre-termination Consideration	192
Promissory Note	234, 273, 308
Purchase Agreement	279
Receipt of Employee Handbook Form	136
Receipt of Idea	120
Reference Check Form	14, 15
Telephone Reference Inquiry	17
Rejection Letter	
From Unsolicited Resume	26
To Job Applicant	25
Release and Disclaimer from Drug Testing	141
Resignation by Employee	225
Review Evaluation Forms	
Alternative Performance Review	167
New Hiring Job Appraisal Summary	171
Numerical Employee Evaluation Form	176
Objective Employee Improvement Evaluation	174
Orientation Period	172
Performance Appraisal	165
Self Performance Review	160
Salary Recommendation Form	158
Sales Employee Agreement Short Version	71
Sales Employee Agreement—letter Version	79
Sales Employee Agreement—long Version	62
Sales Employment	30
Sales Rep Protection Statutes	242
Security Investigation Consent and Release	142, 143
Separation Agreement and Release	202, 206
Settlement Agreement and Mutual Release	230
Sexual Harassment Investigations	185
Shareholder Agreement	262
Standard Employment Agreement	45
Statement on Trade Secrets	123
Stock Purchase Agreement	271
Technical Employment Agreement with a Foreign Employer	288
Termination Log Summary	218
Time Report	152
Trade Secret Concerns	121
Transfer/promotion Log	179
Vacation Request Form	150
Workplace Accidents	182

MORE BOOKS by STEVEN MITCHELL SACK

THE HIRING & FIRING BOOK: A Complete Legal Guide for Employers (Revised Edition, 1996)
390 Pages, 8.5 x 11 inches, Index, Glossary
$149.95 Hardbound (plus $5.00 shipping & handling)
ISBN: 0-9636306-5-2

The definitive reference on hiring, firing, and managing employees, the book interprets complex laws in easy-to-understand language. Discusses pre-employment considerations, employee benefits, on-the-job policies and problems, firing and termination decisions, and more. Contains dozens of contracts, forms, checklists, and hundreds of strategies based on the author's legal experience to save thousands of dollars in lawyer's fees, settlements, and jury verdicts.

"Writing for managers in all industries, Sack has created an outstanding, practical legal guide to help solve employee problems...this single-volume work is a valuable addition to business collections; **highly recommended.**"
— **Library Journal**

"Practical "how to" for employers...a splendid, informative easy-to-use book that all business owners and their lawyers should have at their fingertips."
— **New York Law Journal**

"Sack's book covers virtually every aspect of the employee-employer relationship."
— **Nation's Business**

"Any business that has at least one employee should own a copy of *The Hiring & Firing Book*."
— **The Attorney**

FROM HIRING TO FIRING: The Legal Survival Guide for Employers in the 90's
352 Pages, 6 x 9 inches, Index, Glossary
$34.95 Hardbound (plus $3.00 shipping & handling)
ISBN: 0-9636306-1-X

"The best book on U.S. personnel issues in some time. Sack, a labor lawyer, covers everything between hiring and firing as well... Clear writing and Sack's frequent 'Counsel Comments' energize an already lively book."
— **Executive Book Summaries**

"Will help companies of all sizes avoid legal fees and settlements as well as those who simply want to do the 'right thing.' Clearly targeting the employer's point of view, this book will also help employees who might need to know the 'other side's' strategy."
— **ALA Booklist**

"Worth reading — *From Hiring to Firing* is a comprehensive, easy-to-understand guide on all aspects of the employment process..."
— **Orange County Business Journal**

(Continued)

DON'T GET TAKEN: Protect Yourself Legally from Common Abuses and Rip-Offs!
288 Pages, 6 x 9 inches, Index, Glossary
Price: $12.95 Paperbound (plus $2.00 shipping & handling)
ISBN: 0-9636306-6-0

Step-by-step information on how you can fight back against common consumer scams. Protect yourself from poor products & services, real estate schemes, collection harassment, misleading ads, mail & telephone scams, lending, medical, employment, and insurance fraud, and more... With dozens of sample complaint letters, forms and agreements. This book will give you the edge you need so you Don't Get Taken!

THE EMPLOYEE RIGHTS HANDBOOK: Answers to Legal Questions from Interview to Pink Slip
238 Pages, 6 x 9 inches, Index, Glossary
Price: $24.95 Hardbound (plus $3.00 shipping & handling)

Answers in clear language all the legal questions employees may have about securing a job, acting responsibly on the job and protecting themselves when leaving a job. Easy-to-use, practical and up-to-date, this book provides every employee what he or she needs to know about their rights and how to protect them.

THE COMPLETE COLLECTION OF LEGAL FORMS FOR EMPLOYERS
(ON DISKETTE)
Price: $49.95 for IBM 3.5-inch or 5.25-inch Diskette, WordPerfect 5.1 format
(plus $2.00 shipping & handling)
ISBN: 0-9636306-2-8

Now on Computer Diskette ready for you to customize and print... Over 120 sample Contracts, Forms and Checklists for Hiring, Firing, and Day-to-day Employment that noted labor attorney, Steven Mitchell Sack uses in his daily legal practice. The cost of having your attorney prepare these documents would be enormous.

ORDER FROM:

LEGAL STRATEGIES PUBLICATIONS

1795 Harvard Avenue

Merrick, NY 11566

Phone: (800) 255-2665, Fax: (212) 697-0877